China's Rural–Urban Inequality in the Countryside

Yan Gao · Shailaja Fennell

China's Rural–Urban Inequality in the Countryside

上海交通大学出版社
SHANGHAI JIAO TONG UNIVERSITY PRESS

Springer

Yan Gao
Shanghai Jiao Tong University
Minhang District, Shanghai
China

Shailaja Fennell
Development of Land Economy
University of Cambridge
Cambridge
UK

ISBN 978-981-10-8272-6   ISBN 978-981-10-8273-3   (eBook)
https://doi.org/10.1007/978-981-10-8273-3

Jointly published with Shanghai Jiao Tong University Press

The print edition is not for sale in China Mainland. Customers from China Mainland please order the print book from: Shanghai Jiao Tong University Press.

Library of Congress Control Number: 2018932176

Printed on acid-free paper

This Springer imprint is published by Springer Nature
The registered company is Springer Nature Singapore Pte Ltd.
The registered company address is: 152 Beach Road, #21-01/04 Gateway East, Singapore 189721, Singapore

Contents

List of Figures

List of Tables

List of Pictures

Introduction

China has been experiencing rapid development since its reform and opening up to the outside world in 1978 under the leadership of Deng Xiaoping. From 1979 to 2014, per capita GDP sustained an annual growth of 8.6%, and the country has achieved great progress in poverty reduction. Over the reform years, more than 700 million rural poor have been lifted out of poverty successfully, making China the first developing country to meet the Millennium Development Goals (MDGs) target of reducing the population living in poverty by half ahead of the 2015 deadline.

Along with the process of reform and development, and encouraged by Deng's initiative to 'let some of the people get rich first',[1] egalitarianism under the planned economy has been greatly challenged, and the income disparities have been widening in the reform years. It is estimated that, in 2014, China's richest 10% of the population owned 64% of the total wealth (Stierli et al. 2014). Estimates from the National Statistics Bureau have shown that China's Gini coefficient reached over 0.473 in 2013, a level high enough to set off alarms for development planners as well as academic researchers. It is suspected that, if the trend continues, the widening of the income divide will threaten the social stability and economic development.

Despite the various forms of income inequality, such as differences across regions, between rural and urban sectors, and disparities within both sectors, it is believed that it is the rural–urban divide that drives most of the overall disparities. As identified by an OECD report, one of the most striking features of China's development in the reform period has been a large and growing income disparity between the rural and urban populations (Zwiecinski 2005).

There have been large volumes of studies concerning China's rural–urban income disparities in recent years. These studies have been mostly focused on the political economy and economic analysis of the issue, paying much attention to the magnitudes of the inequality at the macroeconomic level. The analysis at the micro

---

[1] This speech was first known during Deng's meeting with an American delegation on 23rd October 1985. It was mentioned later frequently as one of Deng's famous quotes.

level, especially at the household level, as well as the examination from the sociological perspective is missing in the current literature.

This book has adopted the concept of urban bias in directing resource flow concerning rural and urban sectors. Different from existing literature on intersectoral resource transfers in examining the role of agricultural surplus or extraction in the process of economic development, this book employs the idea of resource flows guided by the state policies, but focuses its influence on individuals. Emphasis is placed on how individual income (especially rural income) has been influenced by such resource allocation. The definition of rural and urban here is also slightly different from that in the urban bias thesis, as the division of rural and urban is based on household registration, the unique system in China. That is, there is urban population in rural areas. The coexistence of rural and urban residents in the countryside not only transcends the spatial definition in 'urban bias' but also helps us to understand the allocation of resources and wealth between rural and urban populations in the rural setting.

Heilongjiang Province has been chosen as a study case because it is one of the important bases for commercial grains, and due to historical reasons, it was established as one of three industrial bases in northeast China. Here agriculture and industry have coexisted since early communist years, which will help with the understanding of the co-development of rural and urban sectors, and income disparities between the two. Given the complexity of the problem, a combination of quantitative and qualitative approaches is selected to explore the rural–urban income disparities at provincial, county and household levels.

Quantitative analysis based on Gini and Theil estimates has been conducted to examine rural–urban income disparities in Heilongjiang Province with data at provincial and county levels, respectively. In addition, the relationship between income disparities and other economic indicators are examined. Limited by local data available, this book has adopted the simplified Gini calculation (Hu 2004); thus, made it possible to estimate Gini coefficients for Heilongjiang Province throughout the reform years. Data for quantitative analysis are officially published by the government, mainly from statistics yearbooks. Due to availability of data, Gini and Theil calculations are estimated until 2012. Data used elsewhere in the book are as latest as possible.

Qualitative analysis has been conducted with data collected from fieldwork by the first author, which was carried out in Qinggang County of Heilongjiang Province from late 2006 to mid-2007, when the author conducted on-site observations and unstructured interviews with villagers, cadres and lowest level officials. Interviews were conducted in private houses and local offices to make sure interviewees were in their everyday surroundings. It is noted that the fieldwork has been supplemented by a follow-up visit in late 2016, with the purpose to understand the changes of income inequality in the county after 10 years.

It is believed that the result of the quantitative study is verified against the qualitative investigation, so that the mix of quantitative and qualitative methods is able to provide a comprehensive understanding of income inequality in rural Heilongjiang.

Chapter 1 of the book gives background information about the rural–urban division and their income disparities. It explains the basic concepts of the division, before examining the development of the disparities. It also provides a brief introduction to the province under discussion. Chapter 2 reviews the theories and existing literature relevant to the study. It surveys not only the economic development models but also approaches from sociological perspectives. Chapter 3 analyses the policies and institutions concerning resource flows, emphasizing the role of the household registration, agricultural tax, pricing and public spending in directing intersectoral resource allocation. Chapter 4 reveals the quantitative results. It calculates the overall Gini coefficient for the province over the reform years before calculating the Theil index with county-level data. In addition, Pearson correlations between rural–urban income gap and other economic indicators have been worked out using county-level data. Chapters 5 and 6 present qualitative evidence concerning rural income growth and local resource reallocation. Chapter 7 provides the discussions and findings drawn from both qualitative and quantitative results. It is followed by Chap. 8 to give a current situation of Qinggang before the book concludes.

It is suggested in this book that the wide rural–urban income gap is the result of considerable stagnation in income growth for the rural sector. From the perspective of individuals and households, too much resource outflow and little inflow have resulted in the low level of rural income growth. Legacies from the planned economy exist in the state policies and institutions during the reform years, which direct the overall resource allocation against the rural sector and, at the same time, influence individual income. It has been such institutions as well as the policies biased against the rural sector that have provided the foundation, which has helped to sustain and further enlarge the income inequality. In addition, the *guanxi* relationships, especially at the county level and below, have played an important role in the local resource reallocation, which in most cases directs wealth away from the ordinary rural residents that increases the income disparities. Therefore, we argue that as long as the state institutions are biased towards the urban sector and against the rural sector, the influence of any policies that aim to support the rural sector will continue to be restricted. Meanwhile, in a less-developed place without sufficient working opportunities, government support and well-established formal institutions, *guanxi* will continue to play a much important role in rural life.

The government has in most recent years introduced a series of pro-agricultural policies to boost the rural income. Such policies are expected to remove the fundamental bias against the rural sector. However, the effects of the recent policies are still waiting to be assessed in further studies.

References

Hu, Z. (2004). A study of the best theoretical value of Gini coefficient and its concise calculation formula. *Economic Research Journal*, (9), 60–69.

Stierli, M., Shorrocks, A., Davies, J., Lluberas, R., Koutsoukis, A. (2014). Global wealth report 2014. Zurich: Credit Suisse.

Zwiecinski, A. (2005). OECD review of agricultural policies. China.

Chapter 1
The Rural–Urban Transition

1.1 Population and Income

When income is examined with regard to the rural and urban sectors in China, the definition of rural/urban has to be clarified, specifically in terms of how the rural and urban sectors are divided.

1.1.1 The Rural/Urban Divide

Geographically, the urban population refers to people living in cities and towns, and the rural population refers to those living in the countryside. The National Statistical Yearbooks define the urban population as people residing in 'cities and towns', while the rural population refers to the population other than the urban population.

Cities and towns are established on the authority of the central government, according to various regulations and standards stipulated by the state at different times. Before 1963, an area with more than 2000 residents, of which more than 50% were non-agricultural,[1] was defined as a town. In 1964, a town was redefined as a place with over a 3000 residential population, of which 70% was non-agricultural, or with over 2500 residents (less than 3000), of which 85% was non-agricultural. After 1984, the definition of a town was readjusted to mean a seat of town or a *xiang* (township) government, if the *xiang* had less than 20,000 residents and over 2000 non-agricultural populations, or an area with a population of over 20,000, of which at least 2000 were non-agricultural. Such regulations were not applicable to some ethnical minority regions, remote places or places of

---

[1]According to the National Statistics Bureau, the rural population refers to all those who make a living from agricultural production. In fact, it also includes those who are the dependents of those engaged in agricultural production. Its counterpart is the non-agricultural population. The division is based on the nature of the work in which people are engaged.

© Shanghai Jiao Tong University Press and Springer Nature Singapore Pte Ltd. 2018
Y. Gao and S. Fennell, *China's Rural–Urban Inequality in the Countryside*,
https://doi.org/10.1007/978-981-10-8273-3_1

interests, where a town was authorized to be established even with less than 10% of non-agricultural population. Since 1986, in addition to population density and percentage of non-agricultural population, more economic indicators such as local GNP have been added to the criteria for town and city identification. Regardless of how a town or city is defined, what remains unchanged is the coexistence of the rural and urban populations in counties and towns (especially since the 1980s, when more of the rural population migrated to the cities), so that such geographic definition is obviously far from precise.

What really divides the urban and rural population is the household registration system. People in China are registered as either urban or rural residents at birth. This institution makes it technically easy to divide China's total population into rural or urban, which will be examined in detail in Chap. 3.[2]

1.1.2   Rural/Urban Income

In terms of income, the definitions of both sectors require further explanation. This book will rely on the most representative surveys of Chinese households conducted by the National Statistics Bureau (NSB) and its local branches. Accordingly, it will adopt the income definitions provided by the NSB, i.e. the per capita disposable income for urban households and per capita net income for rural households.

According to the NSB, urban disposable income refers to 'the actual income at the disposal of members of the households which can be used for final consumption, other non-compulsory expenditure and savings. This equals to total income minus income tax, personal contribution to social security and subsidy for keeping diaries in being a sample household.' (NSB, 2015). That is:

Disposable income urban household = total household income - income tax - personal contribution to social security - sample household subsidy for keeping diaries

Here, the total income of urban households is defined as 'the sum of wage income; net business income; income from properties; and income from transfers of members of the households. Income from selling of properties and income from borrowing are not included.' (Ibid).

As for the rural sector, net income refers to 'the total income of rural households from all sources minus all corresponding expenses' (Ibid). The formula is:

Net income of rural households = total income - household operation expenses - taxes and fees - depreciation of fixed assets for production - gifts to rural relatives

---

[2]By the end of 2014, there are 1789 state farms in China. People working on these farms, however, are considered workers (non-agricultural) rather than peasants, although they are similar to the peasants engaged in farming. Like the workers in the state-owned enterprises, these 'farm workers' receive a state salary; thus, they belong to the category of urban population. In Youyi County of Heilongjiang, for example, there is no rural income published because it is where the Youyi State Farm is located and the people all work on the state farm, so are considered urban.

Here, total income is defined as the sum of income earned from various sources by the rural households and their members during the reference period, and is classified as income from wages and salaries, income from household operations, income from properties and income from transfers. The NSB classifies income from wages and salaries as income from labour earned by the members of rural households employed by other units or individuals, and income from household operations as income by the rural households as units of production and operations. Operations by rural households means economic activities namely agriculture, forestry, animal husbandry, fishery, manufacturing, construction, transportation, post and telecommunications, wholesale, retail and catering, social service, culture, education, health, and other household operations. The NSB has also noted that net income is mainly used as input for reinvestment in production and as consumption expenditure of the year, and also used for savings and non-compulsory expenses of various forms, indicating that reproduction cost/input is not deducted from the rural net income (Ibid). In this book, the income from agriculture will be investigated in great detail, because household income from agriculture remains the major source of income for rural residents in the area under examination.

Unless otherwise stated, the term 'income' in this study refers to the net income of rural households and the disposable income of urban households to reflect the welfare and income level of the two sectors, and to keep in line with the established practice of the NSB.

1.2 The Development of Rural–Urban Income Disparities

The data from the NSB show that rural–urban income disparities existed even before the reform in the late 1970s. The 1978 data indicate that the urban disposable income was 343.4 yuan,[3] while the rural net income was 133.6 yuan. The income discrepancy was large right before the reform, which should not be considered as a new phenomenon emerged during the later reform years. Rather, it might be seen as the legacy from the pre-reform, communist years, while its later development was closely related to the bundle of policies implemented during the post-1978 period.

1.2.1 Pre-1978 Strategy

It is argued that Mao Zedong and other senior communist leaders were claimed to come from peasant backgrounds, but this did not help the government policies to become geared towards the benefits of the peasants, who accounted for nearly 90% of the total population when the country was founded. As (White, 1993): (96) put it,

---

[3]Chinese currency

'state policies towards agriculture…were not designed to encourage rural development merely for its own sake, but to link agriculture and other sectors of the rural economy into an overall economic strategy which benefited industrialization'—the developing strategy of the Soviet Union.

China had adopted the formal Soviet strategy, not only because Mao Zedong believed in the Stalinist development model that industry should be given priority, but also because of China's alienation from many other western countries, which were conceived to be imperialists and exploiters of the working class. Under the guidance of this model, the industry-oriented development strategy was implemented. What happened in China is similar to the summary of the World Bank report:

> There was a strong consensus among the modernizing elite that raising living standards and achieving economic development were major social objectives. That consensus translated, however, into the view that industry was to be highly encouraged … It was further believed that most of agriculture represented 'backwardness', that agricultural output is unresponsive to incentives, and that, therefore, agriculture could be discriminated against in order to raise a surplus for industry without larger economic costs. … This set of ideas, or rationales, for policy was supported, or at least not seriously challenged, by the state of economic knowledge at that time. (Krueger, 1991: 4)

Accordingly, agriculture was designed to be squeezed, while industry was supported. It may be that the rural–urban income disparity was set to be wide at the beginning of the Communist development of China.

1.2.2   Early Reform Years 1979–1985

A glance at the development of rural and urban income indicates that, since 1978, the income for both the rural and urban sectors has been growing rapidly, but the growth of rural income has been slower than the urban one in most of the years. This has resulted in a general widening of the rural–urban gap in terms of income (Table 1.1). A brief examination of the policies concerning agriculture may help to explain the changes in rural and urban income disparity over the years.

In fact, in the early years of reform the rural and urban income disparity had decreased substantially until 1985, when the gap started to widen again. The change is largely attributed to the reform that started from the rural sector. In the early 1980s, a series of fundamental reforms was introduced in the agricultural sector. These reforms, emphasizing the role of the market, quickly expanded throughout the country. As the policies of 'reform and opening up' indicate, since then, China has been gradually opening up to the outside world, on its way to a market-oriented economy.

(1) Institutional reform

Towards the end of 1978, the peasants in some provinces began to try out the Household Responsibility System (HRS), whereby the household was responsible

Table 1.1 Rural and urban income disparities, 1978–2014

Year	Urban	Rural	Urban income growth[a](%)	Rural income growth[a](%)	Urban/rural
1978	316.0	133.6	–	–	2.37
1979	405.0	160.2	28.16	19.91	2.53
1980	439.4	191.3	8.49	19.41	2.30
1981	458.0	223.4	4.23	16.78	2.05
1982	494.5	270.1	7.97	20.90	1.83
1983	526.0	310.0	6.37	14.77	1.70
1984	607.6	355.0	15.51	14.52	1.71
1985	739.1	397.6	21.64	12.00	1.86
1986	827.9	423.8	12.01	6.59	1.95
1987	916.0	462.6	10.64	9.16	1.98
1988	1119.4	544.9	22.21	17.79	2.05
1989	1260.7	601.5	12.62	10.39	2.10
1990	1510.2	686.3	19.79	14.10	2.20
1991	1700.6	708.6	12.61	3.25	2.40
1992	2026.6	784.0	19.17	10.64	2.58
1993	2577.4	921.6	27.18	17.55	2.80
1994	3496.2	1221.0	35.65	32.49	2.86
1995	4283.0	1577.7	22.50	29.21	2.71
1996	4838.9	1926.1	12.98	22.08	2.51
1997	5160.3	2090.1	6.64	8.51	2.47
1998	5425.1	2162.0	5.13	3.44	2.51
1999	5854.0	2210.3	7.91	2.23	2.65
2000	6280.0	2253.4	7.28	1.95	2.79
2001	6859.6	2366.4	9.23	5.01	2.90
2002	7702.8	2475.6	12.29	4.61	3.11
2003	8472.2	2622.2	9.99	5.92	3.23
2004	9421.6	2936.4	11.21	11.98	3.21
2005	10,493.0	3254.9	11.37	10.85	3.22
2006	11,759.5	3587.0	12.07	10.20	3.28
2007	13,785.8	4140.4	17.23	15.43	3.33
2008	15,780.8	4760.6	14.47	14.98	3.31
2009	17,174.7	5153.2	8.83	8.25	3.33
2010	19,109.4	5919.0	11.26	14.86	3.23
2011	21,809.8	6977.3	14.13	17.88	3.13
2012	24,564.7	7916.6	12.63	13.46	3.10
2013	26,955.1	8895.9	9.73	12.37	3.03
2014	29,381.0	9892.0	9.00	11.20	2.97

Note [a]Compared with the previous year
Source China Statistics Yearbook 2015

Table 1.2 Agricultural production and productivity mean annual growth rate (%)

Year	Production	Land productivity	Labour productivity	Total factor productivity
1952–1977	2.10	1.87	0.12	−0.42
1978–1984	6.63	7.37	5.07	4.72
1985–1989	3.17	2.64	1.39	0.95
1990–1995	6.89	6.64	7.50	5.85
1952–1995	3.72	3.57	2.22	1.50

Source Fan (1997)

for its own input and output as well as its tax and sales obligations, and collectively owned land was allocated to individual households under contracts of up to 15 years (Kueh, 1984). This reflected a change from collective farming[4] to an individual household farming system. Although it was first tried secretly on a small scale, because of its great success, it spread throughout China and was officially introduced as the initial stage of 1978 reforms. The proportion of the teams adopting the HRS increased from 5% in 1980 to 67% in 1982. By the end of 1983, the HRS had been essentially implemented throughout the country and the former collective farming system was legally abandoned.

There was great productivity and output growth between 1978 and 1984 (see Table 1.2). From 1978 to 1984, there were increases of 6.63, 7.37 and 5.07% in production, land productivity and labour productivity respectively, while the increases in these three categories were only 2.10, 1.87 and 0.12% respectively between 1952 and 1977.

Many studies have been conducted concerning what caused the production growth (Cao & Birchenall, 2013; Fan, 1997; Lin, 1992; Yao, 2016). According to Lin, the productivity growth for 1978–1984, due to the reform, explained 48.6% of the output growth. Of the productivity growth, 96% was attributed to the change in farming institutions from the collective system to the HRS (Lin, 1992). McMillan et al. calculated that 78% of the increase in agricultural productivity in China between 1978 and 1984 can be attributed to the incentive effects of the new responsibility system (McMillan, Whalley, & Zhu, 1989).

Carter and Zhong, after comparing the different results from various studies, concluded that, even though a smaller HRS effect than that indicated by Lin and McMillan had been found, the estimate that the gross value of agricultural output increased by 55% from 1979-85 remained unchanged (Carter & Zhong, 1991). Results from various studies suggest that institutional change resulted in a one-off economic boost of anywhere from 10 to 33% in terms of output.

---

[4]The 'Great Leap Forward', the strategy for economic development, was launched throughout China in 1958, in which Mao Zedong decided to compete with the former Soviet Union and catch up with Britain and the U.S at a faster speed with greater achievements. The commune system, as a major part of the 'Great Leap Forward' was established in the countryside. The existing cooperatives were amalgamated into larger communes, each with an average of 22,000 peasants.

(2) *Price reform*

Price is one of the important factors influencing agricultural production, but, unlike in the market economies of the West, price plays a different role in improving farm output in China. That is because: (1) under the centralized planned economy prior to 1978, price was controlled by the central government instead of being decided by the market; and (2) China is using its own pricing system in terms of agriculture.

In the agricultural sector, price works through the procurement system. Under the procurement system introduced in 1949, the state would buy products from the peasants for certain quantities (quota) at fixed prices, before shipping them to the state-owned food stores to be sold. Prior to 1963, a unitary price system was used, which means that the peasants had to accept the same prices for both quota and above-quota products. Moreover, only the state organizations were authorized to buy products from the peasants, so the sale of agricultural products was under the complete control of the state. After 1963, a two-tier pricing system was introduced, setting the above-quota price higher than the quota price to encourage agricultural production. Since the quota price was usually set at a low level, the more produce that the peasants sold to the state, effectively the more they paid as an unseen tax.

In the 1978 reforms, in order to increase output, the state raised both the quota and above-quota prices by a large margin. For example, in 1979, the increase in both the quota and above-quota prices for products such as grain, oilseed, cotton, sugar and pork, averaged out at 17.1%, and in 1980, they further increased by 41% (Lin, 1992). It should be noted that the 1978 reforms were not the first occasion when prices rose. Prior to this, the government had increased the procurement prices several times.[5] The difference in the 1978 price reform was that they resulted in a greater increase in procurement prices. The premium paid for the above-quota delivery of grain and oil crops was increased from 30 to 50% of the quota prices. The weighted average increase was 22.1%. If only the above quota prices are considered, the increase was 40.7%.

Meanwhile, in the consumer market, although there were no changes in grain and edible oil prices, with the increase in procurement price, the retail prices for pork, fish and eggs were increased by a third. The government provided subsidies to the urban residents as compensation. As a result, both the consumers and providers benefited but the government became greatly burdened. In 1984, the price subsidies for grain, oilseed and cotton reached 20 billion yuan, equivalent to 14% of the total government revenue (Sicular, 1992).

In this context, compulsory quotas for grain were abolished and replaced with contract purchase in 1985 in order to reduce the burden on the government and increase the role of the market. Thus, the peasants were allowed to sell their

---

[5]For example, the procurement prices for grain and oilseed increased by 14 and 12% in 1953. The increases for both items in 1961 were 25% and 18% respectively. In 1961 the above-quota prices for grain and oilseed rose by 7 and 8%, and the figures for 1971 were 5 and 16%.

produce on the market once the quota had been fulfilled. In the new contract purchase, individual households were required to deliver produce according to the negotiated contract with the state. The purchase price was an average of 30% of the previous quota price and 70% of the price above quota.

Studies show that price changes played a role in improving agricultural performance in China. Lin employed province-level panel data to assess the contributions of decollectivization, price adjustments and other reforms, and found that the adjustment in the state procurement prices had a significant impact on output growth (Lin, 1992). According to McMillan et al., 20% of the increase in productivity in China's agriculture between 1978 and 1984 was due to the higher prices (McMillan et al., 1989).

(3) *Free Market*

Against this background, the central government took the chance to continue reforming the rural economy, allowing the markets to take charge (Huang, Yang, & Rozelle, 2010; Huang, 1998). At the beginning of 1985, the 'No. 1 Document' officially announced a new set of policies that encouraged structural change and introduced market reforms. The aspects of market liberalization mainly included: commodity trading, the limited mobility of labour and the flow of capital.

Commodity trading, which was once monopolized by the government, was more determined by the markets with the help of the dual-price system (purchase price and above-quota price). Accordingly, some limited mobility of labour and capital both within and outside the rural areas became inevitable. There also sprang up a private credit market because of the difficulties that the peasants experienced in obtaining credit from the official credit system, in spite of the high interest associated with unsecured loans. At the same time, a market for hired labour emerged, in response to the needs of private business for labour and that of poor, underemployed peasant households for employment. The private business and new enterprises facilitated the flow of capital and labour from agricultural to non-agricultural activities within the rural sector, and from the rural areas to towns, and even cities.

Even though agricultural production growth rate declined rapidly since 1985 (Table 1.2), the liberalization of the rural market continued to promote the rural economy. The total rural output increased by 13.3% per annum, from 1984 to 1994, which is higher than the average GDP growth (about 10% during the same period).

In summary, the 1978 reform initiated in the rural areas consisted of three main parts. The first was the institutional reform, shifting from a collective system to the HRS. The second part emphasized the price reform with a large increase in the procurement prices for agricultural products. The final part is the market reform, aimed at the freeing up of the rural markets and enlarging the role of the prices and markets. Some further reforms include: (1) in 1984, for the first time since the 1950s, farmers were allowed to move to towns and small cities, provided that they could supply their own food (discussed in Chap. 3); and (2) in 1984, private enterprises were permitted to be established in rural areas (Nguyen & Wu, 1999).[6] Thus, non-agricultural activity was stimulated.

Much has been written about China's 1978 reforms, which contributed to the dramatic growth in the gross value of agricultural output in the agricultural sector as well as in the GDP of the country. Accordingly, great increases in rural household income occurred. The initial years of market-oriented reform resulted in a remarkable growth in the peasants' income. Net rural income nearly tripled during this period, rising from 133.6 yuan in 1978 to 397.6 yuan in 1985 (Table 1.1).

1.2.3 The Mid-1990s Reforms

The mid-1990s saw the introduction of several policies concerning the rural sector. After the continuous decline in grain production in 1992 and 1993, grain prices started to rise sharply nationwide from the end of 1993. In 1994, the market prices for rice, wheat and maize rose by 150, 117 and 157% respectively, compared with the previous year. Because of the high inflation, especially from the declining grain production and rising prices of the 1990s, new policies were introduced in 1994.

Firstly, the central government introduced the 'governor grain bag responsibility system' in 1995, whereby the governor of each province had to take full responsibility for grain production, sales and circulation in order to ensure the stable grain supply within the province (Hou & Liu, 2010). In addition, the government boosted the grain procurement price by 44% in 1994. After 1995, it decided to continue purchasing grain without limitation at protected prices[7] despite the good harvests in successive years. In 1996, procurement prices were raised by another 42%. Thus, within three years, the central government increased grain procurement prices by 105%. From 1995 to 1998, as the succession of four years' of grain production growth continued, the production averaged at 0.5 billion tons per year.

The increased grain production and high procurement prices ensured a rapid increase in rural income. As seen from Table 1.1, from 1995 to 1997, rural income growth for the second time exceeded that of the urban sector.

---

[6]The original statement was in State Council (1984) 'Guanyu Nongmin Jinru Jizhen Luohu Wenti De Tongzhi [A Circular on the Issue of Peasants Migrating to Market Towns]'.

[7]In the early 1990s, rice, wheat, cotton and soybeans were purchased by the state at fixed prices according to the contracts. Any excess above the contracted quota could be sold either to the state at negotiated prices or to other purchasers at market prices, except for cotton, over which the state still held the monopoly. In 1997, the government introduced a 'grain protected price system', with the aim of protecting the grain producers. Protected prices were set by the government, usually higher than the market prices (Zwiecinski, 2005).

1.2.4 The 2004 Reform

It is also indicated in Table 1.1 that rural income growth had slowed down since 1997, and the rural–urban income gap had widened again after a short period of decrease. The disparities had been so remarkable since 2000 that the state decided to increase rural income after its years of stagnated growth.

Unlike in the past, the 2004 reform is household-oriented, aimed at increasing rural income by reducing the tax burden on those engaged in agriculture, especially farming. In 2004, Premier Wen Jiabao announced, in the government work report during the Second Session of the Tenth National People's Congress that, since 2004, the government had decided to reduce the agricultural tax gradually by up to 1% (of rural income) per year, planning to phase it out completely within five years.

Agricultural tax and the affiliated charges were, in fact, eliminated in 2006, three years ahead of schedule. There are some matching policies, including the increase in transfer payments from the upper level governments, the reduction in the staff numbers at the lowest level governments and the practice of 'one discussion over one issue/problem'. The former two strategies were aimed at reducing the financial difficulties of the grassroots governments since, after the abolition of *tiliu* and *tongchou* (local fee collection, examined in detail in Chap. 3), the revenue generation capability of the lowest level governments greatly deteriorated (Takeuchi, 2014).

In order to solve the problem of local public goods provision due to the loss of revenue, the state proposed the policy of 'one discussion over one problem/issue'. The basic rule of such a policy is to introduce democracy into the decision-making, so that, once fund raising is needed concerning public benefits, a discussion should be held in order to reach an agreement among all of the stakeholders. In addition, it is stipulated that such approved fundraising should not exceed 12 yuan per head per year. For villages with a per capita payment of less than 12 yuan, the provincial government would provide half the capital for public welfare establishments as a reward.

Meanwhile, under the central government's guidance to 'extract less and subsidize more', rural households engaged in grain cropping have been given subsidies in order to promote grain production. Since 2004, the peasants have been receiving direct subsidies for growing grain and for using seeds of good varieties, termed as '*liangbu*' (double subsidies). Table 1.1 shows that rural income started to increase more quickly in 2004.

1.2.5 Reforms of the Recent Decade

In fact, since 2004, the Chinese government has issued No. 1 documents focused on rural problems consecutively, indicating the determination of the authorities to regenerate the rural sector (see Table 1.3).

Table 1.3 No. 1 documents since 2004

Year	Theme
2004	Boosting farmers' incomes
2005	Strengthening rural work and improving the overall production capacity of agriculture
2006	Constructing a new socialist countryside
2007	Developing modern agriculture and steadily promoting the construction of a new socialist countryside
2008	Fortifying the foundation of agriculture
2009	Achieving steady agricultural development and sustained income increases for farmers
2010	Speeding up coordinated development between urban and rural areas and further cementing foundation of agricultural and rural area development
2011	Accelerating development of water conservancy
2012	Accelerating the scientific and technological innovation to strengthen supply of agricultural product
2013	Speeding up the modernization of agriculture and further strengthening the vitality of rural growth
2014	Deepening rural reforms and planning the development of modern agriculture

Source Authors' compilation

After the central government decided to boost rural income in 2004, the No. 1 Document in 2005 stressed China should bring into full play the farmers and local governments' initiatives of increasing grain production and boost financial, governmental and technological support for the agriculture sector with an aim to improve agricultural production capacity. Later in 2006, the state emphasized constructing a new socialist countryside was the foremost task facing China in the 2006–2010 five-year period. The central government urged for more efforts in coordinating the development of urban and rural areas, developing modern agriculture, boosting farmers' incomes, enhancing rural infrastructure, promoting social causes in rural areas and deepening rural reforms. Therefore, in 2007, modern equipment, science and technology, industrial systems, management and development ideas were stated in the No. 1 Document to be nurtured to improve the quality, economic returns and competitiveness of agriculture. In 2008, the central government ordered rapid development of an enduring mechanism for consolidating the foundation of agriculture, calling for more efforts to guarantee grain product safety and a balance between supply and demand, and between various grain products. Confronted with the global downturn in 2009, the state highlighted challenges in agricultural and rural development, and urged authorities to take resolute measures to avoid declining grain production and to ensure the steady expansion of agriculture and rural stability. Since 2010, China has claimed to put more investment, subsidies, fiscal and policy supports into rural areas and improve the livelihoods of rural residents. The No. 1 Document also called for more efforts to maintain grain production, increase farmers' incomes and development momentum in rural areas.

In the beginning of the 12th five-year plan, the 2011 No. 1 Document set a target of improving the country's underdeveloped water conservancy works over the next five to ten years, saying the government will double average annual spending on water conservancy over the next 10 years from that of 2010. It highlighted weaknesses in water conservancy infrastructure exposed by floods and drought in recent years, noting the country will finish building effective flood control and drought relief systems by the end of 2020. In 2012, the state issued its first policy document, underscoring the importance of scientific and technological innovation for sustained agricultural growth. Then in 2013, the No. 1 Document listed ensuring grain security and supplies of major farm produce as the top priority in developing modern agriculture. Policies to speed up the transfer of rural land and offer more subsidies to family farms and farmer's cooperatives were promised, in an effort to develop large-scale farming. In 2014, China claimed in No. 1 Document to improve the mechanisms for safeguarding food security, seek sustainable agricultural growth while balancing rural and urban development, deepening rural land reforms and promoting financial support for rural areas.

With years of efforts to promote rural development from various perspectives, rural income has increased at a speed faster than the urban sectors. Table 1.1 indicates that since 2010, rural income growth has outpaced that of the urban. However, the absolute income gap between the two sectors remains large.

1.3 The Case of the Province of Heilongjiang

Heilongjiang[8] is in the northeast of China, at the highest latitude and the northernmost tip of the country (Fig. 1.1). The province is named after its longest river (known as the Heilongjiang River in China or the Amur River in Russia). The province shares its border of more than 3000 km with Russia and is separated from the country by the Amur River in the north and the Ussuri River in the east. In the west, it adjoins the Inner Mongolian Autonomous Region, while to its south lies Jilin Province. The West is used to the term Manchuria instead of northeast China[9] to refer to the region, of which Heilongjiang constitutes the northern part.

1.3.1 Resources Availability

Heilongjiang is abundant with natural resources. Being one of the China's water-rich provinces, it has five water systems composed of major rivers, known as

---

[8]This means the Black Dragon River in Chinese.

[9]Also known as the three provinces in the northeast of China, the other two being Jilin province and Liaoning Province.

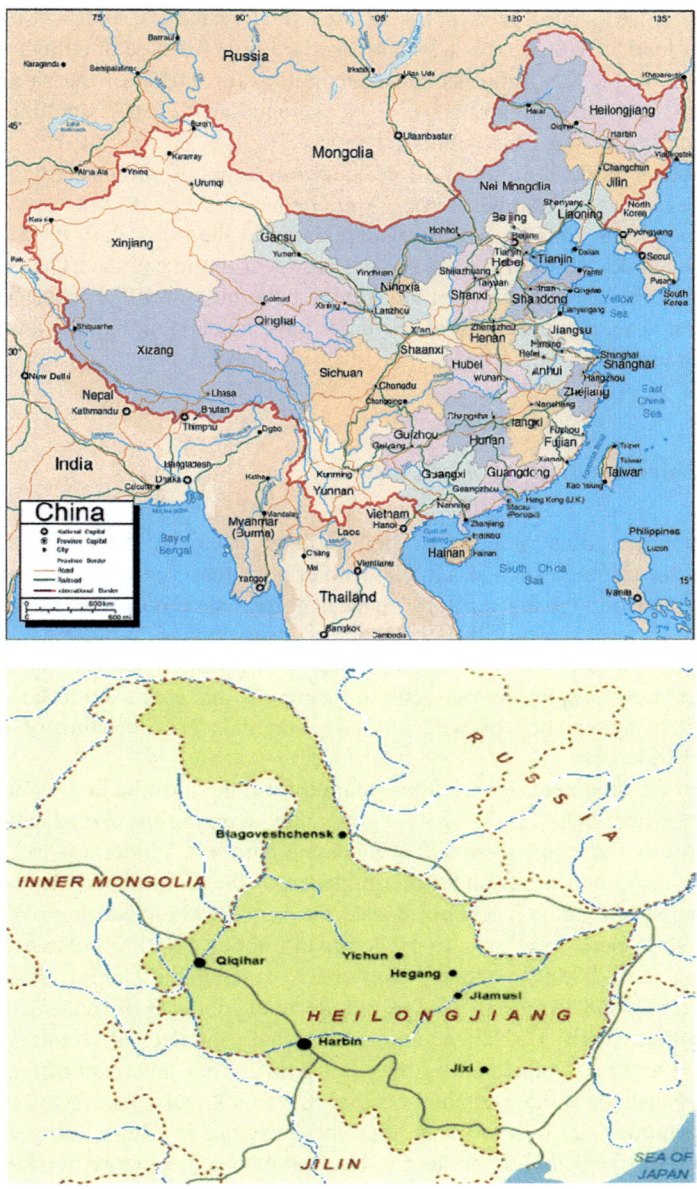

Fig. 1.1 Maps of China and Heilongjiang. *Source* Internet

Heilongjiang (Amur), Ussuri, Songhuajiang (Sungari), Nenjiang and Suifenhe, as well as numerous streams. There are about 6000 lakes and reservoirs throughout the province. Nearly 70% of the rainfall occurs in the warm season, which is ideal for the crops.

The province is also known for its rich land resources. It has 44.4 million hectares of land, of which 40% is suitable for farming. The area of cultivated land in the province is 11.77 million hectares, accounting for 9.05% of the nation's total. The amount of cultivated land per head is averaged at 7.7 mu,[10] the highest in the country, and three times the national average.

Moreover, it ranks the first of all provinces in terms of afforested area, reserves of forest resources and timber output. The Greater and Lesser Xing'an Mountains are its major forest areas. Since oil was discovered there in 1959, the Daqing Oil Field has been developed as the largest oil producer in the country. The province is also rich in coal deposits. Several cities have been built and flourished because of coal mining. The abundant natural resources have made Heilongjiang an important energy base in China since 1949.

1.3.2   Development of Agriculture

The development of agriculture in Heilongjiang is largely due to its favourable conditions for farming, such as sufficient water resources, boundless plains and rich black soil. In Heilongjiang territory, there is a great stretch of fertile plain (one of the world's three major black soil zones), surrounded by three rivers—the Heilongjiang (Amur), Songhuajiang (Sungari) and Ussuri—covering an area of 5.4 million hectares. Despite the rich natural resources, this area used to be desolated, with frequent appearance of wild animals, and thus got its name of the Great Northern Wilderness.

The real development of agriculture started from the introduction of Communist China in the late 1940s. In 1947, two years after winning the Anti-Japanese War, the first group of veterans were sent to the Great Northern Wilderness to 'build up a solid base in the northeast' under the guidance of the Communist Party. The veterans established the first mechanized state-farms in the Great Northern Wilderness. Around 1958, there were sent to Heilongjiang about 140,000 veterans, 100,000 intellectuals and 200,000 youths[11] from cities like Beijing, Tianjin, Shanghai and Harbin. From 1968 to 1976, 540,000 intellectual youths were relocated there as soldier-farmers, with Mao's encouragement that 'intellectual youth go to the countryside and be re-educated by the rural poor'. After the years of reclamation, the Great Northern Wilderness had become China's Great Granary by 1978, with more state-farms (103 in total) than any other province in China. Early wilderness reclamation has helped Heilongjiang to become mechanized more quickly than the other provinces in China, and the province has become one of the country's most important commodity grain production bases, ranking first in terms of both the

---

[10]Measurement unit, 1 mu = 1/15 ha.

[11]Urban youth were encouraged to work in the border areas such as northeast China, known as '*zhibian*' (supporting the border areas) youth.

volume of commodity grains and storage. Unlike other places in China, where farming is characterised as being on a small-scale and self-sufficient, with only 30% of grain output sold out, in Heilongjiang on the contrary, 64% of the grain produced is commercialised (Ho & Lin, 2004; Kako & Zhang, 2000).

Agricultural production, heavily defined by its cold climate agriculture in the province, is traditionally based upon crops such as maize and wheat, in addition to being the nation's largest producer of soybeans. Its exports of soybeans make up two thirds of the country's total. The commercial crops grown include beets, flax, and tobacco, with the output also among the nation's highest. The province's number of dairy cows and output of milk, as well as dairy products are the highest in the country. The grain output of the province reached 67.6 billion kilograms in 2014, leading the country's provinces since 2011 and accounting for one-tenth of the national total.

1.3.3   Development of Industry

Modern industry in Heilongjiang started with the Russian invasion since the Second Opium War (1856–1860), when the Qing government was forced to cut off more than 100 million square kilometres of China's territory beyond the Amur and the Ussiru Rivers, leaving Heilongjiang with the present border. Since 1897, the Siberia Railroad had been under construction, with its eastern branch (known as the Zhongdong Railroad, meaning China's eastern railroad) being built throughout the three provinces in northeast China; namely, Heilongjiang, Jilin and Liaoning. After the reconstructions in subsequent years, it has served as an important railway communication for over a hundred years. Harbin (later the capital city of Heilongjiang), was located at the junction of the T-shaped railroad, which helped it develop from a fishing village into a colonialized modern city, and also greatly influenced the economic development of Heilongjiang Province.

From 1898 to 1918, Russian capital was invested in Harbin with the help of the Zhongdong Railroad. Many of China's largest enterprises and companies were set up in the city, including the General Factory of Zhongdong Railroad (a machinery enterprise), the Zhongdong Railroad Communication Company, and the Sino-Russian Daosheng Bank (a commercial bank). Moreover, the Manchurian Flour Company (China's first modern flour processing factory) and the Ulubulevskij Brewery (China's first beer brewing enterprise) were established. The early industry in Harbin were further developed by some Russian capitalists, especially during the Japan-Russian War in 1904 and 1905, when they obtained large subsidies and deposits from the Russian military organizations and brought many European advanced facilities to the city. Industrial enterprises equipped with modern steam engines were thus established quickly.

After the explosion of the October Socialist Revolution in 1917, the power of Imperial Russian in Harbin was taken over by the Jews. The Jews first moved to Harbin together with the Russians, some provided services for the workers building the Zhongdong Railroad, and others provided loans to businessmen. Gradually, they became more active in business after the October Revolution, and their business extended to vegetable exports and industry. As estimated, until 1926, there were 489 Jewish industrial and business enterprises. Together with Russian and Jewish capital inflow, there was investment from more than 30 foreign countries, such as America, Britain, France and Germany. All of these factors helped the early development of industry in Harbin and Heilongjiang Province, but they all withered after the Japanese invasion in 1932.

When China was invaded by Japan, Heilongjiang fell under the control of Japan and became, in 1932, part of Manchukuo (a Japanese puppet state) until 1945, when Japan was defeated. Also, in 1945, Heilongjiang became the first province to be 'liberated' (with complete control) by the Chinese Communist Party, and Harbin the first major city controlled by the communists. In 1954, five years after the foundation of the People's Republic of China, Heilongjiang was expanded to merge with the former Songjiang Province and became the present province, with Harbin as its capital city.

Being the first province to be liberated by the Chinese Communist Party, Heilongjiang was earlier compared with other provinces in developing under the communist regime, which made it a politically ideal place for consolidating the new power of China. Geographically, Heilongjiang is close to the USSR, convenient for liaising with the first communist country, which was seen as the role model for Communist China and the only foreign alliance of the new political power in the late 1940s. The industrial bases (despite being damaged during the war) and the railroad transportation also helped the Communist Party make the decision to choose Heilongjiang as one of the key regions (the others being Jilin and Liaoning, all in the northeast) to be developed in China. As China decided to follow the USSR strategy of developing heavy industry, Heilongjiang naturally was developed with the focus on its heavy industry. Soon after 1949, its geographical and political convenience helped Heilongjiang become the direct beneficiary of China's friendship with the USSR and receive support from it in terms of technology, experts and management as well as capital.

During the first five-year plan (1954–1958), there were 156 projects[12] built and financed in 17 provinces throughout China with the help of the USSR, with Heilongjiang hosting 22,[13] the most of all the provinces.

These 22 projects in Heilongjiang greatly promoted the development of the region. The hundreds of affiliated projects, together with dozens of relocated enterprises, soon established the position of Heilongjiang as one of Communist China's major industrial bases. The investment in such projects was favourable for urban development and the employment of the urban population.

---

[12]150 projects were finally put into practice, including 106 in civil industry and 44 in military industry.

[13]20 projects were in civil industry and 2 in military industry.

Later, when the Korean crisis erupted in 1950, the central government decided to relocate northwards to Heilongjiang most of the facilities of some factories in cities like Shenyang and Dandong in Liaoning Province. The relocation substantially changed the industrial structure of Heilongjiang and reinforced the heavy industry of the province. Take Harbin as an example; before the relocation, light industry took 82.6% and heavy industry accounted for the other 17.4% of the industrial structure; after the relocation, these figures changed to 44.4 and 55.6%.

1.3.4   Urban Income

For historical reasons, since the beginning of the 20th century, the percentage of urban population in northeast China has been higher than in other parts of the country. In the 1930s, the urban population in Heilongjiang constituted more than 20% of the whole. In 1949, it reached 24.2% in the province, 13.6% higher than the national average. Later, with the development of industry, the percentage of urban population continued to increase, except the reversed trend in the Cultural Revolution, when the urban intellectual youths were encouraged to go to the countryside. The urban population grew rapidly since the early 1980s, and until 1985, the urban population constituted about 42%, which was even higher than the national level of 41.8% in 2004. In 2014, the figure in Heilongjiang reached 58.1% and that for the nation was 54.8%.

In terms of the urban income of the province, data could be found only since 1978, but it is believed that the urban income immediately after 1949 should be high compared with other provinces in the country, because this period was a golden age for the province's development, as explained above. As illustrated by Table 1.4, until 1985, the urban income in Heilongjiang was higher than the national average, but the situation changed soon after, when Heilongjiang lagged behind in terms of urban income. Since 1990, the urban income in Heilongjiang was about 78% of the national average. Since 2000, this gap has been further widening.

If examined in terms of national position, Heilongjiang's has always been ranked below 20th of the 30 provinces throughout the country with regard to urban income. It was 25th in 1995, 27th in 2000, 28th in 2003, and in 2007, it ranked the second lowest, only above Gansu, a province in remote west China. In recent years, urban income in Heilongjiang has always been one of the bottom five.

A question arises as to why the former energy and heavy industrial base of China, with a high level of urbanization, would result in such a poor position with regard to economic development and the low urban income level. The following reasons might be able to explain its economic and urban income development in the post-reform years.

Table 1.4 Urban Income in China and Heilongjiang 1978–2014 (yuan)

Year	National average (1)	Income in Heilongjiang (2)	(2)/(1)
1978	316.0	455.0	1.44
1979	405.0	458.0	1.13
1980	439.4	420.0	0.96
1981	458.0	424.0	0.93
1982	494.5	460.0	0.93
1983	526.0	518.0	0.98
1984	607.6	580.0	0.95
1985	739.1	742.0	1.00
1986	827.9	830.0	1.00
1987	916.0	889.0	0.97
1988	1119.4	1004.0	0.90
1989	1260.7	1138.0	0.90
1990	1510.2	2122.0	1.41
1991	1700.6	1389.0	0.82
1992	2026.6	1630.0	0.80
1993	2577.4	1960.0	0.76
1994	3496.2	2597.0	0.74
1995	4283.0	3375.0	0.79
1996	4838.9	3768.0	0.78
1997	5160.3	4091.0	0.79
1998	5425.1	4269.0	0.79
1999	5854.0	4595.0	0.78
2000	6280.0	4913.0	0.78
2001	6859.6	5426.0	0.79
2002	7702.8	6101.0	0.79
2003	8472.2	6679.0	0.79
2004	9421.6	7471.0	0.79
2005	10,493.0	8273.0	0.79
2006	11,759.5	9182.0	0.78
2007	13,785.8	10,245.0	0.74
2008	15,780.8	11,581.0	0.73
2009	17,174.7	12,566.0	0.73
2010	19,109.4	13,857.0	0.73
2011	21,809.8	15,696.0	0.72
2012	24,564.7	17,760.0	0.72
2013	26,955.1	19,597.0	0.73
2014	29,381.0	22,609.0	0.77

Source China Statistics Yearbooks, Heilongjiang Statistics Yearbooks

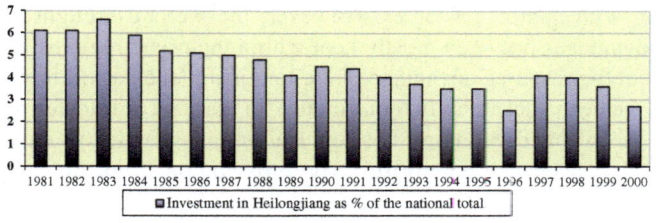

Fig. 1.2 Investment in state-owned fixed assets in Heilongjiang 1981–2000. *Source* China Statistics Yearbooks

Firstly, since the reform and opening up, the national development focus has been switched from heavy industry in the northeast to the market economy, starting in the coastal areas in the southeast. Accordingly, Heilongjiang has lost its privilege in terms of investment. This can be seen briefly from the share of fixed assets in this region during the 1980s and 90s, when the fixed assets in most enterprises in Heilongjiang had been used for more than 30 years, and so needed upgrading on a large scale. However, investment showed a trend of decline, as shown in Fig. 1.2.

The figures indicate that, with the development focus having been shifted to the coastal areas of southeast China, the investment in fixed assets in Heilongjiang had decreased from 6.1% in 1981 to 2.7% in 2000.

Secondly, as an energy source of China, Heilongjiang has been developed or marginalized in terms of energy exploitation. In the official wording, this province has made a great contribution to the state, especially under the planned-economy. According to the Research Centre of Contemporary Heilongjiang, in addition to the grain supply, during the fifty-year period from 1949 to 1999, Heilongjiang had supplied to the state 1.5 billion tonnes of oil, accounting for 45.2% of the national total; 600 million cubic metres of timber, 28% of the national total; and 1.9 billion tonnes of coal, a further 6.9% of the total national output. However, these primary products were supplied at a very low price. Take oil as an example; until the 1990s, oil was delivered to the state at a price lower than 100 RMB (about 12.5 USD) per tonne. It was estimated that, from 1952 to 2002, the amount directly delivered to the state and that supported other provinces indirectly totalled 1400 billion RMB, equivalent to a quarter of its total GDP for those years and roughly four times the state investment in Heilongjiang.

In the early 1980s, supported by the national policy of reform and opening-up, the economy has been developing very quickly in China's south-eastern coastal areas, and the local residents there have benefited greatly in terms of welfare and income. Heilongjiang, on the other hand, was still under the planned-economy at that time, and a great amount of resources and heavy industrial products continued being allocated to other places in the country, which certainly supported the development of other provinces, but that province itself did not enjoy much benefit. On the contrary, it had to bear the cost of resource exhaustion and the environmental problems of excessive exploration. Comparing coastal areas and Heilongjiang, the former is bestowed with a good geographical location and

Heilongjiang with natural resources. However, the welfare brought about by the locational advantages has been mostly kept within their own regions, while most of the gains from the resource advantage of Heilongjiang (such as oil from the Daqing Oil Field) have been substantially 'contributed' to the state or transferred elsewhere.

Thirdly, the planned economy has left Heilongjiang with too many large and medium-sized state-owned enterprises. The gross output from the state-owned or state-controlled enterprises to total industrial output had been maintained at about 80% in the reform years. During the process of reform, more state-owned enterprises have been losing money, despite the state's three-year efforts, from 1998 to 2000, to reform and regenerate state-owned enterprises. Meanwhile, the percentage of state-owned enterprises and their employees remained high. In 2002, for example, there were still 3.7 million state-owned employees in the province, constituting 53% of the urban employment, which is far higher than the national level of 28.9%. Until 2006, nearly 15 years after the state started the market reform of state-owned enterprises, 248 out of the 661 state-owned enterprises in Heilongjiang were losing money, of which 189 were large and medium-sized enterprises and 163 belonged to heavy industry. The high proportion of labour employed in state-owned enterprises and low level of economic benefits of such enterprises restricted the improvement of urban income. Accordingly, in 2007, wage income constituted 67.8% of urban income for Heilongjiang, but the wage level of 19,386 yuan was 5546 yuan lower than the national average. In addition, with the increase in the number of laid off-workers and unemployment in the cities, the number of dependents of each employed urban resident increased from 1.8 in 1995 to 2.0 in 2007. These all influence the urban income level in Heilongjiang.

1.3.5   Rural Income

Due to the reform carried out in rural areas since 1978, rural income in Heilongjiang increased rapidly, improved from 172 yuan in 1978 to 398 yuan in 1985, and 760 yuan in 1990. In 2014, rural net income reached 10,453 yuan. Data have shown that the rural income in Heilongjiang is similar to that of the national average. Before 1998, the national rural income was about 90% of that in Heilongjiang, but, after that, the national income was slightly higher until 2004, when the rural income in Heilongjiang grew faster and surpassed the national level (Table 1.5). This is mainly due to the fact that Heilongjiang was one of the pilot provinces that started to implement the pro-agricultural policies in 2004,[14] two years earlier than most provinces. However, in recent years, rural income growth in Heilongjiang has stagnated again, and become lower than the national average.

---

[14]In 2004, Heilongjiang was one of the pilot provinces that practised a policy of 'one elimination and two subsidies', in which agricultural tax was eliminated and subsidies provided at 10 yuan per mu for growing grains and 15 yuan per mu for using seeds of good varieties.

Table 1.5 Rural net income in Heilongjiang province 1978–2014 (yuan)

Year	National average (1)	Income in Heilongjiang (2)	(1)/(2)
1978	133.6	172.0	0.78
1979	160.2	191.0	0.84
1980	191.3	205.0	0.93
1981	223.4	224.0	1.00
1982	270.1	252.0	1.07
1983	310.0	388.0	0.80
1984	355.0	432.0	0.82
1985	397.6	398.0	1.00
1986	423.8	476.0	0.89
1987	462.6	474.0	0.98
1988	544.9	553.0	0.99
1989	601.5	535.0	1.12
1990	686.3	760.0	0.90
1991	708.6	735.0	0.96
1992	784.0	949.0	0.83
1993	921.6	1028.0	0.90
1994	1221.0	1394.0	0.88
1995	1577.7	1766.0	0.89
1996	1926.1	2182.0	0.88
1997	2090.1	2308.0	0.91
1998	2162.0	2253.0	0.96
1999	2210.3	2166.0	1.02
2000	2253.4	2148.0	1.05
2001	2366.4	2280.0	1.04
2002	2475.6	2405.0	1.03
2003	2622.2	2509.0	1.05
2004	2936.4	3005.0	0.98
2005	3254.9	3221.0	1.01
2006	3587.0	3552.0	1.01
2007	4140.4	4132.0	1.00
2008	4760.6	4856.0	0.98
2009	5153.2	5207.0	0.99
2010	5919.0	6211.0	0.95
2011	6977.3	7591.0	0.92
2012	7916.6	8604.0	0.92
2013	8895.9	9634.0	0.92
2014	9892.0	10,453.0	0.95

Source China Statistics Yearbooks; Heilongjiang Statistics Yearbooks

Table 1.6 Percentage of rural income source in Heilongjiang 1995–2012

Year	Level	Income of wages and salaries	Household operation	Net income from property	Net income from transfer
1995	Heilongjiang	7.38	86.85	1.21	4.56
	National	22.42	71.35	2.60	3.63
2000	Heilongjiang	15.73	79.11	2.82	2.33
	National	31.17	63.34	2.00	3.50
2005	Heilongjiang	14.41	73.38	7.16	5.04
	National	36.08	56.67	2.72	4.53
2010	Heilongjiang	19.99	63.46	5.54	11.00
	National	41.07	47.86	3.42	7.65
2011	Heilongjiang	19.71	63.03	7.18	10.08
	National	42.47	46.18	3.28	8.07
2012	Heilongjiang	21.12	63.15	6.74	8.98
	National	43.55	44.63	3.15	8.67

Sources National Statistics Yearbooks; Heilongjiang Statistics Yearbooks

A closer look at the sources of rural net income reveals that, in Heilongjiang, agriculture has remained the major source of rural income. The percentage of rural income from agriculture has been much higher than the national average. In 1995, household operation (mainly agriculture) accounted for 86.85% of rural income in Heilongjiang compared with a lower national average level of 71.35%. In 2012, it accounted for 63.15% of rural income in Heilongjiang compared with a far lower national level of 44.63%. For the country as a whole, agriculture has been playing a less important role in rural income. However, agricultural income still accounted for over 60% of rural income in Heilongjiang province (Table 1.6).

In terms of wage income, the difference between Heilongjiang and the whole country has been substantial, as the wage income in Heilongjiang remained less than 22% until 2012 when the national average reached over 43%. Since 2000 there has been the trend that wage income has been taking a larger share for both Heilongjiang and the country as a whole. However, the percentage difference between the two has remained large.

Rural income from transfer and property in Heilongjiang was similar to the national average in China before 2004. The major difference lies in that since 2005 its share has been larger in Heilongjiang. This is mainly because the pro-agricultural policies in recent years has transferred more subsidies to the rural sector in Heilongjiang, the agricultural province.

There are at least two indications from the analysis of rural income sources in Heilongjiang. Firstly, as the income from agriculture has been gradually replaced by income from other sources, such as wage income in other provinces, agriculture continues to play a major role in the rural income of Heilongjiang.

Secondly, the share taken by wage income has been relatively small in the province. Wage income mainly comes from non-agricultural labour, and the low level of wage income has shown that the non-agricultural activities and industries in the province have been underdeveloped. To be specific, the township and village enterprises, which facilitate employment and income increase in the rural Heilongjiang, cannot compete with other rural areas in China. This further implies that there is a heavier reliance on agriculture in the province in terms of income.

References

Cao, K. H., & Birchenall, J. A. (2013). Agricultural productivity, structural change, and economic growth in post-reform China. *Journal of Development Economics, 104*, 165–180.

Carter, C. A., & Zhong, F.-N. (1991). China's past and future role in the grain trade. *Economic Development and Cultural Change, 39*(4), 791–814.

Fan, S. (1997). Production and productivity growth in Chinese agriculture: New measurement and evidence. *Food Policy, 22*(3), 213–228.

Ho, S. P. S., & Lin, G. C. S. (2004). Converting land to nonagricultural use in China's coastal provinces—Evidence from Jiangsu. *Modern China, 30*(1), 81–112.

Hou, J. W., & Liu, X. (2010). Grain policy: Rethinking an old issue for China. *International Journal of Applied Economics, 7*(1), 1–20.

Huang, Y. (1998). Agricultural reform in China: Getting institutions right. *Canadian Journal of Agricultural Economics, 46*, 257–258.

Huang, J., Yang, J., & Rozelle, S. (2010). China's agriculture drivers of change and implications for China and the rest of world. *Agricultural Economics, 41*(s1), 47–55.

Kako, T., & Zhang, J. (2000). Problems concerning Grain Production and distribution in China: The case of Heilongjiang province. *The Developing Economies, 38*(1), 51–79.

Krueger, A. O. (1991). *The political economy of agricultural price policy: Volume 5, a synthesis of the political economy in developing countries*. USA: Johns Hopkins University Press for World Bank.

Kueh, Y.-Y. (1984). China's new agricultural-policy program: Major economic consequences, 1979–1983. *Journal of Comparative Economics, 8*(4), 353–375

Lin, J. Y. (1992). Rural reforms and agricultural growth in China. *The American economic review*, 34–51.

McMillan, J., Whalley, J., & Zhu, L. (1989). The impact of China's economic reforms on agricultural productivity growth. *The Journal of Political Economy*, 781–807.

National Statistics Bureau (NSB). (2015). China Statistics Yearbook. Beijing, China: Statistics Press.

Nguyen, D., & Wu, H. X. (1999). The Impact of the Economic Reforms on Agricultural Growth. In Y. Wu & K. Kalirajan (Eds.), *Productivity and Growth in Chinese Agriculture* (2nd ed., pp. 52–99). Hampshire: Macmillan.

Sicular, T. (1992). What's wrong with China's agricultural price policies? *Journal of Asian Economics, 3*(1), 29–56.

Takeuchi, H. (2014). *Tax reform in rural China: Revenue, resistance, and authoritarian rule*. UK: Cambridge University Press.

White, G. (1993). *Riding the tiger: The politics of economic reform in post-Mao China*. USA: Stanford University Press.

Yao, S. (2016). *Agricultural reforms and grain production in China*. Berlin: Springer.

Zwiecinski, A. (2005). *OECD review of agricultural policies*, China.

Chapter 2
Theoretical Background

This book investigates rural–urban income inequality in China, and the existing literature has examined this issue extensively. Whereas the purpose of this book is to explore from the rural perspective we believe the following theories and thoughts are closely related to our research.

2.1 The Lewis Model

In developing economics, the Lewis model has been widely considered as one of the most influential studies concerning the development of agriculture and industry.

2.1.1 Revisiting Lewis

Published as *'Development with Unlimited Supply of Labour'* in 1954, the core of the model is the assumption of a dual structure of the economy. The model argues that economic growth requires a structural transformation between two sectors: a traditional sector and a modern one.

Various terminology has been used to express this dualism, such as urban-rural, industrial-agricultural, modern-traditional, as well as capitalist-non capitalist, of which Lewis himself started to characterize the duality (Islam & Yokota, 2008). He later renamed the two sectors 'modern' and 'traditional' in his 1979 article. Earlier, he believed the two sectors were 'capitalist' and 'subsistence', rather than 'industrial' and 'agriculture', nor 'urban' and 'rural', because 'the urban poor, domestic servants, petty traders, household retainers, were specifically listed among the group contributing to the abundance of labour supply' (Kirkpatrick & Barrientos, 2004).

© Shanghai Jiao Tong University Press and Springer Nature Singapore Pte Ltd. 2018
Y. Gao and S. Fennell, *China's Rural–Urban Inequality in the Countryside*,
https://doi.org/10.1007/978-981-10-8273-3_2

In the model, it is assumed that many LDCs have both a traditional agricultural sector and a modern industrial one. The former is of a subsistence nature, characterised by low productivity, low wages and an abundance of labour (with considerable underemployment), while the latter is defined by a higher marginal productivity, higher incomes and a demand for more workers (initially). Therefore, the workers in the traditional sector would be attracted to the modern industrial sector due to higher wages. Given the wage difference between the two sectors, workers tend to transfer from the traditional sector to the manufacturing one over time, so their general welfare and productivity will improve.

The 'surplus labour' in the traditional sector ensures that, over an extended period, the wages in the modern sector remains constant because the supply of labour to the modern sector exceeds demand at this wage rate. Capitalists capture the surplus of the output over wages 'as profits and growth would occur as the shares of profits in national income rises and are directed to profitable investment' (Kirkpatrick & Barrientos, 2004, p. 4). Growth thus means more jobs and the process of labour absorption is continued.

It is argued that labour transfer from the traditional agricultural sector to the modern one would have no effect on the former, since its marginal productivity is so low (being negligible, zero or even negative), although it would certainly increase the output of the latter. Over time, with the constant labour increase in the modern sector, the marginal productivity would be driven down, but would be increased by reinvestment and capital formation. The process would continue until, eventually, the wage levels of the traditional and modern sectors equalize, as labour leaving the traditional agricultural sector increases the marginal productivity and wages in this sector, but drives down those in the modern industrial sector. This is the time when a dualistic economic structure has been transformed into a unitary capitalistic economy.

2.1.2 The Chinese Case

Arguably, China fits well into the Lewis model of the dual structure. However, what seems to be different in the case of China is that, since the 1950s, the free flow of labour, which serves as an important prerequisite in the Lewis model, has been restricted due to its rigorous household registration system, strictly confining rural labour within the traditional sector. There was only a limited flux of rural labour to the cities during the period from 1961 to 1978 (Chen & Hu, 1994), and it is noticeable that such flows were mainly due to non-economic reasons, such as marriage, reemployment of veterans, student admission, and return to the cities[1] as a consequence of policy changes and the confiscation of rural land.

---

[1]These people used to be urban but were transferred to rural areas during political upheavals.

After 1978, the household registration was relaxed, yet the system continued to play a major role in restricting the free flow of rural labour. Studies have also found that, by the early 1990s, of the rural labour that had transferred, only about 12% were absorbed by the urban sector; the rest all remained in rural areas, simply changing from agricultural to non-agricultural activities locally (Chen & Hu, 1994). The rural marginal productivity could hardly be raised effectively; thus, according to these researchers, the later stage of the Lewis Model cannot be realised. Other researchers further confirm that there is rigidity in China's dual structure, which has become the biggest obstacle to the rural–urban integrated development (Liu, 2014).

Since 2000, there has been further relaxation in household registration and there even appeared shortage of labour in some large cities. Accordingly, more debates have started as to whether China has reached the Lewis turning point, changing from a society with unlimited labor supply to one with labor shortage. Some scholars believe the labor shortfall in recent years does not mean that there is no remaining flexibility in the labor supply (Knight, Deng, & Li, 2011), whereas others argue that China has already passed the Lewis turning point for over ten years (Zhang, Yang, & Wang, 2011). While the debate continues, scholars and policy makers have to consider the future development beyond the turning point.

2.2   The Case of "Price Scissors"

In terms of agriculture-industry relations, it is generally agreed that socialist economies strive for capital accumulation in order to engage in rapid industrialization during their early economic development.

2.2.1   The Mechanism and Evidence

A frequently used method is the 'price scissors',[2] a strategy related to the accumulation of capital in developing, especially socialist countries, first proposed by Preobrazhensky in (1926), i.e. by squeezing the agricultural sector to support industrialization and by lowing agriculture's terms of trade with industry during the early phase of economic development. In the 1920s, the Soviet Union was in its early stage of socialist development. Preobrazhensky argued, in his book, *The New Economics*, that the socialist economy was weak and small-scale, so the resources must be extracted from private enterprises, which was, in the main, the peasantry. The price policy should be designed to compel the peasants to contribute towards

---

[2]The term 'price-scissors' is believed to come from Russia, and is so-called because the diagram of the relative prices of industrial and agricultural goods looks like a pair of scissors.

socialist development, via the process, known in his book, as 'primitive socialist accumulation' (Preobrazhensky, 1926).

In the debate of Soviet industrialization in the 1920s, Preobrazhensky proposed that: (1) the state can increase its capital accumulation by manipulating the terms of trade against peasants; and (2) by manipulating the terms of trade against peasants, the welfare of the industrial workers will not deteriorate (Preobrazhensky, 1926).

Further to Preobazhensky's propositions, Sah and Stiglitz developed a theoretical model based on price-scissors by formalizing the optimal terms of trade against peasants, which encouraged further academic analysis of the issues concerning price-scissors (Sah & Stiglitz, 1984). For example, Cater extended Sah and Stiglitz's framework from a closed economy to an open one, with a consideration of the export of agricultural goods (Carter, 1986). This issue was also noted by Blomqvist with regard to indirect agricultural tax (Blomqvist, 1986). Since the debate, it has been generally believed that the two propositions, in most cases, hold true (Baland, 1993; Blomqvist, 1986; Knight, 1995; Sun, 2001), except for Sah and Stiglitz, who argue that Preobrazhensky's second proposition is invalid (Sah & Stiglitz, 1984).

2.2.2   Price Scissors in China

In terms of capital accumulation in China, it is commonly accepted that Chinese pricing has been implicitly against agriculture, with the prices of farm products set low in relation to those of industrial products (Cao & Birchenall, 2013; Riskin, 1987; Zheng, Lambert, Wang, & Wang, 2013). In addition, China introduced the compulsory procurement of grains through a state monopoly of the grain trade from the very early years under the communist control, and set up communes to ensure grain deliveries. Meanwhile, food rationing was practiced for urban residents. As highlighted by Knight and Song, 'some government policies such as the formation of the communes, compulsory procurement of food, and urban rationing of food could be seen to flow from the price-scissors policy' (Knight & Song, 1999: 25). All of these have ensured that resources would be extracted from the rural sector for capital accumulation in the cities, in line with the price-scissors model of socialist industrialization.

For years, researchers have also carried out empirical studies on price-scissors in China. For example, Li and Tsui noted that, when testing Preobrazhensky's first proposition, the relative agricultural price is correlated positively with the capital accumulation, contrary to their theoretical prediction (Li & Tsui, 1990). In a more recent study on price-scissors, Lin and Yu adopted Sah and Stieglitz's model, but extended it to include an open economy that allowed agricultural rationing. Their empirical study has found that, based on panel data from 1949 to 1992, the importance of peasants in China's governmental objective function is less than the importance of workers, and that the importance of consumption is also less than that of capital accumulation (Lin & Yu, 2008).

Similar to the conclusions of most studies, Lin and Yu's study provides empirical evidence that the price-scissors theory is consistent with the reality in China, especially in the central planned period (Lin & Yu, 2008). However, since the late 1970s, reforms have been implemented, causing huge changes in China. The communes were deformed, food rationing was eliminated and state procurement has played a less important role as the economy has become marketized with less state intervention. The producers' price, for example, has been increased substantially. Under these circumstances, it is noted that the price-scissors theory has been a less appropriate description of China in the period of decentralization.

2.3   Urban Bias

After the price-scissors theory, in analysing development concerning the rural and urban sectors, Michael Lipton observed the presence of 'urban bias' in various policy decisions.

2.3.1   The Rationale

Lipton's major argument is that the rural sector in developing countries receives too little funding for education and healthcare, and, in a broader range of public spending decisions, disproportionate to its population size, but rural people are taxed more, paying an unfair share. In addition, urban bias is aggravated by the governments' 'price twist', by which he means that the prices of products are distorted substantially from what they would be under free market conditions, by the state and its agents, who are working against the interests of rural dwellers (Lipton, 1977).

'Urban bias' thus means that the scarce resources are invariably and disproportionately allocated to the urban (or industrial) sector, which aggravates rural poverty. As Lipton put it, 'resource allocations, within the city and the village as well as between them, reflect urban priorities rather than equity or efficiency' (Lipton, 1977: 13).

2.3.2   The Objections

The thesis of 'urban bias' has received much criticism since its birth. Byres attacks 'urban bias' from a class-analytic perspective, asserting that the rural sector is not composed of an undifferentiated mass of rural paupers, but that there are differentiated entities in different developing countries, which not only influence government and its policies but also define the effectiveness and results of such policies (Byres, 1979; Lipton, 1977).

Following Byres, in a more recent article, Karshenas challenged the political economic foundation of the 'urban bias' thesis, emphasizing that the major shortcoming of this approach is that the comparative static analysis of standard general equilibrium theory cannot explain the complex dynamic interactions in the process of agricultural surplus transfer (Karshenas, 1996). To be specific, Lipton's 'urban bias' theory is based on the neo-classical model of equilibrium, which is more concerned with the efficiency of sectoral resource allocation. Such a framework would regard the factors of production and sectoral output as 'substitutes' rather than 'complementary' during the development process. Thus, the theoretical base is misguided, since it asserts that the gains of one (industrial) sector must be at the sacrifice of another (rural sector). This neglects the dynamic interactions between agriculture and industry, as industrial growth is necessary for the progress of agriculture (Karshenas, 1996), so that the successful development of the urban sector contributes to its rural counterpart, contrary to Lipton's proposition. In this way, the 'urban bias' thesis neglects the blurring boundaries between the rural and urban sectors, and the services as well as the benefits that the rural migrants have enjoyed by crossing the rural and urban areas.

Critics of the 'urban bias' theory also attack its embedded problems of definition and measurement. Although it is common practice to identify rural or urban divisions by the population densities, such practice varies greatly across countries. Even within a single country, in defining rural and urban areas, the political elements must be considered. As explained in Chap. 1, in China, there are exceptions in the designation of cities and towns, and the cut-offs are subject to change due to development of society. Meanwhile, through the process of urbanization, a rural area can be easily re-designed as an urban one when the borders of the cities are extended. Jones and Corbridge also disagree with Lipton about counting members of the rural elite as members of the 'urban' population, and members of the urban poor as part of the 'rural' population, in order to account for the differences within the rural sector (Jones & Corbridge, 2010).

What might be more important, despite some evidence and facts about developing countries, the scale of the distorted allocation of services and goods is difficult to specify. Eastwood and Lipton noticed reduced price twists against the countryside decades later. Yet, such a correction of the price distortion has not helped the rural/urban welfare ratios falling towards unity (Eastwood & Lipton, 2002). They attribute this to the offset effects of other factors, due to 'urban bias'. However, this also reflects the difficulty in measuring the 'urban bias'; hence, the question arises of whether the 'facts' indicate an 'urban bias'. According to Overman and Venables, the biases in outcome may not always be the result of wilful distortions by the state. Instead, the apparent 'urban bias' in public expenditure and provision might have become an efficient allocation of resources (Overman & Venables, 2005). According to Jones and Corbridge, not all bias is bad (Jones & Corbridge, 2010).

In addition, there is the problem of potentially underestimating or even ignoring the urban poverty, under the conceptual framework of 'urban bias'. As noticed by Haddad, et al., 'the number of urban poor is increasing; the share the urban poor in overall poverty is increasing; the number of underweight preschoolers in urban areas is increasing; and the share of urban preschoolers is increasing' (Haddad, Ruel, & Garrett, 1999: 1897). In the context of urban poverty, urban bias has lost is its self-evidence.

2.3.3 Urban Bias in China

With regard to China, researchers seem to be more interested in the primitive motivation of distorted polices than the simple applicability of 'urban bias' to the country.

Nolan and White argue that the case of China should be described as a 'state bias', because the underlying reason for the policies is the state's decision for its own sake, rather than the urban sector wielding sufficient power to influence the government decisions (Nolan & White, 1984). This is because the original bias comes from the state's decision to adopt strategies to develop heavy industry in the cities. Later policies could be mostly seen as a flow to achieve this goal. In fact, the Chinese have been taught by the Communist Party for years that 'the state's benefit is superior'.

Oi argues that China's failure to narrow down the income disparities between the urban and rural areas is due to its concerns about the survival of the party-state legitimacy. She believes that 'the improvement in the economic condition of China's rural sector is the result of the efforts of local officials who have been driven neither by urban nor rural bias but by concerns similar to what Robert Bates terms the revenue imperative' (Oi 1993: 131).

Knight and Song offer an explanation that the policies reflect the latent political power of the urban residents, since the government would have to ensure that the urban workers will refrain from political unrest, so that they will not threaten production and the state's revenue as well as its political regime, which is termed by these researchers as 'insurance policy' (Knight & Song, 1999).

Yang and Cai believe that, prior to the reform, there was seldom any political pressure on the state. The sectoral divide was due to the industrial development strategy, which ensured the presence of a constant urban bias, but, since the reforms, the politically powerful urban group has pressurised the government to foster rapid income growth. Since then, the state has maintained urban bias to for the sake of regime stability and political legitimacy (Yang & Cai, 2003). They conclude that urban coalition and their political activities are not necessary conditions for the existence of urban bias. It was the pursuit of industrial development strategies that started the sectoral divide.

2.4   Intersectoral Resource Flows

Closely related to 'urban bias' and 'price scissors' is the concept of intersectoral resource flow.

2.4.1   Implications for Capital Accumulation

The central issue concerning intersectoral resource allocation is the role of agricultural surplus in the early stages of industrialization. Karshenas explains that 'at this level of analysis, the issue of intersectoral resource flows has often revolved around the role of agriculture in generating or releasing resources for rapid industrial accumulation' (Karshenas, 1995: 9); furthermore, he argues that resource flow should be analysed within a dynamic framework, in which technological changes, innovation and interactions between the two sectors should be considered (Karshenas, 1995). Hence, he criticises 'urban bias' as a highly static and generalized notion that cannot capture these. Drawing on the experience of Japan and Taiwan, he finds that 'in a technologically dynamic agriculture, productivity growth can help maintain relative profitability, and hence the inducement to invest in agriculture, despite high taxation and adverse terms of trade movement' (Karshenas, 2004: 188). Therefore, the macroeconomic implications of different agrarian relations are much more complex than suggested in the 'urban bias' thesis.

Existing research has also been interested in the directions of resource flow. However, 'there is a wide gulf between different authors' interpretations of the optimum magnitude and direction of resource flow and the appropriate transfer mechanisms' (Karshenas, 1995: 179). It not only depends on the country and period selected for empirical tests, but also the methodology employed in these tests, as well as the definition of sectors and resources (Nakagane, 1989).

2.4.2   The Direction of Resource Flows in China

In the case of China, complex as the problem is, researchers tend to obtain various results. Ishikawa, in the 1960s, studied the development procedure of underdeveloped countries in Asia, including China. Contrary to the common conception that the early development of industry depends on resource outflow from the agricultural sector, he argues that such a pattern is inappropriate for the 'present day' underdeveloped countries of Asia, as the low productivity in such countries needs a net inflow of resources into the agricultural sector for infrastructure investment in new technologies, such as irrigation (Ishikawa, 1967). He took China as an example of funds inflow into agriculture. In a later study, he finds that, if the 1957 price is adopted, which heavily discriminated against farm goods, then the net resource flows out of agriculture is positive but decreasing in the 1950s and increasingly negative during the 1960s and 70s, indicating an increasing net inflow to agriculture (Ishikawa, 1988).

In Lardy's early work, he is uncertain about the effect of the policies on intersectoral resources flows since 1978, but he believes that significant resources were transferred out of the agricultural sector before 1978 and that this transfer contributed to a remarkable increase in the rate of investment after 1949 (Lardy, 1983). Knight and Song suggest that there has been a substantial net capital flow from the rural to the urban sector, both in the planning and reform periods (Knight & Song, 1999).

Whereas most Chinese scholars generally believe that price-scissors created a net resource outflow from agriculture, Sheng's study reveals that calculated at different base-year prices, there are different import-export balances to be found of the agricultural sector for the period 1952-83 (Sheng, 1993). Yet, more studies agree that in almost the entire reform era, China has been extracting large amount of capital, from agriculture in particular, and the rural sector more general (Huang, Rozelle, & Wang, 2006).

It should be noted that it is difficult to calculate the net intersectoral resource transfer, as once argued by Huang et al., it highly depends on the approach, definition of the sectors under examination and the data sources (Huang et al., 2006). However, recent studies have reached agreement that China once sacrificed agriculture for the development of the manufacturing sector by large amount of intersectoral resource transfer (Cao & Birchenall, 2013; Knight & Ding, 2010; Zheng et al., 2013).

2.5 State-Local Relations

The models and theories discussed above presuppose a core-periphery dualism that society is composed of the modern core and traditional periphery, represented by the rural and urban sectors. Yet, such a dichotomy tends to overlook several noneconomic characteristics (Huang, 1996; Murphy, 2002).

2.5.1 The Centre-Periphery Relation

Shue, a researcher who has studied issues related to China from a sociological perspective, also adopts the centre-periphery model in *The Reach of the State*. However, instead of the typology itself, she pays great attention to the core-periphery relation, as well as the relationship between central and local.

Her centre-periphery model tends to accept that the centre is the social zone possessing the authority, while the periphery is the hinterland on which the authority would be exercised; and the centre has the tendency to extend so that social integration will be achieved to a greater extent (Shue, 1990). This is linked with the Lewis model that, in the course of development, the traditional sector (or the periphery) is gradually modernized and the peasants will be turned into a proletarian, wage-earning class. Shue highlights the central penetration of the periphery of society, and emphasizes the political/administrative integration.

However, the Chinese case is more complicated than the theories and models. The rural sector, after years of development under the Communist Party, is still highly dependent on agriculture, far from completing the modernization transformation, and the central-periphery relation cannot be simplified to in-control and under-control.

2.5.2 The Nomenklatura System

Some researchers have tried to demonstrate the central-periphery relation by examining China's *nomenklatura* system (Edin, 2003b; Oi, 1999; Shue, 1990; Wishnick, 2014). It is clearly that there is horizontal (*kuai*) rule first. Then, each bureaucratic agency is subject to vertical (*tiao*) ministerial rule. Finally, the Chinese Communist Party is in control of both *tiao* and *kuai* rule (Cartier, 2011; Oi, 1999; Smith, 2010). Shue describes the sub-national political structure of Chinese governance as 'criss-crossed' and notes that 'horizontally based and vertically linked offices and authorities met and contended with each other at each tier of state administration' (Shue, 1990).

Administrators at each level are subject to the direct control of their superiors at the upper level. The ministerial control penetrates from the centre all the way down to the county, and the party holds power at all levels (including villages). There is an unwritten rule that officials and leaders at any level (even village cadres) should be Party members. Meanwhile, those at higher ministerial or administrative positions, in most cases, also hold political titles. For example, a county governor might be the secretary of a county Party committee at the same time. This has ensured the comprehensive and effective control of the Communist Party.

2.5.3 The Principal-Agent Problem

Some studies resort to the agency theory to explain central-periphery (or state-local) relations (Edin, 2003b; Huang, 1996; Oi, 1999). They accept the notion that local governments and officials are acting as the agents of the state principal, because they act as administrators who are directly responsible for the local implementation of state policies. As the agency theory holds, the incentives for the agents are the residual or the payments they get from the principal. The theory is, in the Chinese case, translated that local officials are motivated by the profits remaining after the fulfilment of the state tasks. Therefore, the failure of economic growth in the Maoist era is believed to be due to the system in which the localities are denied the right to obtain the residual they have produced (Oi, 1999).

It is believed that the local agents play an important role in China's state-local relations. Such agents were represented by the local gentry class before 1949. Since the foundation of Communist China, the families of the gentry have been replaced by party-led officials and cadres at the lowest level of governments (Shue, 1990).

The conflict between principal and agent seems intrinsic, since the principal needs the agent's full compliance for its interests, but the latter is more interested in what is left by semi-compliance or even defiance. As the lower level officials are from the local areas, they tend to defend the local benefits by deflecting or reducing certain central demands made against them (Oi, 1999; Shue, 1990). Therefore, they will facilitate some beneficial policies but block others(Yang & Yu, 2012), or implement policies selectively (O'Brien & Li, 1999). Undoubtedly, this means that 'the overall impact of state-sponsored social programs and goals on the peasant family was neither deep nor lasting' (Bernstein, 2011: 374).

In China, it is necessary to consider both the criss-crossed governance structure and the *nomenklatura* system, because the lower level government bureaucracy is characterised by a 'nested principal-agent model', so that there are various principals and agents (Oi, 1999). For a local official, his position is decided by the state in the *nomenklatura* system, while his salaries and general well-being are under the direct control of his administrative superiors. The benefits of those principals and agents are interwoven with each other. As a result, 'the effectiveness of central regulations depends on who the regulatory agents are, on their ability to carry out their tasks, and most important, on whose interests are affected when they process the information they unearth' (Oi, 1999: 143).

2.5.4 Local Relations and Central Control

In this complex context, local officials have developed the skills to behave in a temporizing way. They are perfectly clear what attitudes they should adopt towards the centre in different situations. When applying for funds from the state, they take a low profile, emphasizing the difficulty of their financial condition. During inspection for achievement, they will be proud enough to show the work team how much progress they have made. As depicted in Bernstein and Lü, an official from a well-off county dresses in rags, pleading for emergency relief funds, while the one from a poor county wears a suit jacket, reporting fake good news to his supervisors in the hope of obtaining promotion (Bernstein & Lü, 2000).

In most cases, it is common for the localities to show a façade of compliance in order to avoid monitoring by the principal, while also trying to satisfy the local needs. In order to keep more resources within the localities, officials will under-report agricultural production or industrial profits. Unreported funds are not rare among local governments. As researchers find in their studies, local government officials will conceal misconduct that violates central rules and regulations in order to help their enterprises (Lin, Liu, & Tao, 2013). In this sense, the local regulatory agencies are of corporate nature, with the purpose of keeping information from the principal and so avoid its detection (Oi, 1999).

There are also studies that employ economic incentives and an evaluation system to understand the behaviour of local cadres. For example, Whiting has found out that, encouraged by the revenue incentives to keep more profits within the localities but constrained by the cadres' evaluation system, cadres were 'aware at all times of where they stood in terms of fulfilling their key performance targets and where they stood relative to leaders of other townships and villages in their areas' (Whiting, 2006: 101).

During the reform years, debates never stop as to whether the central control is strengthened or undermined. There are concerns that the state's penetration into China's village periphery is 'seldom' and 'undedicated', less complete than could be anticipated from the socialist political models during the Mao period, and that, under the condition of decentralization, the central capacity has been greatly undermined. However, it is commonly believed that Beijing retains the absolute power in the state-local relation, as the centralized appointment system is sufficiently effective to prompt compliance (Mok, 2013; Oi, 1999; Shue, 1990). For example, having examined the cadre responsibility system, Edin concludes that the capacity of the state to control and monitor the lower-level agents has increased in China, corresponding to Huang's findings concerning central local relations (Edin, 2003b; Huang, 1996). During the process of reform, the state has delegated some responsibilities to the localities, which has relieved the financial burden of the centre, but strengthens the overall strategic control. Thus, it is withdrawing its functions in some areas in order to have a broader, more effective control at the macro level (Edin, 2003a).

The state-local relations provide another framework for understanding resource distribution. While the localities are trying to find as much leeway as possible to keep resources within the local area, the centre has been trying to exert effective surveillance for better control. The 1994 fiscal reform, for example, has demonstrated the centre's dissatisfaction with its control of finance.

It might be safe to say that the state and the local area, under the relationship of principal and agent, are in constant battle over resources. Reform and marketization might leave the localities more freedom for operation, but the state retains the powerful tool for the control of the lower-level agents via the *nomenklatura* system (Huang et al., 2006). Meanwhile, the local agents still depend on the principal as its patron for resource allocation. Therefore, the real power of resource distribution still lies with the state. The localities' (agency) capability to negotiate for more resources might, to some extent, depend on its *guanxi* (relationship) with the state (principal), but the question of how many resources can be distributed is ultimately decided by the state's overall strategic development plan.

2.6 Local *Guanxi* and Its Effects

Large volumes of media stories and research have noted the tense relationships and conflicts between cadres and peasants (Cai & Zhu, 2013; Guo, 2001; Walker, 2006). Oppressive taxes and fees, as well as rights over rural land are all among the major reasons for the tense relationships (Cai, 2003; Guo, 2001). Corruption at the local level increased the burden of the peasants (Bernstein & Lü, 2000, 2003), which has worsened the relationship between the two.

2.6.1 Cadre-Peasant Conflicts

Some researchers have conducted community-based studies that shed light on such relations. These studies consider the roles of the local cadres in both affluent and impoverished rural areas. For example, in prosperous regions like Jiangsu, township officials and village cadres take active roles in economic development. The township industries are developing rapidly and the local officials appear to be a strong and increasingly active economic force. In such areas, the cadres are endowed with substantial assets such as production materials, job opportunities, and profits from local industries, which can be used to 'elicit behavioural responses from peasants such as delivery of obligations of agricultural products and payment of taxes' (Rozelle, 1994: 123).

In less developed areas, on the contrary, agriculture remains the dominant industry. As the economic development is largely limited to the land, there are fewer available resources for the cadres. Since the cadres are in actual control of the scarce resources also needed urgently by the peasants, the cadre-peasant relations will deteriorate easily. In these areas, the local leaders have to give directives in a more coercive way, which can worsen the situation. This is consistent with Oi's view, that:

> The key is the sources of income that officials have under their control. In most villages, the determining factor is the degree of local industrialization. Local governments that control a primarily agricultural, particularly grain-based, economy have few options other than to levy ad hoc surcharges and various other fees and penalties...The greater the level of industrialization, the more likely that the local government will act in a corporate manner to intervene, extract and redistribute income'. (Oi, 1999: 191)

Or as found by O'Brian:

> Wealth and a flourishing collective economy appear to ease completion of state tasks and help prevent paralysis of local political organizations by lubricating inherently conflictual relationships and altering cadre and peasant interests. In more developed villages, where many cadres broker semi-marketized relationships and sometimes operate highly profitable enterprises themselves, cadre spirit and energy are generally higher. (O'Brien, 1994: 47)

O'Brien makes the summary that, in flourishing rural areas with more local revenue, the villagers are subject to fewer charges and levies, and the villagers appear to be more dependent on the local cadres at least, because of the working opportunities in the profitable industry and the village public sector. This helps to ease the cadre-peasant tensions and direct the local public sector to develop in a more cooperative way. In contrast, in poorer villages, the cadres would pay more attention to their own benefits and less to the village public affairs, except for the tasks assigned to them by the state. Studies indicate that, at least in post-reform China, resources are a major factor in the formation of cadre-peasant relations (O'Brien, 1994).

This has also confirmed that the local cadres' real intention in protecting the local area is, in fact, closely related to their own benefits instead of those of the local area as a whole. For example, some local cadres are believed to be out of sight and out of range of the peasants' frustration. They usually would not exhibit any strong concern to raise productivity and peasant living standards (Unger, 1989).

Scholars have also studied cadres' intensions. Rozelle, for instance, categorizes the cadres' goals into six types, being their status promotion, job security, independence from officials at higher levels, personal profit and commitment to the village. The top five goals are all related to the safety of their personal well-being, and he puts commitment to the village as the last goal for the cadres (Rozelle, 1994). There exist other research findings that the local agents are responsive to their superiors only in order to meet the performance targets but refuse to comply with regard to burden reduction, as extraction from the peasants is believed to be necessary in order to meet other performance goals, and such performance is in direct relation with their promotion and job security (Bernstein & Lü, 2000).

The current study will avoid the tendency to make the hasty conclusion that the lower level officials are devoted to their locality and the benefits of the peasants, or that the local cadres are ignorant of the villagers, but will derive its understanding from first-hand data. At the same time, the authors believe that cadre-peasant relations will be better understood with the help of the *guanxi* network.

2.6.2 *The* Guanxi *Network*

Literally meaning relation or relationship, *guanxi* is closely related to social capital (Qi, 2013; Smart, 1993). In studies exploring social capital in China, *guanxi* is often depicted as its Chinese variant (Knight & Yueh, 2008). It is believed to be 'a form of social network that defines one's place in the social structure and provides security trust and a prescribed role' (Hammond & Glenn, 2004), and also described as a 'mechanism by which individuals are able to achieve personal, family or business objectives' (Bell, 2000). Without a universally accepted definition, however, *guanxi* is usually treated as the simple term of 'social connections'.

The *guanxi* network in China is unique in the following aspects. First, it exists within the context of a gift economy, and such '*art of guanxi*' extends into the economic and political realms. Yang believes 'it has the sense of social connections, connections which must be carefully initiated, preserved and renewed through the giving and receiving of gifts, favours and dinners or banquets' (Yang, 1988: 411). Therefore, gift giving is an important way of maintaining the existing *guanxi*, and there has been a congruence between the size of the gifts and the pre-existing relationships. Meanwhile, apart from managing the existing closeness of *guanxi*, gifts are also used to establish new *guanxi*. Therefore, a gift reflects how the *guanxi* was, how it is and how it is expected to be developed (Kipnis, 1997).

Second, *guanxi* is closely linked with 'face' (*mianzi*) (Au, 2014; Chan, Song, Wright, & Wright, 2015; Chen & Kim, 2013). Without a pre-existing relationship, nonrelated parties lack the *mianzi* to face each other in gift giving (Kipnis, 1997). Therefore, intermediaries must be used, and they are usually friends or friends of friends who connect the two parties. The giving at the beginning of relationships acts as a starting point for *guanxi*. It is also believed that developing *guanxi* aims at building up symbolic capital. In China, this symbolic capital takes the form of *mianzi*. In gift giving, the giver increases the *mianzi* and thus 'becomes the moral and symbolic superior of the recipient and can thus subject to the latter to his or her will' (Yang, 1989: 43). Therefore, a good *guanxi* relation is based on the Chinese style of reciprocity (Graham & Lam, 2003). Favours have to be remembered and returned, although not always very quickly, and all these reciprocal gift giving is based on maintaining of *mianzi*.

Third, and most important, it is the feature of Chinese society that *guanxi* is also imbedded in everyday work, apart from general social connections. In fact, the existing literature has widely discussed the use of *guanxi* to acquire power, status and resources in China. Officials generally believe that, without a good *guanxi*, especially with those in charge, they can never do a good job. Scholars have noticed that the cadres' power depends not on their office but on their own ability to mobilize resources (Oi & Rozelle, 2000). It is believed by the local cadres that resources cannot be mobilized without good *guanxi* with the upper-level officials. This was confirmed by Tsai in her fieldwork, where, according to a village head in Fujian: 'Whether or not you get money from the township after you write up a report for a public project depends on whether there are good connections (*guanxi hao*) and good feelings (*ganqing hao*) between you and the township Party secretary…' (Tsai, 2002: 3).

Accordingly, the local cadres and officials will spare no expense in mainstreaming a good *guanxi* or developing a better one with the superiors. In poorer areas, such *guanxi* is maintained sometimes at the expense of the peasants' rights and shares of resources. It does not rule out the possibility that some local cadres may embezzle the public funds as gifts for the convenience of their future work or for their potential promotion, or even for success in gaining more funding. For them, a good *guanxi* will facilitate a funding application from the above and accrue more resources for local use. Therefore, in a society with a long tradition of rule by men instead of rule by law, having good *guanxi* with officials has always been vital (Ying, 2002).

Moreover, *guanxi* networks help members to manage and survive in an adverse economic environment, i.e. a political hostile or discriminatory environment. Therefore, *guanxi* networks are seen as a response to and substitute for weak state and economic environments (Hendrischke, 2004). It has been found that, with the support of networks, 'one group of actors positively discriminate "outsiders" and in favour of members of their own group' (Krug & Hendrischke, 2003: 132). This has made cronyism and nepotism a network-based form of corruption. Therefore, *guanxi* supports nepotism and discriminates against those without it, particularly those without any connections or access to power (Zhang & Li, 2003). Ying even argues that 'there is no business *guanxi* network that is not tinted by corruption and no corruption without using *guanxi*' (Ying, 2002: 377). As a consequence, *guanxi* can be taken as a synonym for corruption and other wrongdoing, such as bribery and fraud (Ying, 2002), and therefore, is closely related to corruption.

2.6.3 The Role of Corruption

If the state, officials and peasants are placed on the same network, a principal-agent-client framework is set up, with the state at the top being the principal, the officials in the middle as the agents and the peasants at the bottom as clients. Of course, this is the simplified relationship network, as, between the state and peasants, are the officials at different levels with various embedded patron-client relationships. Such a principal-agent-client model is adopted by Klitgaard when analyzing corruption (Klitgaard, 1988). Contrary to the common analysis that there are two parties involved in corrupt transactions—the briber and the bribed for example—Klitgaard suggests that there are always three actors in such transactions. This is because, in most cases, the corruption not only involves transactions between agents and clients but also an abuse of the relationship between the agents and principal, such as in internal fraud. It is also noted that agents have to be involved for corruption to be defined, so that in a corruption transaction at least one would hold a post of public trust or exercise a public role (LaPalombara, 1994). On the other hand, if the clients abuse their relationship with the principal, such as in tax fraud, it is not considered as corruption, as it does not include an agent of the state (Galtung, 1998). In this sense, agents or state officials play a vital role in corruption.

In China, with the process of market reform and corresponding decentralization, the state officials have been given more authority not only in terms of the direct control over the implementation of the state policies and resource allocation, but also in terms of the decision-making and local management. It is argued scholarly that the greatest beneficiaries of decentralization in the context of marketization have been the party-state authorities at the middle and lower-middle levels of the system (Shue, 1994). Studies have shown that, since the 1990s, the officials in China have been exposed to more opportunities to accrue wealth by illegal means, because official power has the potential to create tangible wealth and, for many people, power becomes meaningful only when it creates wealth. According to Gong's comments, 'as the relationship between power and wealth draws even closer, the utility of political power as a means to acquiring assets still holds.

Wealth holds a stronger influence over power than before' (Gong, 2002: 101). As devolution occurs from the upper levels, the local officials have been granted more opportunities yet fewer constraints for using and abusing their power. In many areas of resource allocation, the local officials have become the ultimate authorities in deciding who will get what and how and when. Gong believes that decentralization has little accountability and results in the localization of corruption (Gong, 2006).

In terms of resource allocation, it is generally agreed that corruption distorts the government decisions. Corruption is found likely to benefit those who are better-connected in society and who belong mostly to the high-income groups (Tanzi, 1995). It is also noted that corruption undermines poverty reduction by reducing the social services available to the poor, directing higher investment in capital-intensive projects and lower investment in labor-intensive projects (Rose-Ackerman & Palifka, 2016). Empirical studies have also confirmed that corruption increases income inequality, and that its impact on income and poverty is huge (Gupta, Davoodi, & Alonso-Terme, 2002).

Scholars have also been interested in whether the influence of corruption undermines economic development. The general view is that corruption is harmful to economic performance in investment, government expenditure and foreign aid, thus reduce growth. So far, it has been indicated that the South Asian countries fit the concept better that corruption is associated with slow growth (Khan, 1998). However, there are examples of countries with both high corruption and a high growth rate.

Khan has attributed different economic performances across countries to their differentiated patron-client relationships (Khan, 1998), arguing that the relative political power of clients determines the type of payoff they will offer to the patron. If they are weak politically, the patrons are inclined to take the maximum economic payoff exchange of the right being created. In his words, 'the payoff to the patron in this case is not just the value of the bribe paid to state officials and politicians but also the political support (or absence of political opposition) which is often also offered' (Khan, 1998: 26). Thus, the critical factor in determining the difference in the rights transacted between patrons and clients in different settings is the relative power of competing groups of clients and their patrons in the states. Such different patterns help us to understand the different performances of the countries as well as the economic impact of the corruption.

This book adopts the concept of urban bias and resource flows. The urban bias argument emphasizes that resources have been transferred out of agriculture under urban-biased policies, resulting in rural poverty in these countries. Different from existing literature related to urban bias on intersectoral resource flows in examining the role of agricultural surplus or extraction in the process of economic development, this book employs the idea of resource flows, but emphasizes its influence on individuals. Here, focus is place on resource flows guided by state policies in and out of rural and urban sectors, rather than the interactions between the two; and on how individual income (especially rural income) has been influenced by such resource allocation. The definition of rural and urban is also slightly different from that in urban bias thesis, as the division of rural and urban is based on household registration, the unique system in China. That is, there is urban population in rural areas. The coexistence of rural and urban residents in the countryside not only transcends the spatial definition of 'urban bias', but also helps us to understand the allocation of resource and wealth between rural and urban populations in the rural setting, thus provides a new perspective in examining rural–urban income inequality in China.

References

Au, A. K. M. (2014). Influence of Shouren Guanxi, Mianzi and Renqing on ethical judgement of Chinese professionals. *World, 5*(1), 54–61.

Baland, J.-M. (1993). The economics of price scissors: A defence of Preobrazhensky. *European Economic Review, 37*(1), 37–60.

Bell, D. (2000). Guanxi: A Nesting of Groups1. *Current Anthropology, 41*(1), 132–138.

Bernstein, T. P. (2011). *The reach of the state: Sketches of the Chinese body politic, By ShueVivienne*. Stanford: Stanford University Press (1988. x, 175 pp. $25.00. *The Journal of Asian Studies, 48*(2), 373–375).

Bernstein, T. P., & Lü, X. (2000). Taxation without representation: Peasants, the central and the local states in reform China. *The China Quarterly, 163*, 742–763.

Bernstein, T. P., & Lü, X. (2003). *Taxation without representation in contemporary rural China* (Vol. 37). Cambridge: Cambridge University Press.

Blomqvist, A. G. (1986). The economics of price scissors: Comment. *The American Economic Review, 76*(5), 1188–1191.

Byres, T. J. (1979). Of neo-populist pipe-dreams: Daedalus in the third world and the myth of urban bias. *The Journal of Peasant Studies, 6*(2), 210–244.

Cai, Y. (2003). *Collective ownership or cadres' ownership?*. The China Quarterly: The non-agricultural use of farmland in China.

Cai, Y., & Zhu, L. (2013). Disciplining local officials in China: The case of conflict management. *China Journal,* (70), 98–119.

Cao, K. H., & Birchenall, J. A. (2013). Agricultural productivity, structural change, and economic growth in post-reform China. *Journal of Development Economics, 104*, 165–180.

Carter, M. R. (1986). The economics of price scissors: Comment. *The American Economic Review, 76*(5), 1192–1194.

Cartier, C. (2011). Urban growth, rescaling, and the spatial administrative hierarchy. *Provincial China, 3*(1).

Chan, S. H., Song, Q., Wright, A. M., & Wright, S. (2015). The effects of Mianzi and professional relationship Guanxi on Auditor fraud detection. *Journal of Forensic & Investigative Accounting, 7*(2).

Chen, J., & Hu, B. (1994). China's triplex economic structure and surplus rural transfer. *Economic Research Journal, 3*, 14–22.

Chen, J., & Kim, S. (2013). A comparison of Chinese consumers' intentions to purchase luxury fashion brands for self-use and for gifts. *Journal of International Consumer Marketing, 25*(1), 29–44.

Eastwood, R., & Lipton, M. (2002). Pro-poor growth and pro-growth poverty reduction: Meaning, evidence, and policy implications. *Asian development review, 18*(2), 22–58.

Edin, M. (2003a). State capacity and local agent control in China: CCP cadre management from a township perspective. *The China Quarterly, 173*, 35–52.

Edin, M. (2003b). Remaking the communist party-state: The cadre responsibility system at the local level in China. *China: An International Journal, 1*(01), 1–15.

Galtung, F. (1998). Criteria for sustainable corruption control. *The European Journal of Development Research, 10*(1), 105–128.

Gong, T. (2002). Dangerous collusion: corruption as a collective venture in contemporary China. *Communist and Post-Communist Studies, 35*(1), 85–103.

Gong, T. (2006). Corruption and local governance: the double identity of Chinese local governments in market reform. *The Pacific Review, 19*(1), 85–102.

Graham, J. L., & Lam, N. M. (2003). The Chinese negotiation. *Harvard Business Review, 81*(10), 82–91.

Guo, X. L. (2001). Land expropriation and rural conflicts in China. *China Quarterly,* (166), 422–439.

Gupta, S., Davoodi, H., & Alonso-Terme, R. (2002). Does corruption affect income inequality and poverty? *Economics of Governance, 3*(1), 23–45.

Haddad, L., Ruel, M. T., & Garrett, J. L. (1999). Are urban poverty and undernutrition growing? Some newly assembled evidence. *World Development, 27*(11), 1891–1904.

Hammond, S. C., & Glenn, L. M. (2004). The ancient practice of Chinese social networking: Guanxi and social network theory. *EMERGENCE-MAHWAH-LAWRENCE ERLBAUM-, 6*(1/2), 24.

Hendrischke, H. (2004). The role of social capital, networks and property rights in China's privatization process. *China's Rational Entrepreneurs,* 97–118.

Huang, Y. (1996). Central-local relations in China during the reform era: The economic and institutional dimensions. *World Development, 24*(4), 655–672.

Huang, J., Rozelle, S., & Wang, H. (2006). Fostering or stripping rural China: Modernizing agriculture and rural to urban capital flows. *Developing Economies, 44*(1), 1.

Ishikawa, S. (1967). Economic development in Asian perspective. *Economic development in Asian perspective.*

Ishikawa, S. (1988). *Patterns and processes of intersectoral resource flows: Comparison of cases in Asia.* Basil Blackwell, Oxford: The State of Development Economics.

Islam, N., & Yokota, K. (2008). Lewis growth model and China's industrialization. *Asian Economic Journal, 22*(4), 359–396.

Jones, G. A., & Corbridge, S. (2010). The continuing debate about urban bias the thesis, its critics, its influence and its implications for poverty-reduction strategies. *Progress in Development Studies, 10*(1), 1–18.

Karshenas, M. (1995). *Industrialization and agricultural surplus: a comparative study of economic development in Asia.* Oxford: Oxford University Press.

Karshenas, M. (1996). Dynamic economies and the critique of urban bias. *The Journal of Peasant Studies, 24*(1–2), 60–102.

Karshenas, M. (2004). 'Urban bias', intersectoral resource flows and the macroeconomic implications of agrarian relations: The historical experience of Japan and Taiwan. *Journal of Agrarian Change, 4*(1–2), 170–189.

Khan, M. H. (1998). Patron—Client Networks and the economic effects of corruption in Asia. *The European Journal of Development Research, 10*(1), 15–39.

Kipnis, A. B. (1997). *Producing guanxi: Sentiment, self, and subculture in a north China village.* US: Duke University Press.

Kirkpatrick, C., & Barrientos, A. (2004). *The Lewis Model after fifty years.* Manchester: University of Manchester, Institute for Development Policy and Management (IDPM).

Klitgaard, R. (1988). *Controlling corruption.* California: University of California Press.

Knight, J. (1995). Price scissors and intersectoral resource transfers: Who paid for industrialization in China? *Oxford Economic Papers,* 117–135.

Knight, J., & Ding, S. (2010). Why does China invest so much? *Asian Economic Papers, 9*(3), 87–117.

Knight, J., & Song, L. (1999). *The rural-urban divide: Economic disparities and interactions in China.* Oxford: OUP Catalogue.

Knight, J., & Yueh, L. (2008). The role of social capital in the labour market in China1 *Economics of Transition, 16*(3), 389–414.

Knight, J., Deng, Q., & Li, S. (2011). The puzzle of migrant labour shortage and rural labour surplus in China. *China Economic Review, 22*(4), 585–600.

Krug, B., & Hendrischke, H. (2003). The economics of corruption and cronyism—An institutional approach to the reform of governance. In *Corruption and Governance in Asia* (pp. 131–148). New York: Springer.

LaPalombara, J. (1994). Structural and institutional aspects of corruption. *Social research*, 325–350.

Lardy, N. R. (1983). *Agricultural prices in China* (Vol. 1). Washington, DC: World Bank.

Le Mons Walker, K. (2006). 'Gangster capitalism' and peasant protest in China: The last twenty years. *The Journal of Peasant Studies, 33*(1), 1–33.

Li, D., & Tsui, K. Y. (1990). The generalized efficiency wage hypothesis and the scissors problem. *Canadian Journal of Economics*, 144–158.

Lin, J., & Yu, M. (2008). *The economics of price scissors: An empirical investigation for China*. China: China Center for Economic Research (CCER) Peking University.

Lin, J. Y., Liu, M., & Tao, R. (2013). Deregulation, decentralization, and China's growth in transition. *Law and economics with Chinese characteristics: Institutions for promoting development in the twenty-first century. Oxford University Press, Oxford*, 467–490.

Lipton, M. (1977). *Why poor people stay poor: urban bias in world development*. US: Harvard University Press.

Liu, S. (2014). Characteristics, problems and reform of China's dual urban-rural land tenure. *International Economic Review, 3*, 9–25.

Mok, K.-H. (2013). *Centralization and decentralization: Educational reforms and changing governance in Chinese societies* (Vol. 13). New York: Springer Science & Business Media.

Murphy, R. (2002). *How migrant labor is changing rural China*. Cambridge: Cambridge University Press.

Nakagane, K. (1989). Intersectoral resource flows in China revisited: Who provided industrialization funds? *The Developing Economies, 27*(2), 146–173.

Nolan, P., & White, G. (1984). Urban bias, rural bias or state bias? Urban-rural relations in post-revolutionary China. *The Journal of Development Studies, 20*(3), 52–81.

O'Brien, K. J. (1994). Implementing political reform in China's villages. *The Australian Journal of Chinese Affairs*, (32), 33–59.

O'Brien, K. J., & Li, L. (1999). Selective policy implementation in rural China. *Comparative Politics*, 167–186.

Oi, J. C. (1993). Reform and urban bias in China. *The Journal of Development Studies, 29*(4), 129–148.

Oi, J. C. (1999). *Rural China takes off: Institutional foundations of economic reform*. California: University of California Press.

Oi, J. C., & Rozelle, S. (2000). Elections and power: The locus of decision-making in Chinese villages. *The China Quarterly, 162*, 513–539.

Overman, H. G., & Venables, A. J. (2005). *Cities in the developing world*. London: Centre for Economic Performance, London School of Economics and Political Science.

Preobrazhensky, E. (1926). *The new economics* (B. Pearce, Trans., with an Introduction by A. Nove). Oxford: Clarendon.

Qi, X. (2013). Guanxi, social capital theory and beyond: Toward a globalized social science. *The British journal of sociology, 64*(2), 308–324.

Riskin, C. (1987). *China's political economy: The quest for development since 1949*. USA: Oxford University Press.

Rose-Ackerman, S., & Palifka, B. J. (2016). *Corruption and government: Causes, consequences, and reform*. Cambridge: Cambridge university press.

Rozelle, S. (1994). Decision-making in China's rural economy: The linkages between village leaders and farm households. *The China Quarterly, 137*, 99–124.

Sah, R. K., & Stiglitz, J. E. (1984). The economics of price scissors. *The American Economic Review, 74*(1), 125–138.

Sheng, Y. (1993). *Intersectoral resource flows and China's economic development*. New York: Springer.

Shue, V. (1990). *The reach of the state: Sketches of the Chinese body politic*. US Stanford University Press.

Shue, V. (1994). *State power and social organization in China* (pp. 65–88). : State power and social forces: Domination and transformation in the third world.

Smart, A. (1993). Gifts, bribes, and guanxi: A reconsideration of Bourdieu's social capital. *Cultural Anthropology, 8*(3), 388–408.

Smith, G. (2010). The hollow state: rural governance in China. *The China Quarterly, 203*, 601–618.

Sun, L. (2001). Price scissors, rationing, and coercion: an extended framework for understanding primitive socialist accumulation. *Economics of Planning, 34*(3), 195–213.

Tanzi, V. (1995). Corruption: arm's-length relationships and markets. *The Economics of Organized Crime*, 161–182.

Tsai, L. L. (2002). Cadres, temple and lineage institutions, and governance in rural China. *The China Journal*, (48), 1–27.

Unger, J. (1989). State and peasant in post-revolution China. *The Journal of Peasant Studies, 17*(1), 114–136.

Whiting, S. H. (2006). *Power and wealth in rural China: The political economy of institutional change*. Cambridge: Cambridge University Press.

Wishnick, E. (2014). Chinese state responses to pressures from below: Old methods for new challenges? *International Studies Review, 16*(1), 115–118.

Yang, M. M.-H. (1988). The modernity of power in the Chinese socialist order. *Cultural Anthropology, 3*(4), 408–427.

Yang, M. M.-H. (1989). Between state and society: The construction of corporateness in a Chinese socialist factory. *The Australian Journal of Chinese Affairs*, (22), 31–60.

Yang, D. T., & Cai, F. (2003). The political economy of China's rural-urban divide. *How Far Across the River*, 389–416.

Yang, A., & Yu, Y. (2012). Selective pressurizing-responding: An organizational study of the behavior logic of the community residents'committee. *Sociological Studies, 4*, 1–23.

Ying, F. (2002). Guanxi's consequences: Personal gains at social loss. *Journal of Business Ethics, 38*(4), 371–380.

Zhang, X., & Li, G. (2003). Does guanxi matter to nonfarm employment? *Journal of Comparative Economics, 31*(2), 315–331.

Zhang, X., Yang, J., & Wang, S. (2011). China has reached the Lewis turning point. *China Economic Review, 22*(4), 542–554.

Zheng, S., Lambert, D., Wang, S., & Wang, Z. (2013). Effects of agricultural subsidy policies on comparative advantage and production protection in China: An application with a policy analysis matrix model. *Chinese Economy, 46*(1), 20–37.

Chapter 3
Institutions and Policy Making

Government policies and institutions are the driving forces behind resource flows at the macro-economic level. This chapter examines the major policies and institutions that have directed the intersectoral resource flows, which ultimately have an impact on rural income as well as rural–urban income disparities.

3.1 The Household Registration (*hukou*) System

In China, every household is issued with a registration shown in a booklet (known as *hukou*), which officially identifies the members of the household as residents of an area, giving information such as the names, births, deaths, marriages, divorces and addresses of all of the family members. More importantly, each *hukou* falls into one of the two categories: agricultural or non-agricultural, known as rural or urban. The type of *hukou* determines the public services and benefits to which its holder is entitled. Since the urban *hukou* is associated with many privileges with regard to social benefits, the registration system has become a major determinant of the urban-rural disparities (Whyte, 2010).

3.1.1 Review of the hukou System

The first regulation concerning household registration was introduced with regard to cities in 1951, known as the *Temporary Regulation on Urban Hukou Management*. The purpose of regulation was to maintain social safety, as it stipulated the need to 'safeguard the social order' and 'ensure freedom of residence and migration'. A more restrictive directive was issued in 1955 concerning the

© Shanghai Jiao Tong University Press and Springer Nature Singapore Pte Ltd. 2018
Y. Gao and S. Fennell, *China's Rural–Urban Inequality in the Countryside*,
https://doi.org/10.1007/978-981-10-8273-3_3

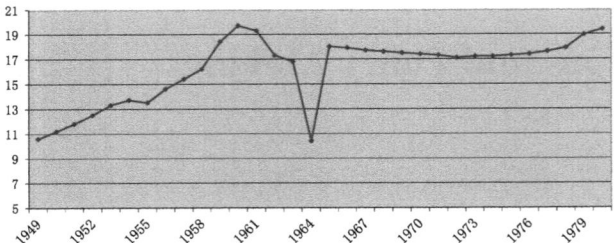

Fig. 3.1 Percentage of urban population against the total in China 1949–1980 (%). *Source* China Statistics Yearbooks

establishment of a permanent household registration system, which unified the *hukou* system nationwide.[1]

Alongside household registration, food rationing was implemented in 1955. Coupons for low-priced food were provided for all urban households every month according to the occupants' age, vocation and labour intensity. With these, the urban residents could buy basic staples, such as grain, meat, edible oil, and sugar from the state food stores.[2] Among other opportunities that the rural residents were excluded from were urban employment and the associated subsidized housing, medical care, pensions, as well as education. The urban-rural divide began to enlarge and the cities became more attractive to rural dwellers, as the purpose of the hukou system was subsequently extended to resource allocation. During this period, a large number of peasants left the rural areas to find work in the urban factories.

As Fig. 3.1 indicates, from 1949 until the early 1960s, the percentage of the urban population rose rapidly, despite a slight decline in 1955, when household registration became more restrictive.

Several considerations of the central government attributed to the tight control of migration after the late 1950s. On the one hand, the government was determined to safeguard the collectivist movement in rural areas to raise agricultural production and support industrialization, and, on the other, the rapid migration to the cities had alerted the government to the problems of food shortages and to the need to reduce the food demand in the cities. The failure of the Great Leap Forward (started in 1958), followed by the Great Famine (1959–1961), finally led the government to exercise strict administrative control over migration.

Despite the fact that, between 1959 and 1961, at least 30 million people (mostly in rural areas) starved to death during the Great Famine, the government took action to send more than 20 million urban dwellers, who had previously been recruited from rural areas, back to the countryside in the early 1960s. This is reflected in Fig. 3.1 that the decline in the percentage of the urban population started in 1962.

---

[1]Some scholars have argued that the 1955 directive was issued in response to the huge influx of farmers into the cities (Liu, 2005).

[2]Food rationing was abolished in 1993.

The stringency of household registration and migration control at the end of the famine segregated the rural and urban sectors.

In 1963, the Ministry of Public Security separated the population into agricultural and non-agricultural, according to whether they were rationed with commodity grains. The government established 'two tough constraints' on the movement from the countryside to the small towns and from the small towns to the cities. In 1977, the State Council stated that a tough constraint on migration to the towns and cities was the Party's important policy during the time of socialist construction.[3] Because of the rigid policies of that period, migration to the cities was restricted,[4] as the percentage of the urban population remained stable from the mid-1960s to the end of the 1970s (Fig. 3.1).

The strict control of migration did not mean that the people could not move. Indeed, they could move anywhere they wished (Yang, 2000). However, without government approval, migrants were unable to register in the cities. Accordingly, they had no access to housing, food or daily necessities. In the central planned era, when the free market did not exist, unofficial migrants were unable to survive in the cities. Migration was thus controlled under the *hukou* system, with the urban residents' benefits well protected.

The *hukou* system did not show any relaxation until after the 1978 reform, when the following factors made it possible. Firstly, the household responsibility system greatly improved grain production and the problem of the food shortage was solved. With the alleviation of the food demand, rationed coupons played a less important role with the emergence of a free market for grains in the cities, enabling the rural migrants to survive in the cities outside the ration system associated with registration. Secondly, the abolition of the collective and commune system freed the peasants to work in the industrial and service sectors. Under the commune system, all adults were required to participate in agricultural production, but now the peasants were able to decide whether to work outside agriculture. Further, the early stage of the reforms in the rural sector greatly improved the efficiency of agricultural production, thus creating a large worker surplus in rural areas (Johnson, 1988; Liang, 2001; Lin, 1988; Yang, 2000).

Accordingly, more rural dwellers were allowed to move to the towns. The Ministry of Agriculture estimated that, in the early 1980s, there were fewer than two million rural labour migrants in the cities. This number had increased to 50–70 million by the early 1990s (Solinger, 1999), or some estimated it to vary from 80 to 150 million (Brooks & Tao, 2003).[5] However, Compared with the total amount of

---

[3]*Regulations on Dealing with Household Registration Change*, Ministry of Public Security, 1977.

[4]Migration did take place during the Cultural Revolution (1966–1976), when many urban cadres, students and intellectuals were *xiafang* (sent down) to the countryside to be re-educated by the peasants. At the same time, peasant labourers were brought in for urban construction and industrialization. Therefore, this was a period of the huge exchange of urban and rural labour (Chan, 1994). As these peasant labourers were usually 'temporary' or 'contract' workers, they were not given an urban *hukou* and not categorized as the urban population, as described in Fig. 3.1.

[5]Estimates of migrants vary in China, as most of them are unofficial and undocumented.

migration, the number of permanent migrants (who had changed their *hukou* status to non-agricultural) was negligible mainly due to the rigidity of the *hukou* system and other corresponding policies.

3.1.2   *The Rigidity of the* hukou *System*

The *hukou* system has been described as an 'invisible Great Wall', which created and maintained the rural–urban divide in China since the mid-1950s, and it has been so rigid that can hardly be changed (Knight & Song, 1999). Zhao points out the stringency of the *hukou* system and the difficulties involved in changing one's status from rural to urban:

> Under the *hukou* system, there are basically three exit routes for rural people, but none is convenient. One route is to unite with spouse or parent(s) or to be adopted by a childless close relative. In each of the three cases, the relationship must be established before the residence can be changed. And the option of spousal migration is relevant only to rural women because rural men are generally considered undesirable by urban women. Furthermore, this is not a guaranteed route – many spouses of urban workers are barred from an urban *hukou* for years. The second route is to wait for urban recruitment. Occasionally when urban factories cannot find enough urban workers to fill jobs, rural workers are hired and given urban *hukou*. However, this type of opportunity is very rare and cannot be predicted and counted on. The third way of changing from rural to urban *hukou* is to be admitted to a college or promoted in the army. College students and demobilized army officers are usually guaranteed urban *hukou*, but these are extremely narrow routes, and competition is fierce. In sum, rural people basically cannot count on the change of registration status to go to cities. (Zhao, 2000: 19)

In addition to the regular methods for changing one's rural status, the government also introduced some special channels for obtaining an urban *hukou*, as the regular procedures explained above are closed to most people. In 1984, the Ministry of Public Securities issued the *Notice on Problems of Peasants' Change of Hukou Registration in the Cities*, which allowed the peasants to settle in the towns and cities, and obtain an urban *hukou* on condition that they could provide their own food. Such an urban *hukou* was called 'food grain self-supplied' (*zilikouliang*) *hukou*. This is equivalent to the fact that such *hukou* holders should either own their own business or be employed in the small towns and cities with their own accommodation. Such urban *hukou* were criticized being of more symbolic than practical value in consideration of the actual benefits received, as the *hukou* holders were ineligible to receive state subsidized welfare and not allowed to move to other areas of higher administrative status. If they wished to move, they had to go through the regular procedures. This did offer peasants another way of moving out of the rural areas, but such an urban status was far from true citizenship.

With the elimination of 'food grain self-supplied' *hukou* in 1992, another type of urban *hukou*—'blue stamp' *hukou*[6]—was introduced according to the *Circular on Application of Locally-valid Urban Hukou Registration* issued by the Ministry of Public Security in the same year. 'Blue stamp' *hukou* was open to a wider range of the population in addition to peasants, and applicable not only to small towns but also to large cities. Similar to a formal urban *hukou*, the 'blue stamp' *hukou* differed only in that, if the holder decided to leave the city, he would revert to his original registration status. The principle of issuing such urban *hukou* was based on local benefits and local needs, and entry fees were required to be paid for newcomers. As it was administered by the local urban government, the fees required for 'blue stamp' *hukou* varied across regions, from several thousand yuan in Shandong to hundreds of thousands of yuan in Shanghai, so it was believed to be open to wealthy investors, the educated and professionals, for the local governments all wished to attract such individuals.

For the ordinary peasants, the transfer from a rural status to an urban one is difficult. The 'food grain self-supplied' *hukou* was aimed at the rural population, but was not comparable to the formal urban *hukou*, while the 'blue stamp' *hukou* was almost equivalent to a formal one, but not affordable by peasants, because they were not designed as the ideal holders to bring either investment or professional skills to individual cities.

In 1997, a pilot policy was introduced to allow rural migrants to obtain urban status in designated small towns on the condition that: (1) they had a permanent job with a stable income; and (2) they had had a settled residence for at least two years.[7] It is stipulated that, with the fulfilment of the two requirements, the peasants would be able to settle in small towns and cities as urbanites, entitled to the same educational and other social services as the local residents. In 1998, the *hukou* system was further reformed so that rural residents could be given an urban *hukou* if they invested in or purchased a commercial residence in the city.[8]

The reforms in recent years have been considered as the gradual relaxation of the *hukou* system, but problems still remain. For a successful transfer of *hukou* citywards, there are certain requirements, such as a stable income, permanent residence (or ownership of accommodation), or high-level educational and professional backgrounds. For example, in Nanjing City, the term 'permanent residency' refers to the ownership of property, or residence in accommodation provided by

---

[6]'Blue-stamp' *hukou* was gradually phased out in different cities since 2003.

[7]This practice was extended to all small towns and cities and, further, to some of the larger and capital cities in 2001.

[8]The State Council and Ministry of Public Security in 1998 published 'Several Comments on Some Predominant Problems Concerning Present Household Registration System', which stipulated that: (1) children's registration will follow either the mother or father depending on the decision of the parents (formerly, the children's registration was with the mother); (2) there would be a further relaxation of the policies concerning separated spouses; (3) parents are able to follow their children by transferring their *hukou* to the cities where their children are living; and (4) investment and property purchase in the cities would be encouraged.

enterprises or government departments.[9] In many cities, a 'stable income' means being employed by enterprises or government departments, or running one's own business, but ironically, there is also a requirement that all employees should have an urban *hukou*.

Largely due to the strict requirements, the influence of the relaxed *hukou* system has been severely limited. For example, in Ningbo, Zhejiang Province, among the total of two million migrants, only 30,000 were qualified, through having a stable income and permanent residency, to become holders of local urban *hukou*. In Shijiazhuang, Hebei Province, only 11,000 of the over 300,000 migrant peasants filled in as urban *hukou* holders (Wang, 2005).

3.1.3 *Discrimination Under the* hukou *System*

The *hukou* system has contributed to a series of policy discriminations against peasant migrants. These policies, usually created locally, vary in details throughout the country, but have a substantial impact on migrant peasants, especially in terms of employment, education, and related social welfare (Wu, 2011).

For example, in Beijing, following the central government's austerity programme initiated in late 1988, the Beijing Municipal Government introduced more restrictions on the hiring of outside workers, including the introduction of quotas. This was later expanded into a system of work permit requirements for outside workers and fines for employers who violated the hiring restrictions. In addition to this, after 1996, the Beijing government issued an annual list of jobs closed off to outside workers. The number of these closed occupations increased from 15 in 1996 to 34 in 1997, 36 in 1998 and 103 in 2000 (Fang & Chan, 2000). Institution have segmented labour market, providing temporary migrants with the least opportunities in the cities.

For rural migrants, the urban demand for their labour is the residual once the supply of labour from among the urban residents has been exhausted (Song, 2000). These are '3-D' (demanding, dirty and dangerous) occupations (Solinger, 1999), unattractive and looked down upon by the urbanites. According to the Fifth Population Census in 2000, peasant migrants supplied 80% of construction workers in China. In 2010, data from the Sixth Population Census show that migration labour increased by 80%, and over 75% were employed in the second industry. Therefore, the leading employment for rural migrants is in the fields of construction, industry and services.

Policy discriminations also made working in the cities expensive for rural migrants. In 1995, Beijing introduced regulations entitled the *Rules on Management*

---

[9]*Interim Regulations Concerning Entry of Household Registration of Nanjiang City*, Municipal Government and Public Security Bureau of Nanjing, June 19, 2004.

of Migrant Workers and Businessmen.[10] Before migrating to Beijing, peasants should apply for a 'certificate of out migration' from the local authorities. Prospective employers could apply for employment permits for workers with such certificates. The combination of a migration certificate and employment permit enabled peasants to work legally in Beijing. Before being employed, however, migrant workers must hold four documents: a temporary resident certificate issued at police stations in Beijing; an employment card issued by the Labour Bureau of Beijing; a health certificate (and marriage and childbirth certificates for women aged between 15 and 49 years old) issued by clinics in Beijing, and a certificate of emigration issued by the police of the sending county. Since all these entailed a fee, the cost was high for a migrant worker.

Accompanying employment discrimination is wage discrimination. There were reports that, in the Pearl River Delta, the major destination of migration and one of the most developed coastal areas in China, there had been an income increase of 68 yuan over the 12 years for peasant workers, making an increase of less than 6 yuan per year.[11] If inflation is taken into consideration, the real wage was decreased. Studies have widely shown the wage discrimination against migrant workres (Lee, 2012; Wang, Guo, & Cheng, 2015; Wong, Fu, Li, & Song, 2007). For example, a study with 2003 data from Tianjin found that migrants earned 51% of the urban-registered wage (Lu & Song, 2006); data surveyed from ten Chinese cities in 2005 showed that migrant workers' hourly wages averaged 45% of registered urban workers (Park & Wang, 2010). Even these low wages were not paid on time. According to the National Economic Research Institute, in 2004, there was an estimated 20 billion yuan of unpaid wages to migrant workers. Moreover, according to the National Statistics Bureau, some enterprises would take 20–30% of their workers' wages as a 'deposit', but this was never returned. Social unrest was frequently reported due to the unpaid or delayed wages of migrant workers.

Another example of policy discriminations was the denial of education to the children of migrants, especially in the late 1990s. Since most migrant workers were not urban *hukou* holders, their children (even though some were born in the cities) could not enjoy equal rights in terms of education. Schools would not accept migrant children unless a large sum of money was paid in the form of a donation to the schools. Here is an example: in the Haidian District of Beijing, the fee was at least 10,000 yuan per year per child to attend primary school in 1996, amounted to more than a year's salary for a construction worker (Zhao, 2000).

With regard to housing, in 1995, the Beijing government decreed that any institution or person leasing houses to non-Beijing residents must obtain a house-leasing certificate from the district or county government, and renew it annually. To be eligible for renting out, the house or apartment must be privately owned and certified by the police bureau as meeting the required safety standards. The owner must sign affidavits with the police bureau and the family-planning

---

[10]This was abolished in 2005.

[11]Xinhua News, The Pearl River Delta Encounters Shortage of Migrant Labour, April 19, 2006.

agency, agreeing to be responsible for preventing the commission of crimes in the house or apartment with regard to over-quota births, and must pay an equivalent of 2% of the annual rent. This regulation undoubtedly raised the transaction cost and discouraged house renting to migrants. It is unsurprising that many migrant workers typically live in tents or temporary buildings on the construction sites where they work.

Due to the biased policies, migrant peasants have been discriminated against by both the urbanites and their governments. The hostility towards rural migrants in the cities primarily originates from the urban residents who are unwilling to share their much higher living standards with rural people, especially when the problem of unemployment arises and there are more laid-off workers in the cities. The urban workers, after decades of almost full employment during the pre-reform era and the high wage growth rates during the reform era, are now feeling the pressure of unemployment during the reform process, and naturally blame the migrant workers for this sharp rise in unemployment, although there are differences between the occupations of the rural and urban labourers, and the number of urban workers who are actually affected by the immigrant workers is negligible. In general, peasant migrants are viewed as inferior and uneducated by the urban residents. They have been treated with attitudes ranging from neglect to scorn, and, occasionally, abuse (by the police and their employers) (Zhao, 2000).

The negative view of rural migrants is also adopted by the government and its media. The press generally portrays migrants negatively, as the source of crime, violence, and overcrowding, and has accused them of violating the family-planning policies. China's media have been criticized for being the mouthpiece of the government, which does not usually reflect the views of the public. However, on the issue of rural migration, the government's views are sometimes in line with those of the urban residents. Scholars argue that it is the urban citizens who have exerted a great influence on the government to form such protectionist policies and anti-migration measures that are urban-biased and reinforce the rural–urban disparities (Fang & Chan, 2000).

From the perspective of the peasants, the limited chance of obtaining non-agricultural work in the cities would hinder their income growth. Studies have shown that, at the margins, the return to rural labour engaged in non-agricultural activities is much higher than in farming. One feature of migration is that it provides an opportunity to generate positive marginal returns from labour input that are much higher than those to be obtained from agriculture, and that the marginal return to rural labour engaged in non-farming could be ten times higher than that engaged in farming (Hare & Zhao, 2000). However, the average returns to rural household capital allocated to farming and non-farming activities are approximately the same, while the marginal return to capital from non-farming activities is thirteen times higher than that from farming. The magnitude difference suggests that rural households are unlikely to choose freely to allocate their labour and capital between agriculture and other economic activities in a more efficient way, indicating the existence of insufficient opportunities for local non-agricultural employment and the institutional barriers inhabiting rural–urban migration (Song, 2000). What might be more important, since the free flows of labour between rural and urban sectors are largely hindered by the *hukou* system and its corresponding policies, the peasants' income-generating opportunities have been greatly limited.

Since the establishment of the *hukou* system, its functions have been extended from simply safeguarding public security in the 1950s, to the allocation and distribution of resources during the central planned years via strict migration control. While the function of the original element has been gradually unseen by the public and academic world since the economic reform, its role in maintaining migration control has been paid much attention and it has been found to have remained basically unchanged, despite all of the reforms over the years. The *hukou* system, after years of reforms, still plays a decisive role in constraining personal free migration and contributes to societal segregation (Chan & Zhang, 1999; Zhao & Li, 2006). This has become the basis for understanding resource flows and the allocation between the rural and urban sectors.

3.2   Rural Tax and Fee Burdens

Taxation was the main method for extracting the surplus from agriculture.[12] In China, taxation on agriculture had a history dating back to 594 B.C. For more than two thousand years, in an agricultural country like China, taxation had been the major source of government revenue. Chinese peasants had already taken it for granted that, as long as farming was practiced, agricultural tax had to be paid. They also considered agricultural tax as the 'emperor's grain and state's tax' (*huangliang guoshui*), indicating that it as an unalterable payment.

In the years immediately after 1949, when the People's Republic of China was founded, the agriculture tax used to make a major contribution to government revenue, which was considered helpful in ensuring the regime stability of the state and industrial development nationwide. Figure 3.2 shows that agricultural tax once constituted 39% of total national tax revenue. But agricultural tax, together with various levies, fines and fees, had become a great financial burden to the peasants, and slowed down their income growth.

3.2.1   Types of Taxation

In rural areas, there were three types of burden imposed on peasants: the taxes collected by the central government; levies and fees collected by the village administration and township governments with the approval and supervision of the state; and various other fines and surcharges collected by the local government and

---

[12]Agricultural and related taxes were abolished officially from January, 2006.

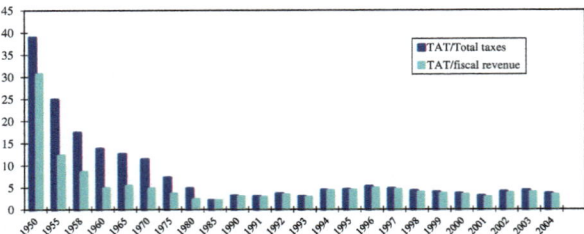

Fig. 3.2 Share of Agricultural Related Taxes in Government Finance. *Source* China Statistic Yearbooks, various issues. *Note* Agricultural related taxes include agricultural tax, animal husbandry tax, the tax on the use of cultivated land, the tax on special agricultural products and the contract tax. The slaughter tax is not included

organizations. While the first category was usually referred to as formal taxes, the other two were 'quasi-taxes', because they were imposed on the peasants by the local administration or higher level governments and, moreover, they were unavoidable (Lu, 1997; Tao & Liu, 2005).

The first type included state taxes levied by the central government. They referred to those agriculture-related taxes, mainly including agricultural tax, animal husbandry tax, tax on the use of cultivated land, tax on special agricultural products and contract tax.

Agricultural tax, also called 'public/state grain' (*gongliang*), was levied on peasants practicing farming proportionally to grain output. An analogous tax was levied on those living by animal husbandry. A special agricultural product tax was levied on certain types of agricultural products from 1994 (Aubert & Li, 2002). This is because with the dramatic changes in production structure, the plantation of certain products, such as cash crops, had been taking the place of grains. The government then introduced a tax to encourage grain cropping in order to guarantee sufficient grain output. Since 1994, the taxes in this category underwent several adjustments. Overall, the rates of taxes had been declining and, after 2004, only tobacco was taxed. Besides, the agricultural-related tax also included a cultivated land use tax and contract tax. These were related to the conversion of cultivated land into non-cultivated land and had less impact on individual peasants compared with the previous ones.

The slaughtering tax was another category imposed on rural households and collected by the central government. It used to levy on a fixed rate per head of cattle slaughtered, but it was not included in the agricultural related tax (Lu, 1997). Because of the strong argument that slaughtering tax constrained the exertion of comparative advantages in certain areas, it was removed from taxation in 2004.

The second type included local levies and fees imposed on peasants. They were the charges that the peasants used to pay to township governments and village administrations. Although not a tax in name, they were considered quasi-taxes because they were also compulsory. At the township level, the peasants paid the *Five tongchou* (unified planned) fees for the following purposes: the nine-year compulsory education, family planning, support for veterans, military training and road construction. The township governments were authorized to pool together the funds for themselves, because the government at higher levels could not provide enough financial support for local development.

At the village level, the peasants had to pay the so-called *Three tiliu* (remained) fees, for the purpose of public accumulated funds, public welfare and administration. Accumulated funds were collected for public use in the villages, such as water conservancy construction and the purchase of fixed assets. The public welfare fund was also intended to support families or individuals with special difficulties, and the administration fees for the daily running of the village organizations (Li, 2003).

The third type referred to the surcharges and fines imposed on peasants for different purposes, such as the violation of rules and regulations, e.g. on family planning. Such fee collections were unauthorized in most cases, but due to financial difficulties, it had become the usual practice for local governments to impose fines and penalties on peasants for the makeup for their revenue shortfalls, and the arbitrary imposition of fines under all kinds of names was rampant in the rural areas throughout China. In 1993, according to the State Council and the General Office of the CPC Central Committee in their joint publication of *Comments on Examination of Rural Fee-paying Items*, there were as many as 122 fee-collecting items to be modified, suspended and immediately cancelled.

Since the 1990s, the informal charges imposed on peasants had been increasing rapidly, and the central government had stipulated clearly that these informal charges (except for government taxes, i.e. *tiliu and tongchou*) should not be more than 5% of the peasants' net income. However, this was out of control in many rural areas.

In addition to the tangible fees and levies, there used to be another burden shouldered by the peasants—unpaid labour. These were usually imposed on the male labourers known as corvees. It was stipulated by the state that peasants should undertake a certain amount of rural voluntary work (*yiwugong*) and accumulated work (*leijigong*).

Rural voluntary work was for public services, like plantations, flood prevention, road construction, the maintenance of school buildings and so on. Each rural labourer should offer five to ten days of voluntary work each year, which would be subject to increase when necessary, such as for flood rescue.[13]

The accumulated labour was for other services, ranging from the construction of farmland irrigation infrastructure to forestation. According to the state, ten to 20 working days should be provided by each rural labourer annually.[14] However, the practice in different regions varied. It was found that, in some regions, the peasants were required to pay the money equivalent instead of offering labour. Some scholars quoted from an internal report of the State Planning Commission: some

---

[13]The State Council, *Management Regulations on Expenses and Labour Undertaken by Peasants*, December 7, 1991.

[14]Ibid.

local governments take advantage of the national corvee labour policy, requiring peasants to contribute corvee labor services, with the real intention of asking rural households to substitute cash for labour (Lin, Tao, Liu, & Zhang, 2002). They also found that, during the 1990s, corvee labour increased rapidly. The average labour contributed 16.4 working days in 1994 and, in 1999, the number increased to 18.2. In some years, it reached 23 working days. The cash equivalent per head in 1998 increased to 89.3 yuan, 130% higher than the 1994 level (Lin et al., 2002).

3.2.2   Features of Rural Taxes and Fees

(1) Small taxes and significant fees

Tax burden for peasants in China was composed of small amount of formal taxes but much of the informal charges. Figure 3.2 indicates shares of agricultural related taxes (formal taxes) paid to the state, in government finance.

Since 1980, there had been a substantial decrease in the ratios of agriculture-related taxes to total taxes collected and to fiscal revenue, which had remained less than 5% during the reform period. Since 1994, the slight increase in both ratios shown in Fig. 3.2 was due to the introduction of other taxes, such as special agricultural products, but on the whole, the contribution of agricultural taxes to the total tax collection and to fiscal revenue had been very limited during the reform years.

For individual peasants, Table 3.1 presents the proportion of agricultural taxes paid to the state as well as *tiliu* and *tongchong*, together with other charges collected

Table 3.1 Rural Burden from Taxes and Fees (billion yuan)

Year	Total tax and fees	Formal taxes	Agriculture related taxes/ rural net income (%)	Informal taxes and levies		Total tax and fees per capita (yuan)	Tax and fees/rural net income (%)
		Agricultural related taxes		*tiliu* and *tongchou*	Other payment		
1990	46.9	8.8	2.3	33.3	4.8	55.8	8.1
1991	51.8	9.1	2.6	36.4	6.4	60.8	8.6
1992	60.3	11.9	3.5	37.3	11.1	71.1	9.1
1993	68.7	12.6	4.0	38.0	18.1	80.7	8.8
1994	95.8	23.1	4.8	46.1	26.6	112.0	9.2
1995	115.4	27.8	4.5	54.8	32.9	134.3	8.5
1996	124.9	36.9	3.8	61.1	26.8	144.4	7.5
1997	137.9	39.7	3.7	70.3	27.9	159.2	7.6
1998	139.9	39.9	3.5	73.0	27.0	161.0	7.4
1999	136.2	42.4	3.6	67.0	26.9	156.6	7.1
2000	135.9	46.5	4.1	62.0	27.4	168.4	7.5

Source China Statistics Yearbooks, various issues

by the local governments. The data show that the informal fees and charges levied on peasants were nearly twice the amount of the agricultural taxes. In 1990, the former was nearly four times the size of the latter. It might be right to say that agriculture-related taxes were only a small part (less than 5%) of the rural net income. But when all of the taxes, fees and other charges were added together, at least 7–9% of the rural net income was taken away.

The total amount of the first category of tax remained fairly stable at about 4% of rural income during the whole period of the 1990s (Table 3.1). The second type included the levies and fees from villages and towns. Although higher than the first group, they were authorized and supervised by a higher-level government. As for the third—the other payment—the official numbers show that it constituted about 20% of the peasants' total tax burden in the 1990s. However, as many local government organizations were in deep financial deficiency, they could neither gain enough funding from the central government nor pool fees in the name of *tiliu and tongchou*, for the state had already mandated that these levies should not be more than 5% of the peasants' net income. Therefore, they took countermeasures by collecting less for *tiliu* and *tongchou*, but much more for all kinds of other names, known as 'other payment' above. Concerning the arbitrary nature of the levies by the local governments and communities, some fees and fines imposed on the peasants were certainly not included in Table 3.1 and difficult to assess.

As a saying goes among Chinese peasants: 'the first tax (from the state) is less, the second tax (fees for *tiliu* and *tongchou*) more, and the third tax (other fees and levies) endless'. In this sense, the peasants' other payments from the official sources are greatly underestimated. This problem has been mentioned in many scholarly studies. For example, Fu drew a conclusion based on a survey of seven counties in Hubei Province that charges (other than agricultural tax and fees for '*tiliu*' and '*tongchou*') were no less than 49% of the total actually paid by the peasants (Fu, 2001). This is consistent with research in Zhejiang Province that such surcharges were 47% of total payments (Chai, Zhou, & Xie, 1999).

Since the mid-1990s, the peasants' burden became heavier due to the arbitrary charges and levies. Especially after the 1994 fiscal reform (which will be discussed in details later in this book), the social contradiction between the peasants and local officials was sharpened. In 2000, a trial reform was first carried out in Anhui Province, with the nature being 'tax-for-fee' (to charge tax instead of fees), merging *tongchou* into an agricultural tax and *tiliu* into agricultural surcharges on it. Apart from agricultural tax and its surcharges paid to the central government, the peasants were not supposed to pay any taxes or fees.

Later, in 2002, the rural tax reform was disseminated throughout China. During 2002–2003, the reform resulted in a drastic drop in the local government revenue. Unfortunately, the most adversely affected area was compulsory education because in the rural areas, education was self-supported, with funding collected from rural households.

Even worse, the transfer payment from the higher government was unable to provide enough subsidies or financial support for the village schools. Soon, in August 2002, a policy was introduced whereby the county government (a higher-level government in rural areas) became responsible for the financial support of rural compulsory education, changing the former practice of relying excessively on peasants and villages. However, it did not offer much help in solving the main problems of financial shortfalls. Instead, the burden was transferred from villages and townships to the county governments in rural areas, which in turn had no alternative but to collect money from the government at a lower level and from the grassroots peasants. Since there was great pressure on the budgets of the local government, there was a rebound of informal fees in some regions. In consequence, a tax reform aimed at reducing the peasants' burden ended up exacerbating it (Kennedy, 2007).

(2) *Regressiveness and Inequity*

Studies show that the tax and fee burden in the rural areas presented a regressive character. Lu studied the tax and fee distribution in five income groups from 1986 to 1999 and found that, the higher the income of the rural household, the lighter the rural tax and fee burden (Lu, 2004). Similar results were found by Lin's study, that poor people were more vulnerable to rural taxation and usually paid higher taxes relative to their income (Lin et al., 2002).

Moreover, regional differences appeared in these studies, in more developed regions rural households had less tax and fee burdens. In regions where agriculture is the leading industry, the rural tax and fee burden of the rural households was heavier than that in regions where agriculture is not dominant (Lu, 2004). In other words, rural taxation rates were found to be higher in low-income provinces than in high-income ones. In more developed provinces, such as Guangdong and Zhejiang, the tax burden was far lower than that of less developed provinces, such as Jilin, Hunan, Henan and Sichuan (Lin et al., 2002).

These studies suggested that people with a lower income in rural areas and less developed regions were taxed more heavily. Usually, the people with the lowest income had the least income from non-agricultural activities, and the less developed areas are more dependent on agriculture; thus, they justify their lower share of the tax burden. The opposite results derived from the studies reflect the regressive character of agricultural taxes.

If we now compare the rural and urban sectors, the divergence will be wider, for the two sectors employ different tax systems.

Firstly, there has always been a tax-threshold for urban residents. Since the 1980s, the threshold had been set at 800 yuan per month, and urban residents would not pay any tax if their monthly income was less than this. In fact, 800 yuan per month was about 20 times the average rural income at that time. This is equivalent to an annual amount of 9600-yuan tax-free for urban employers. Consider that, until 2003, the per capita rural net income was only 3582.4 yuan, far below the urban tax threshold, and most peasants, in fact, should not have paid any tax on their income. According to the policy implemented on January 1, 2006,[15] the urban income tax

[15]*Decision on Amendment of Income Tax Law of the People's Republic of China*, passed at 18th Session of the Standing Committee of the 10th National People's Congress.

threshold had increased to 1600 yuan because of the rapid urban income growth over the years. However, there was no such threshold for agricultural tax, even though a certain portion of rural income is for self-consumption. In rural areas, the agricultural tax was actually paid according to the amount of land acreage cultivated (not as a definition given by the authorities that agricultural tax was proportional to agricultural output), regardless of how much output there was, how much rural income was obtained and whether the income was from selling agricultural products or for self-consumption.

Secondly, the urban residents usually do not have to pay for public services, or contribute a small part of their income for this purpose. For example, when public services are provided in the cities, such as education, libraries, transportation and plantations, the urban residents will not shoulder all the charges, and the construction of the urban infrastructure, such as bridges and roads, will not cost much for urban residents. The administrative outlay for the government and institutions in the cities are subsidized from the state budget. However, in the rural areas, most of the essential services and infrastructure had to be self-financed at least during those reform years before agricultural tax was abolished. The national budget only covered part of the expenditure for rural areas, and the rest had to be collected via taxes and fees by the local government and organizations. For example, since the 1990s, education had become a heavy burden for the peasants. Research by Lin et al. estimated rural and urban household taxation based on data collected from ten provinces and found that rural expenditure on education had become a heavy burden on the peasants (Lin et al., 2002). Table 3.2 confirms the results of the research, revealing the differences between urban and rural taxation in terms of the percentage of incomes for 1995, 1997 and 1999.

The table indicates that, without considering tuition fees, the rural tax burden was slightly higher in proportion to their income, which increased from 11.2 in 1995 to 13.9% in 1999. The urban tax during this time increased from 10.3 to 12.4% of their income. However, when the tuition fee was added, the tax burden

Table 3.2 Urban and rural taxation: comparison in percentage of income

	1995		1997		1999	
	Urban	Rural	Urban	Rural	Urban	Rural
Excluding tuition	10.3	11.2	11.7	12.1	12.4	13.9
Including tuition	10.7	15.4	12.1	17.0	12.8	19.4

Sources Lin et al. (2002)

Note

1. Taxation in the table is composed of indirect and direct taxes for the rural and urban sectors
2. For the urban sector, direct tax refers to personal income tax, while the direct taxation on rural households is composed of agriculture-related taxes, *tiliu* and *tongchou* fees as well as other payments to the local government and organizations
3. The indirect taxes for urban households are value added tax, excise tax and consumption tax. For rural households, indirect taxes are from commodity consumption
4. The taxation for the rural households in the table did not include the corvee service, nor was rural loss from price scissors included

shouldered by the rural households reached 19.4% compared with only 12.8% for their urban counterparts in 1999. Data show that the tuition burden imposed on rural households took 5.5% of their net income.

Therefore, comparing the rural and urban sectors, apart from the common tax paid by both sectors—the value added tax for consumption—more tax was imposed on rural households. This is not only because the directly taxed items for peasants were numerous but they were also proportionally higher to rural income. Taking the widening rural–urban income gap into consideration, the peasants had been earning less but paying more, reflecting the great inequity in its nature.

Meanwhile, there were other problems related to rural tax collection. In some areas, the village organizations once borrowed money or collected funds from the peasants; when they collected tax from the peasants thereafter, the peasants asked for debt-(owed to the peasants by the local organizations)-for-tax. Besides, there were no formal regulations concerning tax collection and no effective measures were therefore taken against tax fraud, deferral and refusal. The rural tax and fee collectors had, in many areas, resorted to coercive methods. The relationship between the local officials or tax collectors and the taxpayers had always been tense, with the peasants complaining about the corruption of the local officials, their embezzlement of the tax paid and the hoodwinking of the higher-level government. Rural riots were repeatedly reported, especially in the less developed rural areas, which became a great hazard to rural stability (Bernstein & Lü, 2000; Lin et al., 2002; Yep, 2004).

3.2.3 Rural Tax and Agriculture

Michael Lipton is an opponent of rural taxation, arguing that, even though a few governments in poor countries could collect as much as 20% of total income in taxes of all kinds, it reflects the governments' most conscious intention to use public policies against the rural sector (Lipton, 1977).

Until the beginning of the 21st century, although China was not less developed than the poor countries in the 1950s and 1960s described by Lipton, nearly 30 years after Lipton's work was published, the rural sector in China was still burdened by taxation, the common practice in those countries. At first sight, the agriculture in China was not taxed heavily because the official figure for agricultural and related taxes was less than 5% of rural net income during the 1990s. However, if informal fees and levies are considered, the number increased to nearly 10% of rural net income (Table 3.1). The above are official estimates, and the real figures could possibly be far higher, as discussed earlier, and the figures for agriculture-dominated regions would certainly be above average. Therefore, an assertion might be made that the rural sector in China was overtaxed, with peasants paying 10–20% of their net income in taxes and fees (Lin et al., 2002). In some poverty-stricken regions, the taxes and fees could be as high as 25% of the rural income (Chen & Wu, 2004).

In terms of resource flows, taxation was clearly intended to extract the rural surplus in the early stage of economic development. Such a purpose was consistent with the Soviet development strategy—to exploit the rural sector in support of industrialization. In present-day China, it is argued in this study that agricultural tax could be better seen as a legacy of previous development policies, as the revenue-generating capabilities of taxation on agriculture has been very limited. Yet, it directed some resources to flow continuously out of agriculture until 2006. As payers of agricultural taxes, the peasants had to shoulder the burden, which impeded their income growth. For *tiliu and tongchou*, as well as other fees and charges, the resource flows were kept within in rural sector. During the process of collecting such fees and local charges, the peasants were extracted, although the rural sector as a whole was not squeezed. However, either way, the peasants became the ultimate target for taxes and fees. They suffered a double burden of resource flows within and out of agriculture.

3.2.4   Tax Abolition

After several attempts at reforming the agricultural taxes, a year after the Prime Minister announced that the taxes would be eliminated within five years, the Chinese government finally decided to scrap all agricultural taxes from the beginning of 2006,[16] thus putting an end to the 2600-year long history of taxation on agriculture.

The central government was certainly concerned about the impact of agricultural tax elimination. The major rationale was the increase in peasants' income. Many scholars welcome a rural tax reform, for it was considered an effective way to increase rural income. They believe that the central government has got the financial ability to bear the loss of agricultural tax elimination, because, until 2001, agricultural tax accounted for only 5.6% of fiscal revenue (Lin, 2003). Moreover, tax elimination would be helpful in reducing the number of tax-collection personnel required, and thus reducing the administration costs and the peasants' relevant burden thereafter.

Other concerns of the central government included expanding the domestic demand once the agricultural tax had been removed. Insufficient consumption has been one of the major problems in China's economy for years. The government thus introduced strategies for increasing domestic demand in order to fuel economic growth. The expanding consumption of the then 900 million peasants was considered an important part of the increasing domestic demand.[17] The central

---

[16]On December 29, 2005, the 19th Session of the 10th National People's Congress Standing Committee passed the *Decision to Abolish the Agricultural Tax Regulations of People's Republic of China*.

[17]Minister of Finance's speech during interview on December 29, 2005.

government hoped that tax elimination would play an active role in the national economic development by increasing the peasants' income and consumption.

In addition, the elimination of agricultural tax would also help to strengthen the stability. Even though Chinese peasants have been considered honest and innocent, far less challenging than intellectuals and workers, they constitute the largest population. If they rioted, the situation would be uncontrollable by the Communist Party. These economic and political considerations made the central government finally decide to eliminate the agricultural tax.

It is estimated according to Xinhua Press that, in 2004, the rural net income soared by 6.8% due to the tax reform and state subsidies for grain production. However, the real meaning of tax abolition lies beyond the absolute value of the tax burden reduction and rural income increase. Lipton believes that the tax in developing countries is small but significant. Agricultural taxes took less than 5% of the total fiscal revenue, and a small part of the rural net income (about 3–4%) in 2005, but provided a policy shield that encouraged exorbitant fees, levies and all kinds of other fines and surcharges to be levied on the peasants; thus, they became the exact source of all rural tax and fee burdens. The agricultural-inclined taxes were destined to be collected at the sacrifice of the rural sector, and therefore, the abolishment of agricultural taxes in China is far-reaching. We argue in this book that its importance is not only in how much the peasants will benefit, but more important in the change in the government's attitude towards agriculture and the rural sector by putting an end to one of the most unequal treatments of the peasants. According to the former Vice Minister of Agriculture, the abolition of the agricultural taxes heralded a new era of 'industry subsidizing agriculture'.[18]

3.3 The Role of Price Setting

3.3.1 The Price System and Grain Procurement

The price system concerning agricultural products in China is complex due to the various categories of products and the existence of different prices. The Chinese government, according to their importance to the economy, has divided agricultural products into three categories, which accordingly fall under different types of procurement and prices, as shown in Table 3.3.

Since 1953, unified or mandatory procurement was applied to the most important category of farm products, including grain and edible oil. As a major agricultural product for export, cotton was included in this category in 1954. Under the mandatory procurement, the producers had to provide fixed quantities (quota) at fixed prices (both planned by the state). Thus, the state could exercise a monopoly over these important agricultural products. As for the second category, the peasants

---

[18]Speech made during interview by the Xinhua News Agency on December 29th, 2005.

Table 3.3 Categories of agricultural products and their procurement

	Category I	Category II	Category III
Products included	Grain, cotton and edible oil	Over 100 products, such as pork, eggs, tobacco, hemp, sugarcane, tea, silkworm cocoons, sugar beet, etc.	Hundreds of local products
Types of purchase	(*tonggou*) unified procurement	(*paigou*) allocated procurement	(*yigou*) negotiated procurement

Source Lardy (1983a), Sheng (1993)

had to sell to the state the quotas allocated to them, also at the state-planned prices, but, unlike the products subject to the unified purchase, which must be sold in proportion to the output, the quantity of sales of these products was fixed in absolute terms at the beginning of each year (Sheng, 1993). In terms of the third category, which was subject to negotiated purchase, the quantity, quality and prices were negotiated by the state departments and the peasants.

In addition to the various categories of products with their corresponding forms of purchase, there were also farm-gate prices in various terms. The first was the procurement/purchase price (*shougou jiage*), the basic price paid for the quota sale of the products in categories I and II. The second was called the 'above-quota' price (*chaogou jiage*), with the premium paid for deliveries beyond the quota sale. 'Negotiated price' (*yigou jiage*) was the third one, and it could refer to either the price of the products in category III or in later development, to the prices decided between the peasants and government for the purchase of the above-contracted products in categories I and II. Finally, with the re-emergence of the free market following the reform, there appeared market prices (*shichang jiage*) decided by the market mechanism (Lardy, 1983b; Sheng, 1993). These prices varied with the development of the procurement system.

Soon after the foundation of the new China in 1949, government central planning was formed to control the national development. Accordingly, the price structure was determined by the government rather than the market forces. In 1953, the state price control was enforced through the introduction of a compulsory sales system for agricultural products,[19] which ensured that there was a state monopoly over the purchase and marketing of rural outputs, mainly grain products (Table 3.4). Since the free rural market was prohibited at that time, the state had complete control over agricultural products, which were collected by the state in two ways—as agricultural tax paid in kind and as grains purchased by the state at procurement prices.

---

[19]In 1953, the Central Committee of the Communist Party of China and the State Council published *Decision on Grain Compulsory Procurement and Sales* and Order *on Planned Procurement and Planned Sales of Grains*.

Table 3.4 Policies concerning grain procurement and prices

1953	Established a mandatory/compulsory grain procurement system. The peasants were required to sell fixed quantities (quota) of products, including grain, cotton and edible oil to the state at the state-determined prices
1979	The rise in the quota price (about 20%) and another 50% above the quota price for the above-quota selling of agricultural products
1985	Mandatory grain procurement was replaced by the state purchase system according to contracts; the rest could be sold at a negotiated price or on the free market. Start of a 'dual track' system
1990	The peasants were allowed to sell any extra produce (above the contracted amount) to the state at negotiated prices, or at free market prices
1994–1996	Sharp increases in procurement prices
1997	End of the 'dual track' in grain procurement and the start of 'protection prices' to support agricultural prices. Subsidies paid to the grain marketing bureaus for grain procurement, storage, and export
2000–2003	Increased reliance on markets; privatisation of grain and cotton marketing
2004	Nationwide direct subsidies to grain-producing peasants and machinery dealers in selected major grain-producing counties, which should pass the savings on to the farmers

Source Author's compilation

At most points during the 20 years before the Reform and Opening-up, agricultural output was not high enough to meet the needs of the entire population. The state exercised strict control over the purchase of agricultural products, and a state procurement system in the rural sector was practiced, largely unchanged, during these decades.

It was after the Third Plenary Session of the 11th Central Committee of the Communist Party in 1978 that major reforms were introduced in China, including the reform of the procurement system (Table 3.4). The measure taken was to increase the grain purchase price in 1979, i.e. the purchase price for grain was increased by 20% within the quota, and another 30–50% was added to this for the above-quota price. Meanwhile, the free market was gradually opened up—in 1979 a total amount of four million tonnes of grain were sold on the free market.

The reforms resulted in a substantial increase in agricultural output and sales. Since 1978, grain sales increased rapidly, from 51 million tonnes in 1978 to a record 117 million tonnes in 1984. Because of the high procurement price for grains over the quota, the above-quota sales grew from 13 million tonnes in 1978 to 77 million tonnes in 1984, the latter constituting 66% of the total grain sold that year. In the meantime, the amount of grain sold to the free markets grew from nil in 1978 to 10 million tonnes in 1984, and the market began to play a more important role (Aubert, 1990).

In 1985, the mandatory procurement system was reformed into a state purchase system according to the contract (Table 3.4). It cancelled the state's monopoly over the purchase and marketing of agricultural products. Instead, the state would purchase produce from the peasants at voluntarily contracted prices. The new contract price was the weighted average of 30% of the previous quota price and 70% of the above-quota price. This price was universal, even after the quota had been fulfilled. This discouraged the peasants from selling more agricultural produce to the state, for they could not get a higher price for the extra products they sold. It also discouraged the peasants from improving their agricultural output. From 1985 to 1988, according to Ministry of Agriculture, grain output had been lower than the 1984 level, resulting in a huge increase in the price of grain. Compared with 1985, the actual market prices for rice, wheat and corn increased by 133, 131 and 94% respectively in 1989.

Meanwhile, another problem arose: due to the gap between the market price and state contract price, the peasants were reluctant to sign a contract with the state, making it impossible to purchase enough grain as planned. In 1990, the system was modified to enable the peasants to sell any extra products (above the contracted amount) to the state at a negotiated price,[20] or at the free market price to other buyers (except for the sale of cotton).

In 1991 and 1992, after a short period of recovery in terms of agricultural output due to government intervention and adjustment, agricultural output continued to drop nationwide. The grain price had increased greatly by the end of 1993. The 1994 market prices for rice, wheat and corn grew by 150, 117 and 157% respectively, compared with the previous year (Ministry of Agriculture, 2001). The state responded by increasing the purchase prices in order to encourage grain production. In 1994, there was an increase of 42% in the procurement price, and, in 1996, there was another 40% increase based on the 1994 price. Thus, by 1996, there had been an increase of 105% in purchase price compared with 1993 (Yang & Qu, 2005). This resulted in the highest level of grain output in history in 1996.

In order to prevent the price from falling after a good harvest, the government introduced a protective price for grain purchase in 1997, promising that the peasants would be able to sell as much grain as possible at state protective prices. Except for soybeans, the protective price was usually higher than the market price, although budgetary constraints meant that the local governments in many grain-producing areas were unable to pay the peasants. Instead of receiving cash in return for their agricultural products, many peasants received paper IOUs (a promissory note without a binding effect). This was against the central government's intention, and, in 2000, the protective prices were cancelled in the main grain-producing regions. Instead, the government decided to rely more on the market. Since 2004, direct subsidies were given to the grain-producing peasants and machinery dealers in selected major grain-producing counties (OECD, 2005). This practice was introduced after the policy in 1997 under which subsidies were paid to the grain-marketing bureaus for grain procurement, storage, and export (Table 3.4).

From the development of policies concerning grain procurement, several conclusions might be drawn. Firstly, since the reform, the market has been given a more important role, especially in recent years, in guiding prices. Secondly, there

---

[20]The negotiated prices were lower than the market prices but higher than the contract prices.

has been an upward trend in grain procurement prices for most of the time. Thirdly, the changes and the policies can be seen as a constant correction to various extents of the discrimination against agriculture that had existed since the early 1950s. The increases in agricultural prices and subsidies reflected the state's favouring of agriculture; the process, however, has been extended over a few decades.

3.3.2 Price Distortion

Since the procurement prices were usually set below the market level, the questions arise: how much did the state extract from the low prices of agricultural produce? How much did agriculture contribute to industrialization? And is agriculture still making a contribution?

It is almost certain that, although agricultural prices have been adjusted and the scissors prices partially corrected since the very beginning of the reform, for a long period of time, the government's principles concerning prices was to ensured that agriculture was to be suppressed in order to continue its contribution. Firstly, high priority was given by the state to preserving price stability. As Lardy argued, price stability was the prime principle of the Communist Party, due to China's very unhappy experience with hyperinflation in the late 1940s (Lardy, 1983a). However, this price stability is sought primarily at the retail level, particularly for urban consumers and staple commodities. Secondly, according to the Price Bureau officials' writing in *Red Flag*, it was necessary to continue underprizing agricultural products in order to transfer resources intersectorally from agriculture to industry via the price mechanism (Lardy, 1983a). Under the guidance of the above principles, it is expected that the price distortion of agricultural products could not be corrected completely after the 1978 reform. This can be proved by the following analysis.

(1) Comparison of state and market prices

There are several ways to measure depressed agricultural prices. One of the approaches to examining the magnitude of the underprizing of agricultural produce is to compare the state procurement price with the market price. There are certainly some drawbacks to such an approach. Firstly, the market price could be substantially higher than the marginal cost because of the insufficient supply of grain within state control, especially in the early years of the reform following poor harvests. Secondly, the market price is expected to be high because the transport and administration cost is added to it. Despite these factors, researchers believe that, considering the price gap between the market and state procurement, the agricultural prices have been set too low.

According to Lardy, in both 1980 and 1981 the average rural market price was 80% above the quota price (Lardy, 1983a). He also found that, in 1981, the wheat

Table 3.5 Terms of trade between rice and selected industrial goods in Guangzhou and Hong Kong

Industrial good	Place of manufacture	Kg. of rice required to buy one unit in		Ratio: Guangzhou/Hong Kong (3) = (1)/(2)
		(1) Guangzhou	(2) Hong Kong	
Portable radio	Guangzhou	14.0	6.0	2.3
Thermos flask	Guangzhou	15.5	3.5	4.4
Sewing machine	Shanghai	616.5	124.0	5.0
Bicycle	Shanghai	582.0	110.5	5.3
Camera	Shanghai	462.5	59	7.8
Alarm clock	Shanghai	75.5	7.5	10.1

Source Riskin 1987 citing Liu 1980: 5–6 (Riskin, 1987)

price received by the peasants in the rural markets was a 39% premium over the average price[21] they received from sales to the state. For rice, the gap was larger, with a 70% premium over the average price for deliveries to the state. The urban market prices for rice were two to three times that of the average state procurement price. The persistence of the gap thus provided a rough conclusion, that the state price for grain purchase had been too low.

Moreover, as the data indicate, since 1978, a higher proportion of the grains produced was sold to the state. The quantities increased from 20.3% of total grain output in 1978 to 34.8% in 1984. In 1989, grain sales to the state represented as much as 34.9% of the total output (Aubert, 1990). The low price of agricultural products and their increasing quantities sold to the state increased the loss of the producers.

(2) *Comparison of prices of agricultural and industrial products*

While the evidence is insufficient to allow an estimate of how far the prices of agricultural produce were depressed, the second approach to the problem is to compare agricultural prices with those of industrial products.

For example, by comparing the terms of trade for certain manufactured goods to rice in Guangdong and Hong Kong, the two adjacent regions (but under different sovereignties at that time),[22] Riskin concluded that the producer prices for the major crops in China were well below the international levels (Riskin, 1987). Table 3.5 shows that the ratios for all of the commodities were several times higher in Guangzhou than in Hong Kong. The lowest ratio is 2.3 for a portable radio, while

---

[21]Price average for the within and above quota prices.

[22]The sovereignty of Hong Kong was handed over to the PRC in 1997.

Table 3.6 Procurement prices and production costs 1980 (per 100 jin)

	Procurement prices (yuan)	Non-labour costs (yuan)	Labour costs		Total costs (yuan)
			Working days	Cost (yuan)	
Grain	12.86	5.19	6.33	8.80	13.99
Rice	11.50	4.71	6.24	8.67	13.38
Wheat	15.72	8.03	9.75	13.55	21.58

Source China Agricultural Yearbook 1980
Note A hundred jin = 50 kg

the highest is 10.1 for an alarm clock, which indicates that rice in China was vastly under-priced.

This method has also been used to assess the agricultural prices before the reform. He examined the relative prices of agricultural produce by studying the price ratios of nitrogen to paddy rice (the over-quota or negotiated price), reasonably homogeneous products, and found that the ratios were relatively high throughout the 1960s and the 1970s in China. In 1976, before the 1979 price increase for paddy rice, the price ratio in China was the highest in Asia, including Thailand, where a rice export tax was believed to depress the domestic price of paddy rice relative to the international price (Lardy, 1983b).

(3) *Comparison of procurement prices and production costs*

In the early stage of the reform, the State Agricultural Committee conducted a survey to analyse the relationship between agricultural prices and production costs. This provides another way of assessing the procurement prices. The findings are shown in Table 3.6. Despite the substantial increase in the state purchase price for agricultural products in 1979, the production cost for grain was still higher than the prices paid to the producers by the state.

Table 3.6 shows that the procurement prices for grains were all below their production cost. Several points deserve further consideration. Firstly, the labour cost for grain production was calculated at 1.39 yuan per working day (8.80 yuan/6.33 working days). This rate was estimated as the cost for daily necessities per labourer,[23] and it is considered higher than the usual practice of using the fixed daily accounting price for labour set by the State Price Bureau.[24] Secondly, from the survey, it is uncertain whether the non-labour cost included the management and other expenditure, such as machinery depreciation. However, as indicated by similar surveys, the total production cost is composed of the cost for the producer goods (non-labour cost) and the labour cost only (China Agricultural Yearbook

---

[23]Labour cost = living necessities for a labourer per year/(365 − days of rest)

[24]It represents a welfare judgement, which cannot reflect the opportunity cost because commune members were paid evenly for their time spent on on-the-job leisure. From 1965–78, a daily labourer's wages were set at 0.8 yuan.

1980: 365). If calculated in this way, the production cost was actually underestimated, because the magnitude of depreciation could be substantial due to the increased use of machinery and new technology since the reform.

Therefore, in the early stage of the reform, despite the increased price of state purchases, the producers were actually losing money by selling products to the state, and this was on condition that the total cost was, to some extent, underestimated.

In general, the above analysis has confirmed that, at least in the early years of the reform, the prices were still set against agriculture, but in favour of industry and the urban sector. The price distortion and discrimination against agriculture, despite the partial correction, had remained in China for a sustained period of time.

3.3.3   Urban Subsidies and Farm Input Prices

Although the official price indices have shown a considerable movement in favour of agriculture since 1978, there appeared to be several other policies against it, one of them being subsidies to urban residents.

Urban subsidies started in the 1950s but accelerated from 1978. Between 1978 and 1981, the price subsidies for cereals and edible vegetable oil more than doubled, adding about 150 yuan per year to the value of the subsidies for each state employee. The direct subsidies for non-staple foods in late 1979 added another 60 yuan per worker per year. These two changes alone increased the subsidies by about 40%, to 740 yuan per worker (Lardy, 1983a). Statistics show that the price subsidies for grain, cotton and edible oil increased from 1% of government expenditure in 1978 to a peak of 12.9% in 1983. In 1988, a survey showed that, if all of the subsidies (housing and other social benefits) were added together, they represented 37.8% of the total urban income (Khan, 1993).

Moreover, the state's favouring of urban residents was also reflected in the retail price[25] they paid for grains. During the reform period, the state retail prices converged with the market prices. The latter was 70% higher than the former in the 1970s, and reduced to less than 35% in the 80s, although the state retail price for grain was the last and least to be changed, as reflected by the state's price priority to preserve stability.

Table 3.7 shows that the mixed average retail price for grain exceeded the mixed average producer prices during the planning period, but, during the reform years, the reverse was the case. In fact, the retail price fell short of the producer price by 11% in 1978, by 26% in 1990 and by 4% in 1995. After 1978, the state supplied urban residents with staple food at retail prices well below its procurement prices. It thus provides evidence that part of the gain from the state purchase of agricultural

---

[25]Retail prices refer to the state retail prices, rather than the market prices. The market retail prices were always higher than the state prices.

Table 3.7 Producer and consumer prices: the mixed average purchase and retail prices for grain, 1952–1993

	Purchase (yuan/tonne)	Retail (yuan/tonne)	As percentage of purchase
1952	138.4	197.8	143
1957	162.0	220.0	136
1965	229.2	237.4	104
1978	263.4	294.8	89
1985	416.1	383.3	93
1990	716.0	528.1	74
1993	825.3	740.5	90
1995	1560.5	1335.1	96

Sources China Statistics Yearbooks, various issues

produce at very low prices were compensated to urban residents in keeping retail prices down. The urban subsidies represented an enormous resource transfer from the agricultural to the non-agricultural population.

Finally, with the rise in input prices, agricultural costs also rose. Input prices first began to rise in 1983 and 1984, when the central government raised the planned prices for the major fertilizers and fuel. The planned prices for urea, for example, increased by about 20% between 1983 and 1985, and those for No. 0 diesel increased by 70% over the same period.

A much more effect came from the state's decentralization of price for extra-plan marketing of manufactured and imported farm inputs in 1983, when the local governments were allowed to import additional fertilizer and sell the extra-planned imports to the peasants at higher, unsubsidised prices. In 1984, the central government allowed local commercial enterprises to purchase farm inputs independently and sell them at prices that were high enough to generate a profit.

The result was the increased prices for farm inputs. In 1985, the chemical fertilizer price was 43% and pesticide price 83% higher than in 1983 (Duan, 1986). In real terms, the price of urea, the principle fertilizer, grew from 450 yuan in 1984 to 700 yuan in 1988, and it could even often be obtained only on the black market at more than 1000 yuan per tonne. By 1995, its prices, adjusted for inflation, had risen to almost 1400 yuan. In consequence, from 1984 to 1988, the production cost of wheat per hectare rose from 650 yuan to 1200 yuan, and that of corn from 450 yuan to 900 yuan (Aubert, 1990).

After 1995, the cost of producer goods had been increasing faster than the state purchase price for farm inputs, resulting in a decline in profits from agriculture.

Table 3.8 shows that since 1995, except for 2001 when the purchase price increased faster than that of producer goods, the price increases for producer goods all exceeded the state purchase prices. Much of the producers' profits were thus squeezed out by the increased costs.

Table 3.8 Price indices for producer goods and the state purchase of farm produce (previous year = 100)

	1995	1996	1997	1998	1999	2000	2001	2002
Purchase price	119.9	104.2	95.5	92	87.2	96.4	101.1	95.7
Price of producer goods	127.4	108.4	99.9	94.5	95.8	99.1	99.1	100.5

Source China Statistics Yearbooks, various issues

China's price policy concerning agriculture was developed from the Soviet model. The Chinese government used it to exercise a monopoly over grain procurement at low, state-planned prices in order to extract the rural surplus. Since 1978, reforms were implemented in the rural sector, including increases in agricultural prices. However, since the agricultural prices were so distorted during the centrally-planned period, the prices in the early years of the reform still discriminated against agriculture.

This can be observed from the sharp gaps between the state purchase prices and market prices for grains, by the unbalanced price ratios for farm and industrial goods as well as by comparing the state purchase prices and total production cost. In addition, the state's pricing principles, to ensure price stability and to continue the resource transfer from agriculture via the price mechanism in the late 1970s, also made the immediate correction of the price distortion unrealistic. These factors ensured that agricultural produce remained under-priced for a sustained period of time over the reform period.

Even though the existing research could neither reach an agreement nor make a precise estimate regarding how many resources had been extracted from agriculture, most scholars believe that the net flow out of agriculture due to the procurement system and price policy would be substantial.

Moreover, the accelerated growth of urban subsidies since the reform greatly enlarged the resource flow, and the sharp rise in agricultural inputs mainly due to the price increases for producer goods had a negative impact on the producers, resulting in a rise in costs.

The price policies have been modified in favour of agriculture, including price increases over the reform years, and subsidies have been provided for the producers recently, but the low level of rural income growth and large rural–urban inequality could hardly be explained without considering the price distortions. They made a major contribution to the resource outflow from agriculture.

3.4   The Role of Public Spending

'Public expenditures are one of the key instruments by which governments seek to achieve their economic and social goals. Through their impact on the allocation of resources, the distribution of income, and on aggregate demand, public expenditure policies play a potentially major role in sustaining sound macroeconomic performance and promoting economic development (OECD, 2006: 1). Here, China's public spending policy especially under the 1994 fiscal reform is examined in order to better reveal the government's development goal concerning agriculture and the rural areas. The focus is placed on the government revenue and expenditure assignments under the institutional framework, and how spending on agriculture and the peasants was affected under this system.

3.4.1 The Centralization of Revenue

Administratively, China has five tiers of governments. Below the national (central) government, there are local governments at the provincial, prefectural, county, as well as town and township levels respectively.

In terms of government revenue and expenditure, China was characterised by a centralized fiscal system before the reform. Taxes and profits were first converged to the central government, and then part of the revenue would be transferred back, according to the permitted local expenditure needs.

In the 1980s, the highly centralized system had been replaced by a revenue-sharing system. Under the new system, the local governments were given more authority over the tax revenue, because they were able to share the tax collection with the centre according to the negotiated quota, and retained the above-quota portion for their own budgets. The local governments were responsible for most of the tax collection, but were not allowed to alter the bases and rates for all taxes.

Therefore, incentives were introduced for local governments to reduce the taxation shared with the central government by concealing their real revenue capability. Their usual practices included the transfer of budgetary funds into less constrained, extra-budgetary revenue and the exercise of discretionary power to allow reduced taxes and grant tax exemptions for local enterprises. Until the early 1990s, more revenue was absorbed by the local governments. Together with the declining contribution from the state-owned enterprises[26] (the main revenue contributor), the 'two ratios' (percentage of government budgetary revenue to GDP, and the central government's share of the total budgetary revenue) dropped substantially. According to the NSB statistics, the percentage of budgetary revenue to GDP decreased from 31.2% in 1978 to 12.6% in 1993. Until 1993, the central government's share of revenue, after gradually dropping, constituted only 22% of the total, which was even less than the 1980 level (Fig. 3.3).

The massive decline in the central government's fiscal health was considered to have endangered its capability for financial control. In 1994, a fiscal reform was introduced to increase the two ratios, with the intention of reversing the central

---

[26]State-owned enterprises were allowed to retain some of their profits since the 1980s.

Fig. 3.3 Ratio of central and local government revenue. *Source* China Statistics Yearbooks, various issues

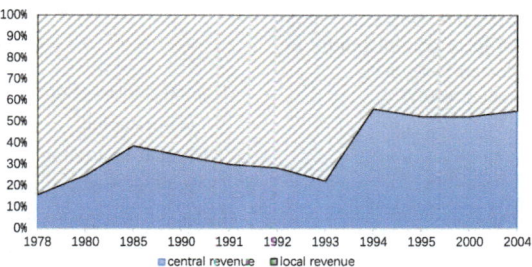

government's unfavourable position of sharing the budgetary revenue. Other purposes of the reform were aimed at simplifying the tax system and stabilizing the fiscal system by replacing the ad hoc, negotiated transfers with a rule-based system.

The core of the 1994 reform was the tax-assignment system. The new system redefined the taxes accrued to both central and local governments, and the revenue sources shared between them. The taxes for the central coffers mainly included custom duties, the consumption tax collected by customs, value-added tax (VAT) and income tax from the central enterprises, turnover tax on railways, banks, and insurance companies, and income tax from the financial institutions set up by the headquarters of the People's Bank of China. The local tax revenue included business tax (excluding the turnover taxes of the banks, railways, and insurance companies), income tax and the profit remittances of local enterprises. The main tax shared would be VAT, with 75% going to the central government and 25% to the local budget.

Another aspect of the reform was the introduction of the national tax services (NTS). Unlike the old system, under which most taxes were collected by the local governments, the NTS was responsible for collecting both central and shared taxes, before 25% of the taxes shared were returned to the local governments. Thus, the tax administration was centralized. In addition to this, the local governments were no longer allowed to grant tax breaks (OECD, 2006; Wang, 1997; Wong, 1995).

All of the above measures had intensified the fiscal central control, that greatly increased the central share of revenue. As Fig. 3.3 shows, from 1993 to 1994, the central share of revenue jumped from 22 to 55.7%. The success of the reform from the perspective of the central government, however, was a blow for the sub-national governments, which deprived the latter of much chance of revenue expansion. Therefore, scholars challenge the core of the reform for not being a real tax assignation, arguing that, even though some taxes were designated as 'local', the central government still dictated their rates and base (Wang, 1997). The sub-national governments could not determine autonomously the aggregate size of their budgets and remained vulnerable to the centrally determined changes in tax base and rates.

Table 3.9 Share of central
and local administration in
selected budgetary
expenditure 2001

	Central	Local
Total	31	69
Capital construction	34	66
Working capital	59	41
Technical upgrading and R&D	25	75
Geological prospecting	31	69
Industry, transport and commerce	28	72
Agriculture	11	89
Culture, education, science and health	11	89
Social relief and welfare	1	99
Defence	99	1
Government administration	3	97
Government debt service	100	0
Policy subsidies	40	60

Source IMF cited Ministry of Finance Data, 2004: 6 (Ahmad,
Singh, & Fortuna, 2004)
Note The local expenditure included earmarked transfers from the
central government

3.4.2   The Devolution of Expenditure

While the revenue was re-centralized, the expenditure became more decentralized,
and was not adjusted in accordance with the change in tax assignment.

China's public spending is characterized by its high level of sub-national
expenditure. In 2001, the local governments accounted for 69% of total budgetary
expenditure (Table 3.9). In 2004, the local share of budgetary expenditure reached
72.3%, while they took only 54.9% of the total revenue.

Table 3.9 shows China's uniqueness in terms of its budgetary expenditure
assignments and also in the fact that the local expenditure accounted for nearly 90% of
agricultural support and the same share of another expenditure category, known as
'culture, education, science and health'. Furthermore, nearly all of the social relief and
welfare services were assigned to the local governments. As noted in a recent OECD
report, 'China is virtually unique among countries in the world in assigning responsibilities for providing vital social services such as social security, basic education,
health care and public safety to local governments' (OECD, 2005: 239).

The same report reveals that the county and township governments (the two
lowest levels) are, together, responsible for providing basic education and public
health for the rural populace—these two levels accounted for 70% of budgetary
expenditure on education, and 55–60% of the expenditure on health.

Take education as an example. As the Compulsory Education Laws (1986)
stipulate, except for some major policies and plans, the management of schools has
been devolved to the local governments. The basic framework is that the central and
provincial governments are responsible for higher education, the prefecture and

county governments for senior secondary education, and the governments at the lowest level for basic education (9-year compulsory education, including primary and junior secondary education), the so-called 'running and management of schools at separate levels' (*fenji banxue, fenji guanli*). This virtually set up a legal framework in which primary schools and secondary schools are the responsibility of the lower-level (township and county) governments. With the reform of school management, finance has also been decentralized. It is also stipulated that different levels of governments should ensure that there is appropriate funding for compulsory education, including school construction and teachers' salaries (Wang, 2003).

Education constitutes the major expense at the county and township levels. Take primary education as an example; almost all expenditure on primary education was met by the local governments. In terms of total expenditure on education, this may represent up to 60–70% at the county level and 70–80% in some townships (Aubert & Li, 2002). It is estimated that by 2000, education accounted for approximately 50% of total financial expenditure at the county level and 75% at the township level (Wang, 2003).

3.4.3   Central Remedies and Their Effectiveness

The devolution of expenditure assignments diverged with the re-centralization of financial control. Since the 1994 reform, the budget deficits of the local governments grew quickly. Figure 3.4 depicts the situation clearly. From 1993 to 1994, there was a sharp decline in the share of revenue for local governments, while the expenditure continued to increase. This resulted in a widening gap between local revenue and expenditure.

Under the condition of lack of funds at the local level, the central government had to resort to intergovernmental transfer as a remedy for continuing its new fiscal system, and three mechanisms were used.

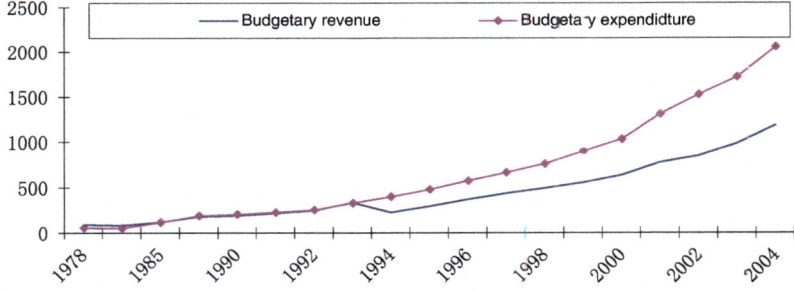

Fig. 3.4 Budgetary Revenue and Expenditure of Local Governments 1978–2004 (billion yuan). *Source* China statistical yearbooks, various issues

(1) *Central remedies*

Firstly, the central government promised to keep local fiscal revenue at no less than the 1993 level by rebating to each locality the amount equal to the reduction due to the new tax-assignment system. That is:

$$\text{Transfer1} = \text{PBR} - (\text{LT} + 0.25 \times \text{VAT})$$

where PBR refers to the province's base retained revenue (1993 as the base year) and LT is the tax revenue for the local budget.

In addition, in order to deal with the problem of local expenditure growth, the central government made a commitment to return 30% of its total increased revenue (IR) from VAT and consumption tax (CT). The compensation amounted to:

$$\text{Transfer2} = \text{Transfer1} \times (1 + 0.3 \times \text{IR})^t$$

where IR = (VAT increase + CT increase) and t is the 1st, 2nd, 3rd … year after the introduction of the new system.

Apart from the tax rebate or tax return, the second type of transfer was earmarked, including specific grants for various purposes, such as disaster relief, important projects and developing poor areas.

The third type of transfer, 'the transitional fiscal transfer scheme', was introduced in 1995. Its aim was to aid poor areas and reduce the regional disparities by assessing local expenditure capabilities and needs. Table 3.10 shows the composition of central transfers to the provinces.

Of the total central transfers, tax rebates and earmarked transfers are the major ones, each category constituting nearly half of the total transfers, while the share of transitional fiscal transfer, a form of general purpose transfer, was less than 5% from 1998 to 2002.

(2) *Effectiveness*

In terms of the remedies provided by the central government, tax rebates, the major component of fiscal transfer did provide much return to the local governments, as shown in Table 3.10. But as its formula indicates, the rebate was based on the tax collection abilities in the various regions. Thus, the transfers were not designed to

Table 3.10 Composition of government transfers to the provinces

As % of total transfer	1998	1999	2000	2001	2002
Tax rebate	62.7	51.8	48.6	38.9	49.1
Earmarked transfer	32.1	43.6	46.3	56.4	42.8
General purpose transfers	5.2	4.6	5.1	4.7	8.2

Source OECD (2006)

address the increasingly important regional disparity issue, but to favour regions with higher revenue generating capability, and to return more to the rich places. In this sense, tax rebates helped to encourage regional fiscal disparities. In the process of expenditure devolution to the sub-national level, the degree of fiscal stress was more intense in the poor regions.

The 'transitional fiscal transfer scheme' was set up to reduce the gaps between different regions. However, its size remained small. In 1996, its size was just 0.5% of the total central government revenue and the programme was applied to only 18 provinces and autonomous regions (Ma & Norregaard, 1998). Even though several modifications were made subsequently, in 1998, it constituted only 1.8% of all central transfers to the provinces (Wong, 2000).

If we examine earmarked transfers, which accounted for virtually another half of the central transfers, some problems also exist. Because of its nature of converting funds to projects with priority purposes, the local governments usually had less control over the management of the funds. Moreover, these special transfers often had to be allocated with matching funds, provided locally. Therefore, in order to gain the central funding, the local governments had to squeeze their limited resources that would have been used for other local priority expenditure. Failing to do so means a failure to obtain central funding, which was the case for many less well-endowed governments. There were reports that local governments had promised to provide matching funds and did gain the central funding, but financial constraints made them fail to keep their promise. The central funding would often end up meeting the local budgetary shortfall or simply being paid as deferred salary to the local government employees (Jiang, 2004). The major problem with this transfer program, therefore, was that the central government lacked the monitoring mechanisms to ensure their effective use.

Considering the above, the revenue transfer system required further modification in terms of both its equity and efficiency. It is argued by OECD that 'a revenue transfer system does exist but has not been able to prevent the emergence of marked variations in public spending across the country. It also gives rise to current substantial gaps between the expenditure responsibilities of sub-national governments and their resources. Such gaps have also been an important factor behind the growing resort to off-budget funds … and they are partly responsible for the relatively low level of public outlays on education and other important development needs' (OECD, 2005: 251).

3.4.4   Local Responses

While the central government were making transfers to the provinces in order to plug the loophole in local government budget, the governments at the local level responded by undertaking less constrained extra-budget or off-budget activities.

An ineffective transfer system (with the result that more than half of its public resources wandered outside its budgetary account) is certainly dangerous for the state's fiscal system, giving the central government less control over fiscal activities. However, its impact on the local governments, especially in rural areas, is immense, partly due to the growing extra-budgetary activities.

The extra-budgetary revenue is derived from the authorized fees, surtaxes, user charges and other levies that are legally sanctioned by the state, but is virtually under the complete control of the local governments, with over 90% of total extra-budgetary revenue being coffered to the local budgets since the mid-1990s. It thus provided access for provinces to generate revenue in situations of local fiscal deficit, and enabled them to support their expenditure tasks and activities. Since the 1994 fiscal reform, the extra-budgetary funds had been growing faster, increasing from 186.2 billion yuan in 1994 to 389.3 billion yuan in 1996.

The off-budgetary funds were collected from illegal charges, unauthorized fees and forced contributions, by the local governments without budgetary control. Scholars argued that virtually all levels of governments—down to the municipal districts and villages—had the capacity to extract payment from the local taxpayers (Wong, 2000), but, because of its illegality, no official data about such funds are available. According to estimates, they ranged from 60 to 200 billion yuan around 1995 (Li & Liu; Wang, 1997; Xu & He, 1995). Meanwhile, it was estimated by Wong (2001) and Ma (2000) that off-budget expenditure rose from around 2% of GDP in the mid-1990s to around 4% of GDP in the late 1990s (Ma, 2000; Wong, 2001).

However, these extra- and off-budgetary activities could be very harmful to agriculture, the rural areas as well as peasants. Firstly, as these funds were derived from fees and charges, they greatly encouraged an arbitrary fee collection and illegal extraction from the peasants. The increase in rural tax and fee collection in the 1990s was largely due to the local government's financial deficit in carrying out expenditure assignments. This partially explains why rural households were exposed to excessive local charges apart from agricultural tax, including *tiliu* and *tongchou*, as well as other fee paying burdens. The existing research confirms that, since 1994, both '*tiliu and tongchou*' and illegal fee collections grew rapidly. For example, in Jiangxi Province, while the rural net income increased by 33.3% in 1994, 25.7% in 1995 and 26.6% in 1996 compared with the previous year, *tiliu and tongchou* increased by 42.9% in 1994, 42.9% in 1995 and 36.1% in 1996. For other fee paying burdens in 1995, the increase was 161.3% compared with 1994 (Guo, 2002). To a great extent, this offset the income growth due to the increased procurement prices in the mid-1990s. These fee charges became a huge burden for the peasants.

3.4.5 Financial Support

With the financial power diminishing down the line and expenditure being delegated to the bottom, there appeared insufficient support for agriculture. Since local governments were responsible for most agricultural support, the local budgets were unable to ensure adequate support without any effective transfer from the central government. Despite the rapid economic growth in the country for nearly thirty years, the government spending on agriculture as a proportion of total expenditure declined from 13.43% in 1978 to 7.12% in 2003.

Within such a framework, the spending also showed an unreasonable structure for agricultural support. Of total support in agriculture, spending on administration occupied a large share. The estimate was maintained at about 60–70% of total expenditure. In 2004, the figure was as high as 64%, leaving a low proportion of expenditure on promoting production.

The overstaffed local governments might be the vestige of a central planned economy, which symbolized the extreme inefficiency and large amount of waste involved in the administration outlay. Scholars argued that 'with a huge basis of extra-budgetary revenue, the government size would expand, and then the government administration expenditure will increase at a rate faster than that of economic growth, resulting in a heavier burden on the shoulder of local citizens and peasants' (Ping & Bai, 2006: 26–27). According to OECD, at the provincial level, such expenditure is almost 15% of the total outlay, rising to 20% at the county level. At the township level, where no official data were available, a large part of the total expenditure was spent on government administration (OECD, 2006).

Apart from the huge outlay for public administration, when we take a closer look at government expenditure on agricultural promotion, much of it was spent on large and medium-sized irrigation infrastructure and environmental constructions, and little was invested in small-sized infrastructure that directly benefits the peasants.

From 1996 to 2000, accumulated capital investment from the central government in the irrigation infrastructure accounted for 70% of total rural infrastructure investment. From 2001 to 2005, national great irrigation infrastructure and ecological projects attracted 70% of the central government's total investment in rural infrastructure construction, while investment directly used for improving the overall agricultural production capability attracted only 11%.

Such expenditure reflected the central government's preference for spending on more visible capital construction and irrigation projects on some of the larger rivers, such as the Yangtze River and the Yellow River, which largely benefited the urban sector with regard to flood control and the water supply, while such flood control for the more directly affected rural areas was greatly neglected (Chen, 2003). Take Heilongjiang as an example, the flooding of small rivers once caused a huge damage of three billion yuan (Jiang, 2004).

The local deficit in many places caused the sub-national governments to under-invest in a small-scale irrigation infrastructure, which would provide direct benefits to the locality. Meanwhile, the local governments had less authority and management over the funds allocated by the state for certain purposes. This resulted in the fact that funds were sometimes not used where they were needed most.

Generally speaking, the public spending policy in China after the 1994 fiscal reform was characterised by the centralization of revenue and devolution of expenditure to the local governments. Such a structure is biased against the rural areas and peasants, since agricultural development, as well as many public services, are the responsibility of the local governments. Due to their lowest position in terms of the control of resources, most local governments were in such financial deficit that unable to provide sufficient support to the rural sector. As a result, the local governments responded by finding other ways to survive the financial difficulties, such as resorting to extra and off-budgetary activities by collecting fees and surcharges from the peasants. In addition, for the limited resources allocated to supporting agriculture, the spending structure made outlays for public administration taking most of the expenditure in rural areas and with the rest of the expenditure in favour of capital construction, greatly benefiting the urban sector. Public spending ensured the state control of most revenue, but deprived the local governments of the resources necessary for economic development, especially in rural areas.

References

Ahmad, E., Singh, R., & Fortuna, M. (2004). Toward more effective redistribution: Reform options for intergovernmental transfers in China (Vol. 4).

Aubert, C. (1990). The agricultural crisis in China at the End of the 1980s. *Remaking Peasant China: Problems of Rural Development and Institutions at the Start of the 1990s. Aarhus University Press, Aarhus*, pp. 16–37.

Aubert, C., & Li, X. (2002). 'Peasant Burden': Taxes and Levies Imposed on Chinese Farmers. *Agricultural policies in China after WTO accession, 5*, 160.

Bernstein, T. P., & Lü, X. (2000). Taxation without representation: Peasants, the central and the local states in reform China. *The China Quarterly, 163*, 742–763.

Brooks, R., & Tao, R. (2003). China's labor market performance and challenges.

Chai, P., Zhou, J., & Xie, J. (1999). Empirical study on the rationale of peasant's burden. *Issues in Agricultural Economy* (12), 41–45.

Chan, K. W. (1994). *Cities with invisible walls: Reinterpreting urbanization in post-1949 China*. UK: Oxford University Press.

Chan, K. W., & Zhang, L. (1999). The hukou system and rural-urban migration in China: Processes and changes. *The China Quarterly, 160*, 818–855.

Chen, X. (2003). *Studies on finance at county and township level and rural income growth*. Taiyuan: Shanxi Economic Publishing Press.

Chen, G., & Wu, C. (2004). *Survey on Chinese peasants*. Beijing: Beijing People's Literature Press.

Duan, Y. (1986). Grain circulating system needs a major reform. *Issues in Agricultural Economy* (11), 37–40.

Fang, C., & Chan, K. W. (2000). *The political economy of urban protectionist employment policies in China*.

Fu, G. (2001). Survey reports on the taxes and fees shouldered by peasants in seven counties of Hubei Province. *Issues in Agricultural Economy* (4), 40–41.

Guo, Y. (2002). The problem of overburden in rural areas in China. *Journal of Peking University (Philosophy and Social Sciences), 39*(1), 47–54.

Hare, D., & Zhao, S. (2000). Labor migration as a rural development strategy: A view from the migration origin. *Rural labor flows in china* (42), 148.

Jiang, C. (2004). The impact of financial difficulties at county and township levels on financial support of agriculture. *Management World* (7), 61–68.

Johnson, D. G. (1988). Economic reforms in the People's Republic of China. *Economic Development and Cultural Change, 36*(S3), S225–S245.

Kennedy, J. J. (2007). From the tax-for-fee reform to the abolition of agricultural taxes: The impact on township governments in north-west China. *The China Quarterly, 189*, 43–59.

Khan, A. R. (1993). The determinants of household income in rural China. In *The distribution of income in China* (pp. 95–115). Berlin: Springer.

Knight, J., & Song, L. (1999). The rural-urban divide: Economic disparities and interactions in China. *OUP Catalogue*.

Lardy, N. R. (1983a). *Agricultural prices in China* (Vol. 1). USA: World Bank Washington, DC.

Lardy, N. R. (1983b). *Agriculture in China's modern economic development*. UK: Cambridge University Press.

Lee, L. (2012). Decomposing wage differentials between migrant workers and urban workers in urban China's labor markets. *China Economic Review, 23*(2), 461–470.

Li, C., & Liu, C. (1997). Difficulties and possible solutions in the circulation of total social funds. *Review of Economic Research*, No. 1007, 2–19.

Li, X. (2003). Rethinking the peasant burden: Evidence from a Chinese village. *The Journal of Peasant Studies, 30*(3–4), 45–74.

Liang, Z. (2001). The age of migration in China. *Population and development review, 27*(3), 499–524.

Lin, J., Tao, R., Liu, M., & Zhang, Q. (2002). Urban and rural household taxation in China: Measurement and stylized facts. *China Centre for Economic Research, Peking University, Beijing*.

Lin, J. Y. (1988). The household responsibility system in China's agricultural reform: A theoretical and empirical study. *Economic Development and Cultural Change, 36*(S3), S199–S224.

Lin, Y. (2003). Several viewpoints on the present rural policy. *Issues in Agricultural Economy* (6), 4–7.

Lipton, M. (1977). *Why poor people stay poor: Urban bias in world development*. London: Canberra: Temple Smith; Australian National University Press.

Liu, Z. (2005). Institution and inequality: The *hukou* system in China. *Journal of comparative economics, 33*(1), 133–157.

Lu, X. (1997). The politics of peasant burden in reform China. *The Journal of Peasant Studies, 25* (1), 113–138.

Lu, Y. (2004). Empirical analysis on differences of tax and fee burden rates of rural households. *Journal of Xinyang Normal University (Philosophy and Social Sciences Edition), 24*(1), 40–43.

Lu, Z., & Song, S. (2006). Rural–urban migration and wage determination: The case of Tianjin, China. *China Economic Review, 17*(3), 337–345.

Ma, J. (2000). *Off-budgetary activities of China governments since economic reform*. Paper presented at the 12th Annual Conference of Association for Budgeting and Financial Management, Kansas City, http://www.use.cuhk.edu.hk/wk_wzdetails.asp.

Ma, J., & Norregaard, J. (1998). China's fiscal decentralization. Unpublished Manuscript. Washington: International Monetary Fund.

OECD. (2005). *Review of agricultural policies: China*. Beijing.

OECD. (2006). *Challenges for China's public spending: Toward greater effectiveness and equity*. France, OECD Publishing.

Park, A., & Wang, D. (2010). Migration and urban poverty and inequality in China. *China Economic Journal, 3*(1), 49–67.

Ping, J., & Bai, X. (2006). Fiscal Decentralization and Local Public Good Provision in China. *Finance & Trade Economics, 2*, 009.

Riskin, C. (1987). *China's political economy: The quest for development since 1949*. USA: Oxford University Press.

Sheng, Y. (1993). *Intersectoral resource flows and China's economic development*. Berlin: Springer.

Solinger, D. J. (1999). *Contesting citizenship in urban China: Peasant migrants, the state, and the logic of the market*. USA: University of California Press.

Song, L. (2000). Diversification of household production in rural China: The determinants and outcomes. *Rural Labor Flows in China*. Berkeley: Institute of East Asian Studies, University of California, pp. 101–128.

Tao, R., & Liu, M. (2005). Urban and rural household taxation in China. Measurement, comparison and policy implications. *Journal of the Asia Pacific Economy, 10*(4), 486–505.

Wang, S. (1997). China's 1994 fiscal reform: An initial assessment. *Asian Survey, 37*(9), 801–817.

Wang, D. (2003). *China's rural compulsory education: Current situation, problems and policy alternatives*: Working paper series.

Wang, F.-l. (2005). Brewing tensions while maintaining stabilities: The dual role of the hukou system in contemporary China. *Asian Perspective*, 85–124.

Wang, H., Guo, F., & Cheng, Z. (2015). A distributional analysis of wage discrimination against migrant workers in China's urban labour market. *Urban Studies, 52*(13), 2383–2403.

Whyte, M. K. (2010). *One country, two societies: rural-urban inequality in contemporary China* (Vol. 16). USA: Harvard University Press.

Wong, C. (1995). Fiscal reform in 1994. *China Review, 20*(21-20), 13.

Wong, C. (2001). *Fiscal Decentralization in China: The problematic outcomes of unplanned changes in transition towards a market economy*. Bangkok: Paper presented at the Asian Development Forum.

Wong, C. P. (2000). Central-local relations revisited the 1994 tax-sharing reform and public expenditure management in China. *China Perspectives*, 52–63.

Wong, K., Fu, D., Li, C. Y., & Song, H. X. (2007). Rural migrant workers in urban China: Living a marginalised life. *International Journal of Social Welfare, 16*(1), 32–40.

Wu, X. (2011). The household registration system and rural-urban educational inequality in contemporary China. *Chinese Sociological Review, 44*(2), 31–51.

Xu, Y., & He, S. (1995). Comments on the current situation of public finance. *Economic Reform and Development* (8), 7–10.

Yang, X. (2000). Interconnections among Gender, Work, and Migration. In B. Entwisle & G. E. Henderson (Eds.), *Red aw ng Boundaries: Work, Household, and Gender in China*. Berkeley: University of California Press. ri, 197–213.

Yang, Z., & Qu, S. (2005). A brief analysis on three policy changes of grain purchase and sales. *Green Issues Research* (2), 13–18.

Yep, R. (2004). Can "Tax-for-Fee" reform reduce rural tension in China? The process, progress and limitations. *The China Quarterly, 177*, 42–70.

Zhao, Y. (2000). Rural-to-urban labor migration in China: The past and the present. *Rural labor flows in China, 15*, 33.

Zhao, L., & Li, J. (2006). China's hukou system: Multifaceted changes and institutional causes. In *Discussion Paper, No. 9 (June), China Policy Institute, University of Nottingham*.

Chapter 4
Quantitative Measures of Inequality

Large volumes of studies have been carried out concerning China's rural–urban income inequality (Chen, Dai, Pu, Hou, & Feng, 2010; Ding, 2002; Li, Sato, & Sicular, 2013; Mukhopadhaya, 2013; Xie & Zhou, 2014; Yang & Cai, 2003). These studies have generally reached an agreement that China's income inequality has been on a rise in the market-oriented reforms. Besides, it is the sector differences between the rural and urban populations that made the dominant contribution to the overall inequality.

However, despite the coexistence of rural and urban populations in the countryside, the rural–urban income inequality in the rural setting has not been paid enough academic attention, although there has been growing literature to study income inequality from the rural perspective (Benjamin, Brandt, & Giles, 2005; Gustafsson & Shi, 2002; Kai-Yuen, 1998; Rozelle, 1994; Wan & Zhou, 2005). These existing studies have revealed rural China is not a homogeneous entity, and the rural–urban inequality as part of the rural heterogeneity deserves further exploration. This chapter aims to give a quantitative analysis on rural–urban income inequality in rural China, in that the patterns of rural–urban income inequality are revealed in Heilongjiang Province at both provincial and county levels. At provincial level, it aims to understand the extent of the overall rural–urban income inequality in the agrarian province by looking at its overall Gini coefficients from 1990 to 2012. At county level, it examines the rural–urban contribution to the overall income inequality in the countryside with the decomposed Theil indices. The relations between the rural–urban income inequality and other economic factors are also examined.

Due to the non-availability of data, the inequality in Heilongjiang Province before 1990 cannot be measured using the methods employed in this book. However, from the available information about income, it can be roughly estimated that, at the very beginning of the 1978 reform, rural–urban income inequality in Heilongjiang is expected to be very close to, or even higher than the national level.

© Shanghai Jiao Tong University Press and Springer Nature Singapore Pte Ltd. 2018
Y. Gao and S. Fennell, *China's Rural–Urban Inequality in the Countryside*,
https://doi.org/10.1007/978-981-10-8273-3_4

This is because, until then, urban Heilongjiang had been developing well, thanks to the national strategy of boosting the heavy industry in north eastern China during the planning era (Table 1.4). Meanwhile, agriculture in Heilongjiang had a better performance than the national level (Table 1.5).

With the help of the greater availability of data in later years, the rural–urban income disparities can be measured systematically. This chapter provides a more detailed examination.

4.1   The Gini Coefficient

In calculating Gini coefficient, the ideal statistical source would be household survey data provided in the statistics yearbooks. To calculate the Chinese Gini, however, the most prominent problem lies in the way that data are organized in the official source provided by the NSB, the Chinese Statistics Yearbooks. The NSB provides two categorical samples from the urban and from the rural areas, rather than the integrated samples for all (Chen, Dai, Pu, Hou, & Feng, 2010).

Due to the technical difficulty in dealing with data, researchers have made various attempts to solve the problem. Among the studies on the overall rural–urban Gini coefficient estimates, some scholars use self-collected but publically inaccessible data (Benjamin et al., 2005; Khan & Riskin, 1998, 2005; Li, Zhao, & Zhang, 1998; Ravallion & Chen, 2007); or/and seek alternative methods that work well when only a limited set of summary statistics by income intervals are available (Cheng, 2007; Wu & Perloff, 2005). However, such studies are generally able to provide snapshots when data in certain years become accessible, or prone to be limited by applicability of the methods.

In 2013, National Statistics Bureau for the first time published the estimates of Gini coefficient officially for the past (Chen et al., 2010) ten years. It rearranged existing data and unified the recording systems for rural and urban income analysis. According to the Chief of the NSB, the computation was based on old data with new methods as the unified system would only be put in use from 2013 onwards. However, at sub-national level especially for analysis of early years, the technical problem for the dual income reporting system still exists as an obstacle to computing the overall Gini. As Li has noticed 'because of problems in statistics data, it is unable work out overall Gini coefficients for the province, but only those for the urban sector' (Li, 2006: 22).

For assessing rural–urban income inequality in Heilongjiang, this book intends to apply a simple framework proposed by Hu so that Gini estimates can be made with existing grouped data (Hu, 2004). Based on the quintile rule, there is the formula below where P_i represents the income proportion of the ith group of population to the total, so that Gini estimates can be made with existing grouped data by the NSB. Therefore,

$$G = \frac{1}{n} \sum_{i=2}^{5} \sum_{j<i} (P_i - P_j)$$

$$= \frac{1}{5} [(P_2 - P_1) + (P_3 - P_1) + (P_3 - P_2) + (P_4 - P_1) + (P_4 - P_2) + (P_4 - P_3)$$

$$+ (P_5 - P_1) + (P_5 - P_2) + (P_5 - P_3) + (P_5 - P_4)]$$

$$= \frac{1}{5} (P_2 + 2P_3 + 3P_4 + 4P_5 - 4P_1 - 3P_2 - 2P_3 - P_4)$$

$$= \frac{1}{5} (4P_5 - 4P_1 + 2P_4 - 2P_2)$$

To simplify the procedure, suppose the proportions of five groups are sequenced according to arithmetic progressions of income with a difference, D, therefore

$$P_2 = P_1 + D$$
$$P_3 = P_1 + 2D$$
$$P_4 = P_1 + 3D$$
$$P_5 = P_1 + 4D$$
$$G = \frac{4(P_5 - P_1) + 2(P_4 - P_2)}{5}$$
$$= \frac{4(P_1 + 4D - P_1) + 2(P_1 + 3D - P_1 - D)}{5}$$
$$= 4D$$
$$= P_1 + 4D - P_1$$
$$= P_5 - P_1$$

Therefore, according to Hu's framework, the Gini coefficient equals the difference between the income percentages of the highest income group and the lowest income group to the total if population are divided equally into five groups. Of course, in reality the differences between the five groups could not be identical, but this is a simplified approach and is proved to be precise. Hu has compared calculation results of the simplified Gini coefficient estimates for 34 countries in the 1990s against those published by the World Bank, and the results are found to be very close, although he has pointed out that the result from the simplified calculation is in theory bigger than the real Gini (Hu, 2004).

What is more important, such simplified method proves to be effective in China, as the large rural–urban inequality makes the two sectors easily separable in terms of income. For example, in 2012, 25% of rural population, or 20% of the total, had an income lower than 6073.9 yuan, which was less than the bottom urban group with an average income of 6092.3 yuan. We thus assume that the bottom quintile income group is from the rural sector. Similarly, 40% of the urban population, or 23% of the total, had an income over 21,411.7 yuan, which was higher than the top rural group with an average income of 18,825.3 yuan. Accordingly, it is assumed that the top quintile income group is from the urban sector. That is, there is reason to believe that the top income quintile is composed of urban residents while the bottom quintile is composed of rural population. By using the simplified method, the problem of dual income reporting systems for the rural and urban sectors is able to be solved, and it is possible to work out the overall Gini coefficient as long as information about the top and bottom quintiles is available.

It is noted that the above is only the simplified estimate of the Gini coefficient. It is based on the assumption that the top 20% income group is composed of urban residents while the bottom 20% is rural only, in order to avoid the problem due to the dual reporting system. In reality, however, there might be exceptions where some rural households are much better off, and some urban residents are in extreme poverty. But considering the large income disparities between the two sectors in China, such exceptions are expected to be very small in number, thus will not be considered in this book.

The measurement of China's income inequality with Gini coefficients has been conducted extensively by social scientists and economists, both domestically and overseas. Some of the results on China's Gini coefficients since 1990 are listed in Table 4.1.

Estimates with provincial data indicate that Gini coefficient in Heilongjiang remained at a level of below 0.30 until the late 1990s. Since then it has shown an increase until 2004 and soon resumed a growing trend in line with the official Gini estimated by the NSB which started to go down after 2009, although still maintained at a high level of about 0.40.

In examining the Gini coefficient result, several time points deserve more attention. Firstly, in the mid-1990s, the growth in income disparities seems to have stabilized or even fallen slightly. In 1994, there was a large increase in the grain procurement prices in China. In Heilongjiang, the price index for grain procurement increased by 30.5% compared with the previous year. The introduction of the GGBRS (governor grain bag responsibility system) gave further support to grain prices. In 1995, the prices for wheat, maize and soya beans were 38.6, 26.2 and 11.9% higher respectively than those of the previous year in this province. This has greatly improved the rural income and helped to narrow the rural–urban income divide.

However, almost at the same time, the state had decided to strengthen its financial control by introducing a fiscal reform in 1994. This ensured that more revenue went to the state coffers. With the delegation of more responsibilities to the lower level governments, the local financial difficulties deteriorated and many local governments resorted to non-budgetary funds to make up for the financial deficits, such as collecting local charges, and the peasants shouldered the burden of such financial difficulties. In addition, since 1997, for three years, the procurement prices constantly decreased. Until 1999, the prices for wheat, maize and soya beans were only 82.5, 92.9 and 79.3% respectively those of the 1998 level. The Gini coefficient calculation result has shown a rapid increase in inequalities since the late 1990s, which continued to 2003.

Table 4.1 Gini index by various sources

Year	Cheng (2007)	Ravallion and Chen (2007)	Wu and Perloff (2005)	Mukhopadhaya (2013)	NSB (2013)	Chen et al. (2010)	Li (2006)	Guo et al. (2005)	Current study
	National Overall						Heilongjiang Urban		Overall
1990	0.3587	0.3485	0.327	0.379		0.3508			0.2717
1991	N/A	0.3706	0.345			0.3646			0.2874
1992	0.3993	0.3901	0.361			0.3832			0.2719
1993	0.4183	0.4195	0.380			0.4070			0.2902
1994	0.4300	0.4331	0.381			0.4154			0.2973
1995	0.4169	0.4150	0.382			0.4112			0.2827
1996	0.3946	0.3975	0.349			0.3913		0.19	0.2818
1997	0.3964	0.3978	0.375			0.3924		0.25	0.3094
1998	0.4001	0.4033	0.378			0.4026		0.24	0.3199
1999	0.4124	0.4161	0.389			0.4092		0.25	0.3406
2000	0.4127	0.4382	0.407	0.465		0.4321		0.27	0.3839
2001	0.4275	0.4473	0.415			0.439	0.296	0.28	0.3888
2002	0.4331					0.4506	0.350	0.33	0.4206
2003	0.4297			0.444	0.479	0.4657	0.313		0.4126
2004	0.4430				0.473	0.4567	0.347		0.3996
2005	0.4419				0.485	0.4573			0.4447
2006					0.487	0.4624			0.4409
2007					0.484				0.4333
2008				0.508	0.491				0.4370

(continued)

Table 4.1 (continued)

Year	Cheng (2007)	Ravallion and Chen (2007)	Wu and Perloff (2005)	Mukhopadhaya (2013)	NSB (2013)	Chen et al. (2010)	Li (2006)	Guo et al. (2005)	Current study
National							Heilongjiang		
Overall							Urban		Overall
2009					0.49				0.4350
2010					0.481				0.4092
2011					0.477				0.4129
2012					0.474				0.3920

Source Compiled by the authors

In 2004, Heilongjiang became one of the pilot provinces to practice pro-agricultural policies. Agricultural taxes were abolished, together with local charges. In addition, subsidies were given to the grain growers. Accordingly, there was an increase of rural income in 2004 (see the last column for current study in Table 4.1). Such policies did have some effects on reducing the income inequality but the impact seemed to be limited because, although income inequality was reined into some extent, it remained at a high level. In addition, inequality resumed the trend of growth in 2005.

Another change started in 2006, that since then there have been more pro-agricultural polices introduced concerning the regeneration of the rural sector (see Table 1.3). The impact of series of such polices seemed to have slowed down the overall Gini coefficients to some extent. However, the effectiveness of the polices are still waiting to be assessed as the Gini remained high until 2012.

Results of our estimates show that compared with other studies, income inequality in Heilongjiang Province is lower than the national level. Meanwhile, at provincial level, this study presents a much higher overall Gini than the urban Gini coefficients of the province worked out by other researchers (Guo, Wu, & Zheng, 2005; Li, 2006).

It should be noted that the low level of income inequality should not be, in any way, related to the 'harmonious development' of rural and urban sectors in Heilongjiang. This is because, as introduced in Chap. 1, such a low level of income inequality is within expectation, as the performance of the urban sector in Heilongjiang has been unsatisfactory compared with the national average. This led the local researchers to believe that the apparently low level of income inequality is, in fact, the result of a low level of development in the urban sector (Guo et al., 2005; Xiangguo & Wei, 2006; Xu & Xue, 2006).

4.2 The Theil Index

The book goes down the administrative level to decompose income inequality in Heilongjiang by measurement of its Theil index. The Theil index is the special condition of generalized entropy measures, when within and between inequality among groups are explained more clearly. Here we use Thiel's T Statistic as it is a powerful tool for analyzing inequality within and between various groupings, written as

$$T = \sum_{i=1}^{n} \left[\left(\frac{1}{n} \right) * \left(\frac{y_i}{\mu_y} \right) * \ln \left(\frac{y_i}{\mu_y} \right) \right]$$

where y^i is the ith individual's income measured in Chinese yuan, and μ_y is the total sample mean. Since population of Heilongjiang can be classified into rural and urban as mutually exclusive and completely exhaustive groups, Theil's T Statistic for the population in the province (T_H) is made up of two components, the between group component (T^B) and the within group component (T^W), known as

$$T_H = T^B + T^W$$

The purpose of analysis at this stage is to examine how large the income inequality is in Heilongjiang province at the county level and contributions of inequality from within rural and urban sectors as well as between rural–urban. Data at the county level come from Heilongjiang Statistics Yearbooks for various years. The results are shown in Fig. 4.1.

It is found in the Theil index calculation that much of the income inequality is due to the sectoral difference, or rural–urban divide. Since the 1990s, inequality has explained more by the difference between rural and urban rather than within individual sectors. In 1991, the rural urban divide explained about 90% of the total inequality, which was reduced to 72% in the mid-1990s but increased to over 80% after 2000, and reduced to the level below 80% only after 2010. This indicates that, even within the rural setting, which is less heterogeneous in terms of income, major difference still emerges between the rural and urban categories.

Similar to the Gini result, the Theil calculation of the study also reflected the impact of the price change on inequality. As explained in Chap. 3, in the mid-1990s, when the central government increased grain prices twice, rural income enjoyed a constant increase, which contributed to the lowest level of income inequality. The 2004 reform produced the same result. Take Qinggang as an example: when the agricultural tax was abolished and subsidies were provided for grain planting, the grain yields increased by 169.4% compared with the previous year, with increases of 30.9% in value added to the first industry, 24.8% for local

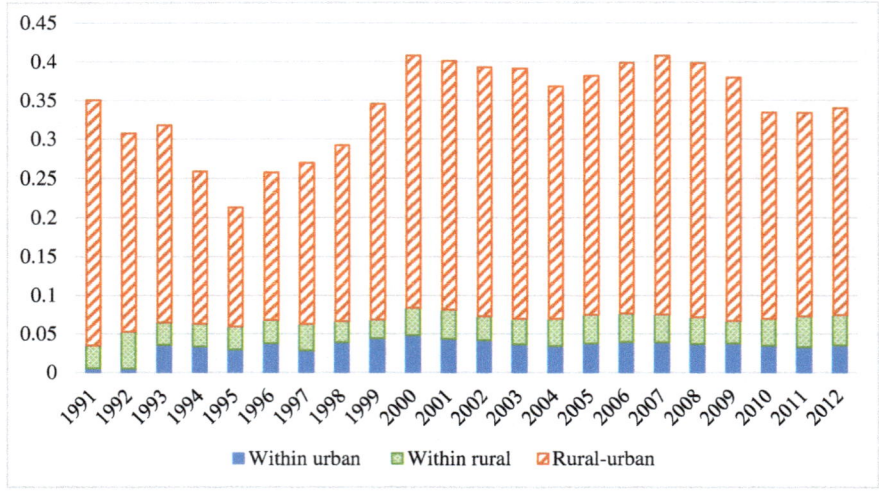

Fig. 4.1 Theil coefficients at county level, Heilongjiang. *Source* Authors

GDP and 36.7% to the rural net income. Taking the province as a whole, the abolition of agricultural tax did work towards the reduction of income disparities, as reflected in the Theil index calculation result, although the effects of such pro-agricultural policies proved unsatisfactory, as the overall inequality remained at a high level. There appear slight decreases of the total disparities after 2007 (Fig. 4.1). As analysed previously, this might have been the impact of the pro-agricultural polices introduced thereafter. Yet, the comprehensive effects need further examination.

It should be noted that, for the Theil index calculation in this study, the income disparities are expected to be lower than the provincial average. That is because the Theil results have been based on county-level data, and the inequality is expected to be lower as, down the administrative ladder, it is generally becoming more homogeneous in terms of income. Counties are places where most of the population is rural. Even for those living in the rural areas but holding urban household registration, their income is not comparable to their counterparts in the cities.

In fact, in Heilongjiang, the urban income in the cities is much higher than that in counties. Take 2006 as an example; the average urban income at the provincial level was 17,760 yuan. However, at the county level, the average urban income was only 14,405 yuan. Moreover, the urban income between the cities varies a lot. The statistical data show that in Heilongjiang, for years, only two cities (Harbin and Daqing) have a higher urban income than the provincial average. Harbin is the provincial capital and Daqing is where the oil field is located. Urban income for the cities in Heilongjiang is not included in the Theil calculation, and there is reason to believe that, if urban income in the cities were considered in the measurement, the inequality could be much larger.

Larger cities are places into which more resources flow. Take Harbin City as an example: in 1979, because of the price increase of more than 20 agricultural products, the urban subsides had increased greatly, from 19.39 million yuan in 1978 to 32.97 million yuan. Since then, price subsides for grains and edible oil in Harbin grew rapidly, due to the increase in the purchase price as well as the rise in the quantities consumed. In 1983, the total subsidies on grain and edible oil reached 72.93 million yuan, more than double the amount in 1979. In 1985, the State Council decided to designate Harbin as one of its separate planning cities.[1] One big change in subsidies is that the standard was improved to a higher level accordingly. The total price subsides for grains and edible oil jumped from 84.67 million yuan to 140.41 million yuan within a year, with the per capita subsidies increasing from 33.59 yuan to 54.83 yuan. In 1986, urban subsidies reached 340 million yuan including price subsides for grains, edible oil, meat and poultry, vegetables as well as subsidies for coal. Subsidies thus constituted about 40% of the city's total

---

[1]'Separate planning city' used to be one of the terms used for China's administrative regions. Its fiscal revenue and expenditure were decided by the central government and the individual city, without the intervention of the provincial government. Until 1993, there were 14 such cities, Harbin being one of them.

expenditure. From then on, subsides grew substantially, based on a new level and, until 1990, the total and per capita subsides both doubled the amount of 1985.

In this sense, the high income level of the provincial average for the urban sector is propped up by two large cities with a very high urban income, indicating a high level of income inequality between cities and a larger income gap between the rural and urban sectors in the province.

4.3 Correlation Result

The Pearson correlations between the rural–urban income gap and related variables have been calculated using SPSS. The calculation was based on county level data in 2006, according to the Second Agricultural Census in 2006. It helps to establish the statistical relationships between rural–urban income inequality and other economic indicators. These include the per capita GDP, rural income, percentage of rural labour transferred out of agriculture against the total, grain production, local revenue, local expenditure, mileage of village roads, high school enrolment, urbanization, and the ratio of urban labour productivity against the rural one. These are believed to include all of the important economic indicators with possible relationships with the rural–urban income gap. The following table displays the correlation results with their statistical significance (Table 4.2).

Some local researchers have tried to establish a relationship between rural–urban income difference and other variables. For example, by using 1978–2006 yearbook data, Meng set up a multivariate regression model to examine the impact of various factors on the rural-income gap in Heilongjiang. He believes that five factors are closely related to the rural–urban income gap. They are the ratio of added value of non-agricultural industry to the added value of agriculture, the ratio of urban labour productivity to rural labour productivity, the growth of the per capita GDP, the percentage of government expenditure on agriculture against the total, and

Table 4.2 Correlation results

		Per capita GDP	High school student numbers	Urbanization	Ratio of urban labour productivity against rural
Rural/ urban income gap	Pearson correlation	0.485**	−0.252*	0.281*	0.255*
	Sig. (2-tailed)	0.000	0.044	0.024	0.042

Source From the author
Note *Correlation is significant at the 0.05 level (2-tailed)
**Correlation is significant at the 0.01 level (2-tailed)

urbanization. The regression result, obtained using SPSS, shows that all of these variables are significant at the 0.05 level (Meng, 2007).

For the current study, among all the variables examined, rural/urban income disparities are found to be statistically correlated with four of them. It is found that, at the 0.01 level, the rural/urban income gap is highly correlated with per capita GDP. At a significance of 0.05, the rural/urban income divide is statistically correlated to high school student enrolment, urbanization and the urban/rural labour productivity ratio.

The high correlation between income inequality and the per capita GDP suggests that the rural/urban income gap is related to development. It seems that the gap is bigger in more developed areas. The correlation result between income gap and per capita GDP is consistent with Meng, who argues that, for a region with a low level of development, the rural/urban income gap will increase with the per capita GDP growth. This continues until development reaches a certain level, when the income gap starts to decrease, with the continued growth of per capita GDP (Meng, 2007). As found by Chen, the growth of GDP at this advanced stage has become an important force in reducing urban/rural income disparity (Chen, 2002).

The results of this study regarding the correlation between income disparity and urbanization is different from others in that it shows a positive relation, while, in other studies (Chen, 2002; Meng, 2007), urbanization is negatively correlated with rural/urban income disparity, indicating that urbanization is helpful in reducing income inequalities. However, the county data in Heilongjiang used for the present study reveals that a place with higher urbanization tends to have higher income inequality. This could be explained by research conducted by Wang that drawing on the concept of an inverted U from Kuznets, he confirmed that the process of urbanization has an inverted U-shaped effect on rural/urban income disparities in a region (Wang, 2006), that income inequality undergoes a rapid increase, and then a stable and finally a rapid decrease process, with labour continuing to be transferred out of the rural sector. This indicates that the counties in Heilongjiang are at an initial stage of development. Urbanization in such areas could only further widen the income gap before it eventually closes up.

The correlation results also show that, for a county with better economic development, higher urbanization and more earning opportunities, more young people of school age will be attracted to join the labour force. Therefore, in such counties, high school enrolment is seen to be lower. But it has to be pointed out that such result does not mean education is a level of income gap. Considering that high school students are between 14 and 18 years old, at the suitable age to start earning for the family, the result could only indicate that more students are simply attracted by income earning opportunities rather than staying at school.

Statistically, a relationship between income inequality and the ratio of urban/ rural labour productivity is set up. As argued by Meng, a higher ratio indicates higher urban productivity or lower rural productivity (Meng, 2007). For the counties in Heilongjiang, this is reflected as a large amount of under- or even unemployment in rural areas, which eventually results in an enlarged rural/urban income gap. On the contrary, a county with a lower urban rural productivity ratio will reflect the higher productivity of the rural sector, which helps to reduce the rural/urban income divide. This is consistent with the Lewis model, that the transfer of rural labour from agriculture will certainly help to reduce the rural/urban income disparities as rural productivity can be improved.

Several points deserve further consideration for the calculation of the Pearson correlation. First, the purpose of this part is to find out the possible statistical relationships between rural–urban income gap and other economic indicators to give a preliminary test on the features of areas with high or low rural–urban income inequality, rather than how much the income difference has been influenced by these variables. Therefore, the result only reports bivariate relationships. Second, statistical relationships between income inequality and some other economic indicators cannot be established with the help of the Pearson correlation. This does not mean that the income gap and these indicators are not related. Rural–urban income inequality is a complicated issue, a simple method like the Pearson correlation calculation may be far from sufficient to explain its relationships with other variables. Finally, the correlation result in this study and those found by other local researchers are related only to the situation in Heilongjiang. Such tentative results cannot be generalized to other parts of China, and their applicability still needs to be tested in the development of other regions. However, the Pearson correlation result does provide statistical indication on the relationships between rural–urban income gap and some economic development indicators in Heilongjiang. The result is helpful for further research.

References

Benjamin, D., Brandt, L., & Giles, J. (2005). The evolution of income inequality in rural China. *Economic Development and Cultural Change, 53*(4), 769–824.

Chen, Z. (2002). *Further discussion on income distribution in reform and development.* Beijing: Economic and Scientific Press.

Chen, J., Dai, D., Pu, M., Hou, W., & Feng, Q. (2010). The trend of the Gini coefficient of China. *BWPI Working Paper 109.*

Cheng, Y. (2007). China's overall Gini coefficient since reform and its decomposition by rural and urban areas since reform and opening up. *Social Sciences in China, 4,* 45–60.

Ding, L. (2002). Rural–urban income disparity: impact of growth, allocative efficiency, and local growth welfare. *China Economic Review, 13*(4), 419–429.

Guo, Y., Wu, X., & Zheng, J. (2005). The economic analyse on the enlargement of the difference of the city residents' income in Heilongjiang Province. *Journal of Qiqihar University (Philosophy & Social Science Edition), 1,* 51–53.

Gustafsson, B., & Shi, L. (2002). Income inequality within and across counties in rural China 1988 and 1995. *Journal of Development Economics, 69*(1), 179–204.

Hu, Z. (2004). A study of the best theoretical value of Gini coefficient and its concise calculation formula. *Economic Research Journal, 9,* 60–69.

Kai-Yuen, T. (1998). Factor decomposition of Chinese rural income inequality: New methodology, empirical findings, and policy implications. *Journal of Comparative Economics, 26*(3), 502–528.

Khan, A. R., & Riskin, C. (1998). Income and inequality in China: Composition, distribution and growth of household income, 1988 to 1995. *The China Quarterly, 154*, 221–253.

Khan, A. R., & Riskin, C. (2005). China's household income and its distribution, 1995 and 2002. *The China Quarterly, 182*, 356–384.

Li, S., Sato, H., & Sicular, T. (2013). *Rising inequality in China: Challenges to a harmonious society*. Cambridge University Press.

Li, S., Zhao, R., & Zhang, P. (1998). Transition of China's economy and change of income distribution. *Economic Research Journal, 4*, 43–51.

Li, X. (2006). Calculation and research on income disparities in Heilongjiang Province *Statistics and Consolation, 5*, 22–23.

Meng, X. (2007). Empirical analysis on rural-urban income inequality in Heilongjiang Province. *Township Economy, 11*, 15–18.

Mukhopadhaya, P. (2013). Trends in income inequality in China: The effects of various sources of income. *Journal of the Asia Pacific Economy, 18*(2), 304–317.

Ravallion, M., & Chen, S. (2007). China's (uneven) progress against poverty. *Journal of Development Economics, 82*(1), 1–42.

Rozelle, S. (1994). Rural industrialization and increasing inequality: Emerging patterns in China's reforming economy. *Journal of comparative economics, 19*(3), 352–391.

Wan, G., & Zhou, Z. (2005). Income inequality in rural China: Regression-based decomposition using household data. *Review of Development Economics, 9*(1), 107–120.

Wang, R. (2006). An analysis of the reasons for rural-urban income disparities: Applicability of the 'inverted-U' hypothesis in China. *Statistical Research, 4*, 14–19.

Wu, X., & Perloff, J. M. (2005). China's income distribution, 1985–2001. *Review of Economics and Statistics, 87*(4), 763–775.

Xiangguo, X., & Wei, X. (2006). Research on rural-urban income inequality in Heilongjiang Province. *Academic Exchange, 145*(4), 98–100.

Xie, Y., & Zhou, X. (2014). Income inequality in today's China. *Proceedings of the National Academy of Sciences, 111*(19), 6928–6933.

Yang, D. T., & Cai, F. (2003). The political economy of China's rural-urban divide. *How Far Across the River*, 389–416.

Chapter 5
The Perspective of Peasants

5.1 The Province of Heilongjiang

The fieldwork for this study was conducted in Qinggang County, Heilongjiang Province. Located in east central Heilongjiang, Qinggang is one of the grain producing counties of the province with maize as its major product if not the only one (other grains and vegetables grown there are mostly for self-consumption). Qinggang County is in the hinterland of the Songnen Plain, 120 km north of the provincial capital Harbin and 120 km east of Daqing, the city famous for its oil resources. No railway service is available in the county, though it is universal throughout China. Its transport link to the outside relies on buses and private vehicles.[1]

5.1.1 The County of Qinggang

As an ordinary county in north China, Qinggang became known to the country for two reasons. The first is its poverty (Picture 5.1). In 1990, it was designated as a 'national poor county'. Designation of poor counties is part of the state's Poor Area Development Program for poverty reduction. In 1994, 592 counties were identified as 'national poor counties' when the state decided that counties with a per capita rural income of less than 400 yuan in 1992 should be designated as poverty-stricken.[2]

---

[1]There are many bus services available from Harbin to other places by way of Qinggang. But when the fieldwork was conducted in 2006, the only one between Harbin and Qinggang was a mini-bus service, which was extremely unreliable because of the poor condition of the vehicles. The first author took twice, and for both times the mini-buses broke down on the way.

[2]See the Eighth Seven-year Poverty Alleviation Reinforcement Plan (1994–2000), issued by the State Council in 1994, available at: http://news.sina.com.cn/2004-08-25/17534137022.shtml. Accessed 12 January 2017.

© Shanghai Jiao Tong University Press and Springer Nature Singapore Pte Ltd. 2018
Y. Gao and S. Fennell, *China's Rural–Urban Inequality in the Countryside*,
https://doi.org/10.1007/978-981-10-8273-3_5

Picture 5.1 A Glimpse of a Village in Qinggang. *Source* Authors

Qinggang was included among the 592 counties as its per capita rural income in 1992 was 299 yuan, well below the 400 yuan national threshold.

Once an area has been designated a 'national poor county' it is entitled to money from the state. State funding came in three forms: a special loan for poverty reduction, work for poverty relief (*yigong daizhen*, to provide working opportunities for local infrastructure construction) and capital investment for local development. There is no way to know without the help of the county government how much Qinggang had been benefited from being a national poor county during the Eighth Seven-year Plan. But the first author's previous trip with the Research Centre of Heilongjiang Provincial Government in 2005 provided some reference.

During the visit to Huanan, another national poor county within the jurisdiction of Jiamusi City, the county governor told the delegation that funding provided by the state for poverty alleviation was more than its annual local fiscal income (84.85 million yuan in 2005). Qinggang is certainly different from Huanan in many ways. However, the Huanan case provided a good reference as to how much financial support a county might get if it is designated as 'national poor'.

The following example given by a local official in the township government of Qinggang illustrates how 'national poor' and 'non-poor' counties were differentiated in terms of disaster relief. After a flood in Heilongjiang, food stuff for disaster relief was given to the flooded counties. Grains were given in trucks to Lanxi (a nearby national poor county) while Qinggang (it was not a national poor county at that time) was only given a few sacks.

This may help to explain why counties have been competing with each other to be designated as 'national poor'. Being 'poor' is thus not a shameful title any more, but something which may lead to substantial financial benefits. In this sense, Qingang's governor was not 'wise' enough to get the title removed in 2001, which was due to the reportedly substantial per capita income increase from 751 yuan in 1993 to 2300 yuan in 1998. Because of the drastic rural income growth, Qinggang got the title of 'national poor' removed. The then county governor had accumulated enough political achievements in poverty alleviation and was promoted as a leader in the Suihua Prefecture. But the removal of the 'national poor' title was against the benefits of Qinggang County, as commented in Liu Chengguo's (former Deputy Head of Ministry of Agriculture) speech during his visit to Heilongjiang Province in 2002,

> There are fourteen national poor counties in Heilongjiang Province with Mingshui and Qinggang excluded, which is in accordance with the state policy of keeping general stability while making minor adjustments. National poor counties in Heilongjiang Province have been designated by way of rigorous calculation and ranking according to four indicators in each county as population under poverty, rural net income, per capita GDP and per capita fiscal income. Although Mingshui and Qinggang were reluctant for not being included, they had nothing to say. The county party secretary told me: 'we cannot blame others, for the figures we reported were too high'. Lanxi had restructured its leading team and did a lot of practical work, it was thus included (designated as national poor) because of its factual and realistic work style.

When the removal of the title 'national poor county' was mentioned to one of the informants, an ordinary peasant, she snapped back with a rhetorical question, 'It is removed. Is our living improved then?' Her reply made people speechless at how realistically and differently ordinary people would see the same issue.

In addition to poverty, what also makes Qinggang famous is a law case from 2005, known as the biggest bribery case concerning post selling in Communist China by that time. Ma De, the then Committee Secretary of Suihua Municipal City (Qinggang is located within its jurisdiction) took large sums of bribes (over 6 million yuan) from officials at municipal and lower level governments before appointing them higher positions. 265 officials were involved including the former head of the Ministry of Land and Resources, who was former governor of Heilongjiang and president of Heilongjiang Provincial Political Consultative Conference. Two officials from Qinggang were involved. One of them once bribed Ma with 500,000 yuan to be appointed as the county governor.

Qinggang, an ordinary county in north China thus became infamous throughout the country, as people were curious about the driving force of buying a position of county governor with so much money and inevitably wanted to know how much money a county governor would be able to accumulate in such a poverty-stricken place where 40% people still lived under the national poverty line with an average per capita rural income below 2000 yuan in 2005.

As for our research, the case of Qingang is worth researching not only because of its economic development but also its special political background. However,

Fig. 5.1 Map of Qinggang
County. *Source* Internet

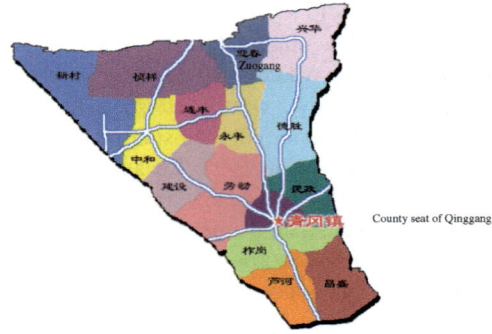

under such circumstances, local cadres were extremely difficult to access and talk to, as they might be more alert and sensitive. During the fieldtrip we did not have the chance to see any of the county leaders in office, except a former secretary who used to work in the administrative office of the county government.

5.1.2   The Township of Zuogang

The difficulty in reaching the county-level officials had forced us to change the field site from the county seat to one of the townships in Qinggang. Zuogang is the location where our fieldwork was conducted. It is a township located 4 km south of the county seat (Fig. 5.1), and a farming community with about 170,000 mu of cultivated land composed of good black soil.

In addition, there is an alkali ditch stretching from the east to the west of Zuogang. Along the ditch spreads 12,000 mu of grassland suitable for animal pasturing. Apart from these, Zuogang is located by the main road with convenient transportation. Despite the comparatively preferential natural conditions, living was still difficult for the local people. According to the secretary, responsible for drafting speeches for the township leaders, when the fieldwork was carried out in 2006, 6–8% of the population had an annual income less than 668 yuan and about 3500–4000 people (about 10% of the total population) had their annual income less than 882 yuan.[3]

Our research from both the perspectives of local peasants and cadres has tried to provide an answer as to why income was stagnated, although we have to admit that contact with cadres proved to be much more difficult than with ordinary peasants.

---

[3]668 yuan was set as the poverty line and 882 yuan as the low income line by State Statistics Bureau in 2004.

5.2 Opportunities for Earning Income

There were three major sources of rural income, from farming, off-farm rural activities and from *dagong* (working for others).

5.2.1 Income from Land

Land is probably the most important asset to which rural households have access. Compared with other parts of China, Heilongjiang is abundant in land resources. On average, cultivated land allocation is 9.3 mu per rural head, well above the national average of 1.39 mu.[4] However, for ordinary peasants in Zuogang, the land allocated is much less than the provincial average with only 5.3 mu per rural head, and land allocation is far from equal among villages.

Historically when the commune system was dismantled in the early 1980s, land was divided among brigades. A large brigade with more people would usually have less land per head. In the villages we visited near the town government, land allocation per head was between 3 and 6 mu. Thus, each household has about 10–30 mu of land allocated as a subsistence field. But for Fanrong Village located further away from the township government, land was scarce with only 2.2 mu per head. In that village, an ordinary household would have less than 10 mu of land. As one of the informants from that village said, 'each family has 8 or 10 mu of land, some 5 or 6 mu of land. The most in our *tun*[5] won't exceed 20 mu.'

Land is a sensitive issue and essential to villagers' living. There are usually disputes over land between cadres and peasants. One of the informants described her experience of taking back her land by 'fighting' with a village cadre. Several years ago, local cadres decided to confiscate her subsistence land together with that of 15 other villagers to 'develop something'. She had a terrible quarrel with one of the cadres emphasizing, 'are you going to starve us to death, after taking the land?' The cadre replied it was for *zaofu* (to benefit). She condemned him by asking: 'how about the big hole (deep debt) in our brigade? How did you make benefits?' She complained, 'a big hole of over one million! how did they make benefits? Make benefits? Benefit whom?' She then continued her story: 'even by fighting I would have to take back my land, the only land I have got, 2.2 mu for each person! Without the land for four, I am not able to make a living! The village head banged the table that hard, almost smashed it to scare me off. I said: You scare me? It won't work if you scare me. I just want my land back! …At that time, he wanted to hit me.

---

[4]It might be worth noticing that there are 103 state farms in Heilongjiang, the largest number in China, accounting for 21.5% of total cultivated land, which is cultivated by non-rural population instead of by peasants, as workers of state farms are non-rural.

[5]Natural village.

I said: You do it!... I am an ordinary person, and what can you do with me? I have to take back my land!' She also went to the county government, where she was asked which level of cadres she would like to denounce. She said: 'cadres at any level would be the same; I wouldn't denounce any of them. I just want my subsistence land back. I just want my land!' According to her, 'without the land, I cannot survive. I grow some grains, whatever they are, coarse or refined, I could keep myself alive'. She finally managed to take her land back with the other 15 people. She said without the 'fighting' the cadres would have sold her land and she would have no way to survive.

We got it from the fieldtrip that no matter how much land was actually allocated to each household, the peasants would always complain that 'land is so scarce in this place, it is barely enough for ordinary people to make a living'. The words that followed would be 'there is no way out!' or 'what else can we do?'

In recent years, many people have migrated to the cities and more land is left behind in villages. The common practice in Zuogang as in many other rural areas is that those who have migrated would lease the land to their fellow villagers if there were no other members (such as parents) of their families able to till the land. One of our informants was working on 70 mu of land. His family had been allocated 15 mu of land for three members. He got the rest of the land by lease. According to him, 'without land lease, there is only several mu for each member of the family. If you rely only on the allocated land, you barely have any income'. He continued, 'the problem in rural areas, although the policy from the state government is really good, it is still difficult living in rural area. There is so little land.'

Theoretically, more land is now concentrated within the hands of a smaller number of people, but few ordinary villagers are able to rent much land. Of all the people we interviewed only the one mentioned above rented much land for farming. There are two possible reasons for this. Firstly, land rental is getting more expensive, with some good land as high as 260 yuan per mu in 2007, which was not affordable for ordinary villagers as they had little money in hand and a bank loan was difficult to get.[6] Besides, ordinary people do not have powerful enough social networks to acquire much land and they would at most get a few extra mu from their fellow villagers or relatives. The first author was told by a villager, 'let me tell you the truth, some with certain rights[7] would have dozens of mu'. The above-mentioned person with 70 mu of land acknowledged that he was the accountant[8] in his village.

---

[6]Peasants have to pay off the loan on time. Otherwise it is harder to get a loan for the following year. There was a story during an interview that because one family did not pay off the loan on time, the credit association would not lease loans to the whole village the following year.

[7]The author once asked about the meaning of 'someone with certain rights', and got the answer that 'the cadres and those who have relationships with brigade (village) leaders in terms of kinship and friendship...those who get along well with leaders'.

[8]One of the three major village positions, the other two being village head and party secretary.

During the visit to Fanrong Village, while an ordinary peasant was allocated with only 2.2 mu per rural head, several villagers said that the former party secretary Old Fifth Han was in post for about two years and got 300 mu of land. The present party secretary Han Chunlei (Old Fifth Han's nephew) had over 100 mu of land. What attracts people's attention is that their land was neither allocated nor rented, but according to the villagers the land was 'their own property', as the land used to be flexible land in the village, but somehow fell into their own possession.

In each village, there used to be some *jidongdi* (flexible land). Such land was reserved as village property and was supposed to be allocated to 'new members' of a household such as a bride from another village or a new born baby of the family. However, villagers complained that there was no such land left. For the families visited, children under the age of 10 were usually not allocated with any land. The reason, as we were told was that for years much land had been sold and occupied by some private owned businesses such as factories, pig farms and chicken farms. In the words of a villager, 'in the past there was a lot of flexible land, and now it has been sold out (to individuals) by the brigade.'

The following examples illustrate how the flexible land went to individuals. In Fanrong Village, there was a Zhang who somehow lent a substantial sum of money with high interest to the village. After a year the village was unable to pay off the principal with interest and the party secretary decided to give him 40 mu of land as compensation. There was another one who was the owner of a local brick factory. The village once bought bricks from him on credit, but ended up returning 30 mu of land to him in lieu of money.

Since it was the local cadres' decision to sell flexible land to those who had various deals with them, villagers were very angry about it, complaining that 'the land has all been occupied, and flexible land is all under the control of the cadres'. This made some peasants nostalgic about the past, as a villager remembered, 'in the production team era, before…say 1975. (There was) a lot of land to grow crops. But now the good land has all been lost!'

With little land local peasants were unable to earn much from farming. Apart from production cost, the average net income from each mu would be 200 to 300 yuan. If the land was rented, the net income would be about 100 yuan. This was on the condition that no labour was hired. People with a lot of land would certainly earn more from comparatively large-scale farming, but for most peasants earnings from land were barely enough for living.

Research by the World Bank has found that, 'unlike other developing countries, landlessness is not a significant determinant of poverty in China. The incidence of poverty is higher among the landless, but not dramatically so, and most of the landless are not poor' (Atinc, 1997: 35). However, at least according to our findings from the field, land remained the most powerful protection for villagers in Zuogang, and landlessness became one of the main reasons for poverty. What is more important, both land allocation and land acquisition were found to be highly unequal. It has been established that land allocation was determined by endowment of individual villages, but land acquisition was much more manipulated.

5.2.2   Income from Off-Farm Activities

As mentioned above, maize is the major product in Zuogang. When asked, all villagers said they only plant maize and they gave the following reasons. The first reason might be related to the natural condition of the locality. There is no river in Qinggang, and droughts are frequent as the saying goes, 'there is a drought nine out of ten years', which is especially serious in spring during the ploughing season. This makes it difficult for the local people to grow paddy rice, a more profitable product. In addition, maize planting is simple as it is easier to take care of and unlike soybean, maize usually produces stable if not always high output. According to the villagers, 'compared with soybeans, maize is much easier to grow and easy to look after', while 'soybeans are not like maize, (which have) low production. (For maize) after pesticides are spread, you just shovel the land, and that's it.' When asked how long they would work in the field every year, the answer was that it took more time in the past. At that time, people had to shovel the field manually, but it is not necessary nowadays because of the mechanized farming implements. The following question was asked as what kind of implement it was, and the answer was 'just a shabby *silunzi* (four wheels).[9]'

In general, nowadays farm work takes less than a month in total, as one of the informants said it would take 'no more than a few days' and her daughter-in-law exaggerated that it 'could be finished within a day', as the farming is 'only for a couple of mu of land.' Besides, winter in north China is long, cold and dry. Unlike in south China, crops are harvested only once a year in Heilongjiang. Therefore, there is much off-farm time for peasants.

During the visits we discovered that local people had been trying every means to earn money, although not everyone could find enough work to do. Some villagers participated in various off-farm household activities including raising chicks, pigs, growing and selling bean sprouts, grain and vegetable collecting and selling, and goose egg incubation. Some families had their own business to transport goods or to run a local store.

Animal raising might be one of the common off-farm activities to earn extra money, but the scale was very small. For the households visited, villagers would have only a few small animals raised in their backyards. Raising chickens was the most popular way to supplement everyday living. As one of the villagers said she would 'sell the cocks when they grow up and keep the hens for eggs', because 'eggs can be sold for cash'. However, even though Zuogang is famous for goose raising, nicknamed as 'township of the white geese', no family visited made a living from it. The first author was told goose raising used to be a good business by the alkali ditch

---

[9]Local people used the term 'four wheels' (*silunzi*) to refer to any four-wheeled motor vehicles (except trucks and cars requiring a proper licence to drive). In most cases, these vehicles are more like tractors with trailers.

in west Zuogang, but there was no place to herd geese when the fieldtrip was made, because the public grassland had been sold out by the cadres. As one of the informants commented,

> Now there is no husbandry here, the marshy grasslands were all sold. Nothing is left. If you graze animals, you have to pay money. A certain amount (is charged) for a goose and a certain amount for a sheep. If you raise some small animals you just couldn't find a place to graze them…Without paying money, you don't think of the graze. You raise something but have nothing to feed them. (Interview conducted on 04/07/2007 with Wang, female, peasant)

One of the families made a living from growing and selling bean sprouts. When the family was visited, the woman was washing bean sprouts. She apologised for not being able to stop working and the interview was conducted against the background of water splashes. She constantly complained how hard living had been for her family because of landlessness and lack of social welfare. Over the past ten years, she had been living on selling home-grown bean sprouts. In her opinion, growing bean sprouts was not easy work at all because sprouts had to be washed regularly even at midnight. This meant she would work almost all day and night. Since she had to get up at about 2 a.m. every day, she barely had time to sleep. In explaining why she had to work that hard, she asked in reply, 'how can we earn money without working? What to spend then?' She said she never calculated how much exact she would earn each month.[10] Usually the more beans were grown the more money earned, but it was also necessary to deduct the cost of diesel expenses and tax for selling sprouts at market. Taxes were about 100 yuan in total each month at the time of the interview, which used to be much higher about 200 yuan per month.

Rural off-farm activities also involved something unusual. An old couple interviewed helped the family by hatching goose eggs. This was a practice requiring special techniques as the temperature had to be strictly controlled and maintained. The couple had one room only with half of their *kang* (bed) occupied by two big basket trays filled with goose eggs. The man was proud of his skills saying that this was actually an easy way to earn money because once the skills were acquired, selling the newly hatched geese was out of question. The problem is there was limited space at home and his earnings were not good enough. If he had a larger room he would certainly earn more.

One of the families interviewed had their own truck (bought with bridewealth and some borrowed money). The wife took care of the land at home while the husband was usually away from home transporting goods and fruits between Harbin and Qinggang. With about 18 mu of land for the family and income from

---

[10]The first author tried to calculate according to the information gathered from her. As bean sprouts were sold at 0.6–0.7 yuan per jin and every jin of beans (at the price of 3.5 yuan) would produce 10 jin of sprouts, she would earn 2.5–3.5 yuan for 10 jin of sprouts sold. Taking tax and diesel into consideration, she had to sell at least 70–80 jin of sprouts before she could earn money. This did not include other expenses such as lunch outside home during the sale, room heating and water boiling as temperature was needed for growing bean sprouts. Considering the room size needed to keep the growing sprouts, it would take her at least a week to produce 80–100 jin of sprouts.

goods transport (the debt had just been paid off), the young family was better-off than many of the others. Unfortunately, not many families would be able to afford a truck even with borrowed money. In most cases, they would use their own *silunzi* to collect (purchase) grains during the harvest season or to buy vegetables from households in one place and sell them at slightly higher prices in another, usually within the same county.

There were such people who would always keep themselves busy. According to one such villager, in winter he would 'lead' some people to 'collect' grains with his shabby vehicle.[11] He could earn 300 yuan for the winter, but he joked, 'will the money help a lot? Well, it's enough to pay the phone bill'.[12] His fellow villagers seemed to admire him. One of them commented that 'you are something! You are able to be a grain dealer!' and 'wise enough to think about money'. He replied, '(but for thinking about money) you say what else to do? A little will help if you could think of any....That's better than staying at home.' He also went to collect fish and vegetables in summer. He termed this as 'doing business' and such business would last half a year.

During the talks with local peasants we also found out that ordinary people could hardly afford any failure or risk because of poverty. Two examples provide good illustrations. One was told by the woman growing sprouts. She mentioned another woman whose bean sprouts were all rotten and lost a lot of money. The woman worried so much that she was sick and was seen constantly rubbing her eyes because there was a lot of gum in them. The other example was given by the man hatching eggs. According to him, there was a family who bought some piglets from others. The second day there was a swine disease, the boars, sows and over 30 piglets all died. He said, 'that is so terrible!' The woman's husband kept scolding her for buying piglets from others and the woman had been ill since then.

This made local villagers risk-averse. On the one hand they had no money to invest in anything on a large scale. What is more important, they would rather do something safe on a small scale than lose any money. There were various off-farm activities for villagers, but in most cases they were for survival only as considering the scales peasants could only rely on these activities to supplement insufficient income from land.

5.2.3 Income from Non-agricultural Activities (Dagong)

The term of *dagong* (working for others) has usually been related to migration work in the cities. But in Qinggang, *dagong* had two basic connotations: migration work in the cities and local casual work. Both shared the meaning of working for others and both were seen as important supplement to household income.

---

[11]He said his 'four-wheels' was old enough to be sold as wasted iron.

[12]His phone bill for that winter reached 159 yuan due to his contacts with grain dealers.

(1) *Migration work*

For the families visited, most had members migrated to work in the cities. These migrant workers included teenagers as young as fifteen and those in their fifties, although most were in their twenties and early thirties. Their destinations were mostly in north China, but young people tended to locate in further cities. Some even migrated to Guangzhou, the most southerly end of China. Even though it is reported in local media that Qinggang was successful in transferring rural labour to the cities, for the households we visited, none of them found their jobs in the cities under the guidance or with any help from government agencies. All of them were introduced by relatives, fellow villagers and friends to the places they work. Often these migrated people would group together in the new place taking care of each other so that their families left behind in their home village would feel reassured about their safety. An old woman with four bachelor sons told the first author that her sons were not able to work outside because they had no social network outside the village, thus no one would introduce any job opportunities to them. This seems to indicate that rural labour transfer/migration work is still very much dependent on individual villagers and their social networks.

Similar to findings of other studies, people from Zuogang who went to work in the cities were all making a living as factory/construction workers or in the service industry. Young males could work in the factories making sofa, jewellery boxes, and some work on construction sites. Those with special skills would work as chefs. For young girls their destinations were usually hotels and restaurants where they could work as waitresses. The youngest migrant worker had been working in a factory making clothes. She would work from 6 am to 12 pm for 300 yuan per month with food and accommodation provided.

Like most of the migrant workers, those working outside the village were still registered as rural no matter how far they had been away from home and had land entitled to them. Of all the migrant workers we heard of, only two had permanently settled in the cities, both by way of marriage. One of them started as a waiter in a hotel of Dalian (a city in Liaoning Province) and was later promoted as supervisor. He married a local girl and they bought their own apartment, which was considered as a great success among his fellow villagers. The other one was a woman who was working as a cosmetic sales girl in a department store in Beijing and got to know her future husband, a young man from suburban Beijing. By marriage, these two young people were allowed to transfer their household registrations to the cities. But according to the girl's mother, the girl's registration had not been transferred yet. That would cost her thousands of yuan for immediate transfer unless they could wait for another three years. Her daughter said she would rather wait than pay the money.

Without an urban registration peasant workers were not entitled to any benefits or welfare in the cities, such as a pension, medical care and insurance against unemployment. Even so, those who had already been working in the cities for a while would like to continue working there for a few years before they could decide whether to come back home. When asked why they decided to stay in the cities even though no corresponding welfare was provided, two reasons were provided.

First, some villagers believed the work in the cities was not as hard as in their home village.[13] Contrary to the research and media reports about migrant work, the villagers in Zuogang described the work in the cities as less harsh. During the visits there, the first author never heard anyone complain about the harshness of the migrant work even for construction jobs.

Instead, some of them were quite satisfied with working in the cities because the work there was long-term, which was the second and perhaps more important reason. For example, one of the villagers was working in Manzhouli, a medium-sized city in north China close to the Sino-Russian border. He had been working there as a bricklayer seasonally (he came back for the autumn harvest). When the first author asked his wife if he earned more there than back home, she was frank that the income there was almost the same as back in his hometown. But the work there was long-term and he would go there to earn more when there was no work in the village. She commented that, 'were not working like this, we would be all begging in the street.' A mother of two sons believed, 'it is just not that hard…In addition, there is work throughout the year. There is work in both winter and summer, and make money every month.'

To earn 'more' money was the aim of all migrant workers and all hoped to save some by migrant working. But as far as we got to know in the interviews, few could actually save anything after a few years' work. According to the mother whose son had been working in a fabric factory for about 6 or 7 years, '(he) cannot save any. Every year they (her son and daughter-in-law) would just *nianchi nianyong* (make ends meet).' Another young man was 25 years old and went to Beijing to be trained as a cook when he was 17. His mother remarked, '(he is)…unable to save any money! He earns money but can't save a penny. He hasn't saved any money since he left.' A young woman mentioned her brother-in-law had just started to earn some money after his apprenticeship for a few years. On average, peasant workers would usually earn about 300 yuan to slightly more than 1000 yuan each month, some with food and accommodation provided. Apart from maintenance in the cities, they barely had anything left for themselves, let alone to support their families back in the home village.

In order to save money, most of them were not able to go back home every year because of the travel expenses. If they were working in another province, they would go back home once in every few years, depending on the actual distance. A mother was even concerned about the money her daughter would spend when the girl called back home. The mother of the youngest migrant worker[14] described the time when her daughter called home one day. She asked, '*guniang* (girl), did you spend a lot making the phone call?' and that, 'don't call back so often if it is costly.'

---

[13]This refers to casual work in the village, i.e. working in a local brick factory. It will be discussed later.

[14]The girl was 15 when she went to work in a cloth factory.

The girl answered, 'it is three *mao* (0.3 yuan) per minute.' Her mother said: 'don't waste the money even it is only three *mao*.' The young girl was sensitive enough not to call back again. The mother said to her fellow villagers, 'look at my child! I said it is costly, she will never call back again.' One of the villagers remarked, 'she cried when the child didn't call, but when the child did she would say it costly'.

Sometimes wages for migrant workers could not be paid on time. One of the villagers said his elder boy was working in Suihua City, earned 3000 yuan in total for road construction, but still got 1000 yuan unpaid. He believed his son was able to get the rest of the money, but the money was given a little (about 300 or 500 yuan) each year. For him, delayed payment for migrant workers seemed normal as we could not tell any complaints from his words other than statements of facts.

Another villager was not so lucky. He once worked as a construction worker in Harbin. He said, 'my temper wouldn't allow me to do that. I wouldn't listen to others. In addition, working in the cities… I used to work in the cities years ago… money was not paid! …(Is the payment) on time? Did they actually pay? What they said was good, payment would be given on the seventh day. On the seventh day, nothing was given. Damn it! Wouldn't work anymore! When I decided to quit the job and came back, I didn't have money to return. Later I was really cornered, wearing a pair of unlined shoes,[15] it was almost in winter! And I had my foot pricked. I said what I should do? I was not able to work like that. I asked the boss for help. He hemmed and hawed, and agreed reluctantly to lend me 20 yuan. How much money would it take to come back from Harbin? Only about ten or twelve yuan! It was cheaper at that time…At that time, I would say I begged him for the 20 yuan in order to come back home. Then how much money shall I get for the seven days of work? …He didn't give me that money! …(I only) worked there for a month and came back…'.

These were the only complaints we heard about migrant workers. There were certainly harshness and unfairness to migrant workers in the cities. But people from Zuogang would take it for granted. They liked the work mostly because they could earn money at any time of the year, and compared with the casual work back in their home villages, migrant work was considered lighter.

(2) *Local casual work*

Local casual work has been another important way to supplement family income. It was believed in the villages that migration was for young people only. Therefore, people in their late forties would seldom think of going out. As one of the informants said, 'how can we migrate? Being in our fifties, we cannot be hired by anyone.' However, it does not mean that people at such an age would stop working. Instead, such 'old' villagers would keep looking for working opportunities.

---

[15]The temperature in winter in Harbin could reach −30 °C. Therefore, fully-lined shoes are a necessity in winter.

Villagers who did not migrate would normally work as casual labour in local brick factories. In fact, when asked what kind of local jobs they were doing in addition to farming, the answer from peasants would always be: working in the brick factories! Workers there included people of all ages from as young as fourteen to as old as over seventy. We did not meet the fourteen-year-old boy[16]—he was described as a child labourer by an old couple. The boy's mother left home to escape the poverty leaving only the child and his father in the village. The boy did not do well at school and was sent to work in the brick factory. Some villagers pitied the boy. A woman said, 'now he is trapped there. He might as well study hard at school! I said to him, if only you could work hard at school. Now he has to leave home at 4 a.m. and come back at 8 p.m....There used to be nobody watching him. Now he has been watched closely in the factory.' Her husband sighed, '*Eiyamaya* (interjection)! 14! Child labour!' During the fieldtrip, the first author did meet the 71-year-old man working in the brick factory. According to the villagers he had just been diagnosed with cancer, but he preferred to keep working rather than resting at home despite the hard work in the brick factory.

Any outsider would be curious about what kind of job would attract so many people, old and young, healthy and sick in a factory According to the villagers, local people would mostly depend on the money earned by kilning in the brick factories, which would last 6 months every year. The task in the factories was simply—carrying bricks with bare hands and money was paid by job units. Usually one could expect to earn 30–50 yuan for a day's work. Thus for half a year, one would earn about 4000–5000 yuan.

The work in the brick factories was in fact only suitable for healthy young males, because brick carrying required great strength—a single piece of flan would weight seven *jin* (3.5 kg) and people had to carry these back and forth for a whole day. But there were also women working there. As one of the villagers described:

> Women would pass bricks and men would fill in kilns – to push the trolley with bricks and lay them inside kilns, working as hard as donkeys.... When you get in, there is all dust in the air. When the bricks are drawing out, dust is red. You just think about the hands, how to bear the heat! (Interview conducted on 29/06/2007 with Li, female peasant)

In describing how hard the work was, a woman talked about how exhausted her husband was after each day when coming back from work.

> Every day the person in my family[17] is so tired and upset. He comes back like that every day (scored): 'Damn it! Don't know the point of doing this every day!' ... (We could) just make a living by drudging and we've got such a donkey (her husband). That person I would say is a *tuyibalü* (a donkey without a tail), working there every day. Whenever he comes

---

[16]He was actually less than 14, might be 13 or even as young as 12 years old. As in rural areas of north China, people would add one year to their real age. For example, the child's age is equal to the present year minus the year he was born plus one, regardless in which month the child was born.

[17]Her husband. Local women would never use 'husband' to address their spouses. They would rather say 'the/that person or the/that one in my family'.

back, he is always extremely dirty all over, with his vest and his coat all soaked. In that kiln, haven't you seen it before, baking bricks? The dirt was blown everywhere because of the fans and he sweats a lot. Once the clothes are put in a basin, the water becomes mud immediately (Ibid).

The working time in the factory seemed to be totally dependent on the mutual agreements between the owner and workers. When asked how long the 71-year-old man was working in the factory, his fellow villagers said 'for 24 h' because he was living there except the time he came back home for meals. Sometimes when there was rain someone had to cover the flans at night. Others did not have to live in the factory, but they got up extremely early to work. According to a woman, 'that person (her husband) in my family would get up at 2:00 a.m. Get up to prepare some meals to take to the factory.' During the night the first author stayed over in that village, she was woken up by loud noises of engines, tractors, and dog barking at about 2 or 3 a.m. She was told the next day that villagers were about to set to work at that time including those working in the brick factories.

Physically one could only work in the brick factories for two days and rest for the next two. A young woman was complaining how stiff her fingers felt after a few days' work. Her mother-in-law said people were 'knocked down' (collapsed) one after another after working in the brick factories for a while. But for those able to work, they still took every chance. After all, there was only half a year that they could work there. During the summer when the fieldtrip was made, there were more workers than needed and villagers had to take turns to get hired. In their words, 'we all rely on the brick factories. Let me put it this way, work for half a year there and stay at home for the other half. If the factories close down, it's all up for all of us'.

Underdevelopment of local industry was considered one of the reasons for stagnated rural income growth according to villagers. Besides, villagers believed there was no suitable local work for women. Instead of earning more money out of the family house, most of them could only stay at home.

5.3   Rural Expenditure

In addition to daily necessities, field research revealed that there were several major expenditures for people in Zuogang, and these became great financial burden for peasants.

5.3.1   Agricultural Tax and Local Charges

As one of the few provinces to carry out new pro-agricultural policies, agricultural tax in Heilongjiang was abolished in 2004. However, when it was mentioned, peasants still had much to say. Actually, it was not agricultural tax itself, but the affiliated local charges that had much influence on peasants' income.

Agricultural tax in Zuogang was collected based on the area of land allocated. The amount was not much (about 15 yuan per mu).[18] It was usually paid by cash, but could be paid in kind if cash was not available. Obligatory as tax was, most villagers would consider the amount reasonable and the ways of collection flexible.

On the contrary, local charges were more arbitrary in nature. It was the local charge that had aroused much resentment, as villagers still remembered that much more money was charged by local authorities instead of the state. According to the interviews, local charges ranged from 55 yuan per mu to about 100 yuan per mu, which varied in different places and years. But in any case it would far exceed 5% of rural income considering that net income per mu could hardly be more than 200 yuan during the tax-charging years, as the price of maize was only raised to a higher level of 0.5 yuan each jin in 2006. For a farming household, the contribution to local charges was substantial.

Ordinary villagers could only tell that the money was paid as state tax or paid to the local authorities, and were unable to discern whether it was for *tiliu* or *tongchou*. But they did remember that the purposes of money collection and the fee-charging items were various, and almost all of them were charged according to land area contracted. The most common purposes were tree planning and road building, and there were a lot of complaints. Peasants' comments could generally be summarized as two points: (1) trees were all contracted to individuals; (2) villagers carried earth with their own vehicles for road repair. Therefore, fees paid for these purposes were both unreasonable.

Apart from *tiliu and tongchou,* the other purposes for fee collection were various. Some of them were charged consistently for a few years and the collection was extremely arbitrary. An example was the charge for self-owned vehicles. Since 1999 for a few years all self-owned vehicles in the county were charged twelve yuan annually. In 2006, there was news that part of the money collected could be returned. One of the informants happened to be in the local credit association to pay back the loan when he asked whether the money was returned. When he got a positive answer, he asked for the money to be credited to his account. He thus got the money partially returned. But for most villagers the money was still not paid back. What is more, some people had never paid the fee at all. It seemed without asking in person no one would return the money back and no one would care about the money uncollected years ago. As villagers said, those who had paid would keep the status of 'having paid' and those 'haven't paid' also kept in status quo.

In addition, villagers were once asked to pay 25 yuan for house insurance before 2004. Sizes of houses and yards were measured, and the extra areas were charged. One of the informants remembered it was 2.5 yuan for an extra square metre. Once the money was collected, it was the end of the story as the houses had never been

---

[18]Some remembered the number as twelve yuan per mu.

insured. The insurance money was collected for that year only, and in the villagers' words, 'they charged in this name this year, and in that name the next.' Because money charged was in different names, villagers were greatly confused. For them, 'there was only money collection, no explanation.' Therefore, when asked about the other purposes of the local charges, peasants would answer 'who knows? In most cases ordinary people wouldn't ask much about it.'

For most local charges villagers would seldom get receipts. A woman interviewed once asked a cadre, 'you collected the money, but we didn't get anything (proof)!' After she asked quite a few times, the cadre got impatient, 'why are you always asking while others don't?' He later advised that the higher authorities had not instructed him to provide proof of payment. The woman said ordinary people like her were quite confused because they knew nothing. A similar story was told by another villager that a few years ago each household was charged 20 yuan for a 'land use certificate'. It had been three or four years, but he had not received any proof. When he asked a village cadre about it, he got the reply that 'you still remember that!' This indicated that most villagers did not ask questions—they simply paid when required no matter how reluctant.

Their attitude towards the local charge, to keep disagreement to themselves, might be related to the ways that fees were collected. According to the villagers, payments of the local charge had to be paid in time and in cash, otherwise they would get caught. One of the villagers said, 'we really don't understand the policy and who made the policy. Anyway, if you didn't pay you would be caught; you dared not say you didn't have money.' Another one complained, 'in those years, when you were unable to pay the land charges, they took away whatever you had at home'.

Among the local charges, 'voluntary labour' might be an item with the most bewildering nature. To understand it from the term itself, it seemed voluntary labour would be given once needed. However, such an understanding is wrong for at least two reasons. Firstly, it was not voluntary at all. Secondly, the service was not always paid by offering labour, but in most cases in cash. Villagers explained how 'voluntary labour' was converted into money. It was stipulated that voluntary labour should not exceed 15 working days each year. In one of the villages visited, peasants gave half of the labour service according to the labour number of that family. The other half was paid in cash according to the land area. At that time, it would be 80 or 90 yuan each mu. In another village, peasants were asked to pay 150 yuan per male labour; it was not necessary to pay for females, and the payments had to be in cash. In this village, 'voluntary labour service' thus became an item simply for fee paying purpose and no labour service was required, as villagers said, 'they wouldn't let you work'.[19] Putting 'voluntary labour service' aside, when villagers were needed and were asked to offer free labour in the real sense, this was

---

[19]According to the villagers, the roads wouldn't be repaired by anyone, and nothing was done (with the help of 'voluntary labour service'). They continued, 'you see the road has been dug up and no one would care.'

not considered relevant to their cash payment under 'voluntary labour service'. Even after 'voluntary labour' was exempted together with agricultural tax in 2004, villagers would still provide some free labour, simply because 'once asked, how can you not go?'

Even though state tax was not much according to villagers, the local fees and charges placed a heavy burden on peasants. Villagers complained that they were working in vain with only a little straw left to burn.[20] When agricultural tax was abolished, villagers felt very relieved as one of them said, 'after agricultural taxes were abolished, no leaders dare charge anything on our land'. They expressed their gratitude that they hoped the state leaders who made such preferential policies could live up to 200 years old.

It is noteworthy that after the exemption of agricultural tax together with local charges and voluntary labour, fee-paying items were replaced by 'yishi yiyi' (one discussion over one problem). However, for the 12 yuan collected for yishi yiyi every year, no discussion was ever held in Zuogang and villagers usually had no idea how the money collected was actually used even though they did get a receipt each time indicating the use such as road maintenance. When asked about discussions over fee collection, a villager gave the following answer, 'once money is collected, what to discuss? Problems and trouble would all come out during the discussion!'

Villagers said there were rarely any meetings in the village. They hardly ever saw the village heads or party secretaries except for fee collection. For peasants, there seemed to be no outlets for complaints. Therefore, dissatisfaction gradually built up. That further explains why no discussions over important issues would be arranged by village cadres.

5.3.2 Medical Expenses

In rural China, illness has become one of the main reasons for rural poverty. Once a member is struck by a serious disease the whole family would no doubt fall into poverty, because for peasants nearly all the medical expenses would be paid by themselves.[21] Chances are few that once back in poverty they could get out of it again.

Of the villagers interviewed, there was a 13-year-old girl who was diagnosed as having leukaemia in 2006. About 10 years ago, her father Guan was involved in a car accident, during which he lost his right leg. Medical treatment after the accident immediately put the family in debt. Over the ten years, the Guan couple had been

---

[20]Local people use maize straws as fuel.

[21]Rural medical cooperation system started to be carried out in late 2006. For the villages visited during the fieldtrip people had not got any benefit from it.

working hard to pay off the debt. But hard work had destroyed their health. Guan had liver disease and his wife various illnesses but she never knew what the problems were because she could not afford to see a doctor in a proper hospital. When their debt was almost paid off, their younger daughter was found ill. The initial medical treatment for about 70 days took them 80,000 yuan. Further treatments were expected to cost 16,000 yuan every year, lasting about six years before the disease could be cured. The figure was a fortune for the family considering that their annual income was mainly dependent on the total 6 mu of land. Their fellow villagers contributed as much as they could. The family also applied for some disease relief fund from the county government. Even so they had to borrow 20,000 duplicate yuan with a high interest rate from loan sharks, as the local credit association would not release a loan to them because 'they had no capability to repay'.[22] The interest rate was said to be 30% and interest each year was as high as 6000 yuan, more than their income from land. Their older daughter was soon forced to drop off school and work away from home as the youngest migrant worker in the village.

The family was living an extremely frugal life. Apart from a sack of flour given by the government the only food to be found in the house was maize. When the first author stayed in their home for dinner, she was treated with pancakes, corn porridge and runner beans (grown in their backyard), the best food they could prepare. Villagers said there was usually only staple food for the family. Apart from the runner beans, their only vegetables were leeks and cucumbers grown in the backyard during the warm season. They spent every penny on the child's treatment, but could not afford anything nutritious for her. The girl was much loved and pitied by the fellow villagers, who would always take her to their homes for something delicious at dinner time. This, according to the villagers, was the only way they could continue helping the family as they were not rich and could not keep donating any money.

Guan once asked for help from the local government. He kneeled down in front of the township governor until he was told to go back, and ask the brigade (village) secretary to take him house to house for fund raising. However, the village secretary[23] refused by telling him, 'there are so many families with difficulties. Once I raise funds for you, there are others who are ill. Who shall I help?' A local woman gave the following comments,

---

[22]Rural credit cooperatives are financial institutions in rural areas which collect rural residents' savings and lend mainly to agricultural projects and township and village enterprises. The lending decisions are highly influenced by local governments (Cousin, 2011).

[23]It was known from the fieldtrip that when there was election in the village, Han Chunlei's (the village secretary) father went house by house to lobby. When he came to the girl's home, he said to her father, 'you vote for my son and we won't forget you in the future.' Later, we happened to find out, via the internet, that soon after the fieldtrip, Han Chunlei got an award for nomination as one of the ten outstanding youths of Qinggang County. According to the description, his major achievement was helping villagers increase income thus reduce poverty.

No one cares. He did go to ask for help from brigade, commune[24], and county. (He) visited all of them. Who else could he resort to? There are only two characters waiting for him there: *bu xing* (no way). What else can you do? There is no way out. The family's condition is like this. You came this year, the house looks better. There are some plastic sheets covering the ceiling, given by this or that one in the *tun* during the past spring festival. If you came last year, without those plastic sheets, I doubt if you could come in being such a tidy young lady. It seems the house is going to collapse because of the big cracks and is leaking. The open windows couldn't be closed. And the doors! Who would buy such a house? Last year, they said they would sell the house at whatever price, as long as someone would like to take it. Even for only two or three thousand (yuan), we would save our child. Who would take it? No one! You see how pitiful they are. (Interview conducted on 30/03/2007 at the Guans with Zhao, female, peasant)

After having tried as many sources as possible, they got financial help from the county government, with a total amount of 7000 yuan in two allocations, the first time 4000 yuan and the second 3000 yuan. Guan went to the civil affairs office in the county government where he was told the government would offer some help and the local civil affairs officer in his home township would send the money to his home.

But when the local officer arrived with the money, he asked the girl's father to give him 500 yuan and said as civil affairs assistant he had expended a lot of effort on the family's behalf, indicating that he had used his *guanxi* with the upper-level government to get the money for them. Guan said: 'you cannot take the money! This money is to save the life of my child!' But the local officer would not leave, lingered and said: 'you give me the money this time and in the future, if there is anything good I won't forget you.' Considering that he was the local officer and the family would have to ask for his help, Guan gave him 500 yuan reluctantly. The next time, when the 3000 yuan was allocated, the officer took away another 500 yuan without asking for the Guan's permission.[25]

From the view point of most villagers, Guan should give up the medical treatment simply because it was not affordable and there was no guarantee that the child would survive the treatment or recover completely. However, Guan and his wife said they could not see such a teenage girl die without doing anything. Even by selling their house and land they would continue the treatment. They did sell the land (rented out with young crops).[26] But for the house, even for 2000 or 3000 yuan, no one would take it (Picture 5.2).

---

[24]Communes were dismantled in the early 1980s in Heilongjiang, but villagers in Zuogang would keep using the terms they once used in the planning era, such as commune and brigade. Commune was generally referred to the town government, and brigade the village.

[25]The father did not say anything about the commission when he was interviewed during the day. It was the girl who told the first author about it during a night-time chat in her room. She also said that, as a civil affairs assistant, the local officer would take commission for all the money he applied for on behalf of villagers. If a villager received more than 1000 yuan, he would take 500 yuan; if the total amount was less than 1000 yuan, he would take 100 yuan. The next morning, the author confirmed this with her father.

[26]It was considered extremely unwise to lease land with crops as investment had already made for seeds and labour.

Picture 5.2   The Guan's House (the Back). *Source* Authors

When talking about illness with other villagers, most took the attitude that for a minor ailment they would simply take some common medicines without seeing a doctor. If there was a serious disease, they would wait to die. A villager said, 'we seldom buy any medicines, some for common problems at most. That would cost 200–300 yuan (every year).' Another old woman said even for serious illness she would not go to see a doctor, 'people like us would hold on without seeing a doctor. Usually when we get to the hospital the doctors would be surprised and say: how could you rural people hold out for such a long time! But, what else can we do except this? Cannot afford the treatment… If you go to have a medical examination (let alone treatment), how much it would cost from head to feet? 1000 yuan won't make it! Things like CT…(are all expensive)'.

When the first author visited the villages in 2006, the rural medical cooperation had been introduced for over six months. According to the new system, peasants were encouraged to participate on a voluntary basis. Both the state government and local government (provincial) would subsidize 20 yuan for each participant, while the latter would pay 10 yuan each year for a subscription. Once subscribed, peasants were expected to get a partial refund for medical expenses over the thresholds of 50, 500, 1000 yuan at township, county and above-county level hospitals respectively. A certain percentage of expenses could be reclaimed according to individual situations.

As far as we know from the fieldtrip, participation in the new medical system was about 50%. In some villages all members of the family were required to participate (perhaps for the easy collection of subscription fees) if they would like to do so. For other villages where there was no such regulation, only some of the family members chose to join. For those who did not subscribe, some thought it would be no use because they were still young and healthy. For example, there were families who only subscribed for parents and very young children. Young people in their twenties usually believed it a waste of money. There were people who would like to subscribe, but did not because they had no money in hand when local cadres came to collect subscription fees (the payment had to be in cash). Whether subscribed or not, the rural medical cooperation became something known to all; a success to some extent.

But when asked how much they actually reclaimed for medical treatment, none of the informants said they did, because most of them did not know how to initiate the claim and all of them said they did not know exactly how the system worked. Therefore, their understanding about the system varied. Some thought once they participated, they would get 20 yuan back if they were treated in a village clinic, about 50 yuan back in the township and more in the county. In fact, one should first consider the village clinic, if it was not capable of dealing with the problem, he should go to the township and then the county hospitals. Based on this, there was a saying, 'an ill person would die if he had to go through the process'. Some did the calculation saying that the payment from one's own pocket under the new system would be almost the same as before. Some said there might be 400 yuan refundable, but one had to spend more than 900 yuan at first. In particular, one had to pay the whole amount himself and get some refunded with the receipts. However, it was not refundable for all hospitals, and people had to go to the designated ones. According to the peasants, one of their villagers was trying to claim back some of the expenses. He presented all the documents, which had to be checked and endorsed by the upper authorities, i.e. signed and stamped before the partial refund could be given. He had been waiting for over half a month and there was no news.

If pieced together the information from all of the villagers, people would get a general idea as how the system worked. However, individual villagers usually had some misunderstandings about it. One of the informants said he paid the subscription fee about six months ago, but the booklet (membership certificate) was given a few days before the first author visited his home. He was worried that six months had passed and if his membership expired his money was paid in vain. He thought the membership was for six months only because the bank loan he got was usually due in six months. It seems apart from the introduction of the rural medical cooperation, no one ever told villagers how the system worked, how to ask for refund and how much could be reclaimed. Some villagers would say, 'it is said you can get refund with this, but no one would bother to go.' Some people believed, 'there is too much trouble to see a doctor under the new system.'

5.3.3   Expenditure on Bridewealth

Economic studies have examined the impact of agricultural tax on rural income extensively, but the impact of bridewealth seems to be less focused. During our field trip in Qinggang, we got to know that the influence of bridewealth on rural households had been substantial.

The first author was told repeatedly by local people that *quxifu* (marry a girl into the family) nowadays cost a fortune. The normal price would be 60,000–70,000 yuan, and the least would be 40,000–50,000 yuan. Take an ordinary family with four members as an example. It would take the family at least five years to earn so much. However, in the villages visited where ordinary peasants could only struggle to make ends meet, so that to save up to 60,000 yuan for the son's marriage would be almost impossible. As one of the informants said, 'in rural areas, it is just *nianchi nianyong*. Who, for how many years, could save 40 or 50 grand?' This was echoed by the words of another, 'you see, the price (bridewealth) at the moment is so high. 60,000 *kuai*! Where can we get so much money? Apart from food and living, which family is able to save money?'

Some of the villagers interviewed felt very relieved if their sons were married some years ago. In 2002, bridewealth would cost the groom's family 20,000 yuan, and in 2006, it went up to over 40,000 yuan. Then it soared in 2006 and 2007 when the first author visited the villages, which reached 60,000–70,000 yuan.

Villagers told stories of some families with more than one son, and they were too poor to get married. When a villager just mentioned there were two families in his village, both having three sons, but only one in each family was married, the response from the audience was, '*eiya*! Must be worried to death!' There was a woman with three sons, all in their thirties. When asked whether they were married, the mother answered, '*eiyamaya*! How can they get married in such a difficult situation? Now it is worse.' In the single village of Fanrong, there would be 30–40 bachelors. The old ones were in their 40s and many in their 30s. One of the villagers was kind enough to take the first author to a family with two unmarried sons. According to the father, the young men had to find ways for themselves, because it would be impossible to depend on their parents. The two young men in their late 20s were working in different cities. According to other informants, they were forced to migrate because of the pressure of bridewealth.

The man mentioned above who was complaining about the harshness of work in the brick factory had a newly-wed son. The wedding took place in September 2006. His wife said the bride's family asked for 43,000 yuan. The groom's family also paid for clothes, flowers and other expenditures for the wedding including two feasts. The total cost was 45,000 yuan. That was the reason why the groom's father had to work in the brick factory every day. When he was complaining that he had been 'working like a donkey' his wife would retort, 'what to do if you don't work like a donkey? After *quxifu* (their son got married), shouldn't you repay the money you owe?' She said, 'to earn some by working would pay some off.'

As for the destination of bridewealth, in the above case, the groom's mother gave the money to the bride. She said she had no idea whether the girl gave the money to her mother. The mother-in-law did not seem to care about the destination of the bridewealth. She emphasized that, 'all that matters was, the person was married in...Who knows whether she gave it (bridewealth) to her mum?' It might be indicated from her words that she could not make further inquiry about the destination of bridewealth as long as the she had got a daughter-in-law at home.

But according to the information from others, the bride's family usually would not take bridewealth. One of the informants had a son and a daughter, married almost at the same time. The son's wedding cost them 20,000 yuan, and the bridewealth for his daughter was 19,000. When his daughter got married, the new couple took the money and when his daughter-in-law came to his home, the money (bridewealth) was hers. In this way, neither the bride's nor the groom's family would benefit from the bridewealth, and the beneficiaries were the young couples as new conjugal units.

The groom's parents were supposed to pay off debts from the wedding. Even worse, in addition to the financial corner, they were sometimes forced into a physical one. There was a story about a family. After two sons were married, the debts were as high as 70,000 yuan, but the two daughters-in-law did not care. In addition, according to their agreement, the house should be occupied half and half by the two young couples. This meant that the parents had nowhere to live. The first author happened to interview an old couple with a son and a daughter. After the children were married, the couple left the family house to their son, and moved out into a rented one. There was still 10,000 yuan of debt from their son's wedding. When asked whether they were supposed to pay off the debts, the father said: 'that's right. Otherwise, who will pay it for him? That is, you (should) help your son set up some financial foundation...but I am not able to work these years. It is not fair for the son (if you cannot provide him with a good foundation), and you don't even pay off the debt for him... That's what everybody will do as a parent, isn't it?'

In terms of resource flow, bridewealth is still within the rural community even within the same family, passed down to the next generation. It is reasonable to say that for an ordinary rural household, after the sons are married the parents would have no money left, sometimes with the giving of house and in most cases paying off the debts. Rural parents have been struggling for life to save enough for a decent bridewealth and probably together with a house to leave for the children (sons). The bridewealth has certainly helped some young couples set up something they could make a living with. It, together with the house, might be taken as the heritage young people take from their parents in advance.

5.3.4   Gift Money

Gift money is another important issue for villagers. It has become one of the major expenditures although in the long run almost all the gift money given out is expected to come back, because gift money is given in a reciprocal way, as the proverb goes *lishangwanglai* (etiquette demands reciprocity).

In terms of the amount, gift money given out each year was appalling considering rural income, which ranged from 1000 yuan to over 5000 yuan for the families in the field site. The occasions for money giving varied from birthdays, weddings, school admissions to births of new babies. For each occasion at least 50 yuan was given for a normal *guanxi* (relationship), and for close relationships up to 200 or 300 hundred yuan would be given (for example, a relative's wedding).

Villagers considered such money giving obligatory, while their role in the process of giving was passive. They were giving because they 'owe other's *renqing*'. Literally *renqing* means human emotions, even though it has very subtle shades of meaning. It could be taken to mean a kind of sociable emotion between people which needs to be nurtured and maintained by certain social exchanges. More simply, it can sometimes be exchangeable with *guanxi* or social network. When explained why they had to give gift money, villagers indicated it had to be given because they were in *renqing* debt, most probably because they received money as gifts from others on previous occasions. According to a villager, 'isn't there a saying of *lishangwanglai?* They give us 500 (yuan) for my son's wedding, I cannot give back 400 (yuan).'

It is interesting to note that there were times when the villagers were invited for an occasion, yet they had no special relationship with the family, as one villager explained:

> The other day, I …met Chen xx, Chen xx asked me to have a drink (for a family occasion. You see we are not relatives, cannot say we are friends, just acquaintances from the same *tun*, the same brigade. He told me to have a drink, and I said OK, OK. (Interview conducted on 30/03/2007 with Peasant Li, male)

For such an invitation, he had to pay at least 50 yuan to be 'presentable'. In addition to his conservation with the invitation, it is likely that he went for the 'drink' not only because he agreed to go, but also because Chen was someone he was acquainted with in the *tun*. Local people consider their fellow villagers as *tunqin* (relatives based on living in the same *tun*).

The first author was at first surprised when she heard one of the informants address everyone he met as if they were relatives such as auntie, brother-in-law, and of course he was called by some young children as 'grandpa' although he only had two teenage daughters. He later explained that was because they were *tunqin*. He had referred to people in this way since he was young, and for generations villagers automatically established a 'quasi-relative/kin' relationship, which seemed complicated in a way, but people would know their corresponding positions in the network. Observation and interview data showed that villagers had established a close network based on the relationship of *tunqin*. Apart from their address to each other, villagers visited each other whenever they liked and they felt at home whichever household they visited. When a mother was cooking but could not find any leeks, she simply told her daughter, 'pick up some from your auntie's backyard!' The auntie here was not a relative, but a *tunqin*. When people were in real need, villagers would offer help straight away. The sick girl's initial emergency treatment was supported by donations of villagers. A woman whose husband went out for migration work often asked for help from her neighbour. Such a close *guanxi* did help peasants out of difficulties in poor areas.

Let us go back to Chen's invitation. By going to Chen's drink, a closer relationship between the two was thus established. Chen's case also gave us more information that such invitation was usually followed by a feast, where people got together to eat and drink. It might be safe to say that a certain amount of gift money was consumed as food and drink during the feasts, although some might not enjoy the events considering the money they have paid reluctantly. Villagers seemed to feel it a waste, as a woman said, 'you see, if we could use the money for the family...the several thousand yuan. Isn't it good enough?' But she also indicated that it was a tradition and custom, and nobody was able to change.

In rural areas, there are quite a few money-giving occasions. In most cases villagers felt reluctant to give because it cost 'quite a lot of money'. In some extreme cases, some would think of ways to take back the money. A story was given by the villagers about a person who was really angry about giving out so much gift money. He then invited his fellow villagers for a feast for his newly-built henhouse. The story teller was not sure whether this really took place as this was not a story in his village. In addition to the desperation of the feast holder, it at least indicates that the impact of gift money on rural households had been great.

In recent years, gift money has been increased with the rise in living conditions. In the early years, people would give gifts to others, but now all gifts to be given have been converted into money. One villager used to be the village head many years ago. He still remembered the time when one of the villagers was about to marry. As village head, he collected 47 yuan from 47 households and bought a clock for 49.5 yuan for the couple (he contributed the extra 2.5 yuan). According to him:

> This (gift money) is really...you say, is it a custom or problem? I am not sure. It has been handed down from our ancestors. What is the point? It is just unable to overcome! You see it is voluntary...but something like: hi Old Zhang, Old Wang, my child is getting married and I would like to invite you for a drink (to the wedding). He is not actually saying he is asking for money! (Thus unable to refuse)...ordinary people would say that's the most important moment of my family and I just invite you for a drink... you see this... cannot find a cure for that! (Interview conducted on 27/03/2007 with a retired village secretary, male)

No matter how pointless and wasteful in nature the villagers found the gift money, or how much they were reluctant and obligatory to give. Gift money played a vital role in the establishment and maintenance of local *guanxi*. For ordinary villagers however, their *guanxi* was confined in a small range compared with cadres. It also seemed the *guanxi* network was hierarchical as ordinary villagers were not involved in the social network of cadres. When asked whether they gave gift money to village cadres, villagers replied, without *renqing* debt they would not have gift money exchange with cadres.

According to villagers, one had to have money and power before they could establish friendship or close relationships with cadres. As commented by a woman, 'people like us with both the elderly and the young in the family, who would like to rap to you?'

In terms of resource flow, the destination of gift money, similar to bridewealth, still remains within the rural communities. Although what is given out is expected to be returned in a long enough period of time, it does impose a great financial burden on peasants' current life. Over the years, taking the rural community as a whole, more resources have been taken away as gift money, much of which will be spent on food and drinking on the special occasions.

References

Atinc, T. M. (1997). *Sharing rising incomes: disparities in China* (Vol. 5). World Bank Publications.
Cousin, V. (2011). *Banking in China*. Springer.

Chapter 6
The Officials' Perspective

Our first 'official' knowledge about peasants was from the Director of Rural Affairs Committee of Daoli District, Harbin City. While driving the first author to do a pilot study, he commented that peasants were both 'pitiful' and 'hateful'. It is easy to understand how pitiful they are. By having a brief look at the poverty they have been living in, one could not help sympathizing with them. As to why peasants are hateful, according to the Director, it was extremely difficult to talk them through any policies. One of the examples was the compensation for land confiscation. It was stipulated that if there was any building or construction (such as a well) on the land confiscated, a higher compensation would be given by the government. However, many peasants would only pay attention to the latter half of the sentence without thinking of the condition. This meant that many peasants went to the government offices asking for higher compensation without listening to the explanation. This has made working with the peasants difficult especially in the implementation of a new policy. In the following chapter, we will explore the views of local officials on various issues.

6.1 Through the Eyes of Local Officials

As confirmed by local officials and people who used to work there, Qinggang used to be a poverty-stricken county, and the title was later removed. The designation of a 'national poor' county depends on various indicators, such as the local GDP, and per capita income. According to Wan,[1] a former officer in the county government,

---

[1]He used to work in the county government as a secretary, mainly responsible for drafting articles for inspection of upper level governments or speeches for local leaders. Once he was found good at writing articles by one of the directors from the provincial government, and was later transferred to work in a research centre of the province.

© Shanghai Jiao Tong University Press and Springer Nature Singapore Pte Ltd. 2018
Y. Gao and S. Fennell, *China's Rural–Urban Inequality in the Countryside*,
https://doi.org/10.1007/978-981-10-8273-3_6

'the first round of designation seemed to be fair, and was dependent on nothing but the economic indicators.' It might be inferred from his words that (1) later rounds of designation might not be fair enough and (2) the designation could possibly depend on something else besides the economic factors.

This reminds us of an earlier trip in late 2005 to other counties in Heilongjiang. In one of the 'state poor' counties, its governor told us that his county was able to be designated as 'state poor' mainly because there was a person working in the decision panel in Beijing, who happened to be native of that county. He did a lot of 'work' to help his home county, as a title of 'national poor' would entitle much financial support. The county looked really different from the rest in the local areas, even better developed than the city (the fifth largest in Heilongjiang) to which it belonged administratively. Its advanced infrastructure made it stand out as a modern small city rather than a 'national poor' county thanks to the financial support from the central government. As according to the same governor, the central financial support amounted to over 100 million yuan, more than the local revenue.[2]

As a 'national poor' county, Qinggang certainly received financial benefits. According to Wan, such benefits were mostly reflected in 'work for relief' funds. 'Work for relief' referred to funds from the state for specific projects, such as road building, well digging and bridge construction. He later emphasized that 'work for relief' was different from transfer payment in that the former was from the state, not the provincial government, and more importantly 'work for relief' was project specific, not used for general purposes. In terms of amount, Wan believed 'work for relief' from the state exceeded transfer payment from the provincial government.

In Wan's words, transfer payment was a complement to the finance capability of a poor county, thus alleviated financial difficulties of the poor county. It came in various forms that some were project specific while others were not. The tax-sharing system was carried out in 1994. Since then the central and local governments have been separated in terms of finance revenues. However, Wan believed that the tax-sharing system had little impact on county finance, as it was a poverty-stricken county with little fiscal income. Separated or not, its fiscal income was scarce.

As a native of Qinggang, Wan was nostalgic when introducing its industry. The industry system in Qinggang used to be complete with its own bicycle factory, air conditioning foundry, machinery factory and processing industry, such as sugar refinery and solvent plant. They were all founded by the state during the central planned economy. However, the switch to the market economy was the changing point for the county, as 'everything was over once they (the state factories) were embraced by the market because there was no market for the products.' These factories were later transformed into enterprises (the transformation was not complete for some of them during the fieldtrip). But many became 'empty shell' enterprises, with no factory buildings, no equipment and nothing else but a pile of debts.

---

[2]This figure was reported by a local official during some local researchers' earlier visit.

According to Wan, 'poverty-stricken counties all lack industry. All the poverty-stricken counties are based on agriculture, except those mountainous areas'. Qinggang was one such county with many of its townships having no industry at all so that they had to depend on transfer payment from the above. Zuogang Township was one of them that its major fiscal income was from business taxes. According to Wan, it was as little as 100,000 or 200,000 yuan around 2006.

In terms of agriculture, soil is good in the south but bad in the north. Zuogang is located near the south end of Qinggang, and there is good soil for planting maize. Production would reach up to 1300–1400 jin per mu for a good year. But in other townships the best production would be 1200 jin. Therefore land rental in Zuogang is higher than in other places. When the fieldtrip was made, the rental for good land could reach 200 yuan per mu, and for bad land the rental would be from 150 to 160 yuan. In addition, Qinggang is a place with many natural disasters. The most common is drought, which happens in nine out of ten years. That partially explains why only maize is planted, as its production is least affected by bad weather.

There is 700,000 mu of grassland in the west of the county suitable for grazing. In this sense, Wan believed Qinggang should be considered as half farming and half husbandry. But husbandry had not made much of a contribution to peasants' income except for some villages specializing in it. There used to be several villages famous for raising pigs, such as Tongxin village of Yincheng, where villagers started raising pigs many years ago. However, husbandry was considered more risky. For example, the price of pork decreased in some years, and it was affected by epidemic problems such as swine fever. As a result, fewer people would like to do it. Such epidemic problems were also applicable to the raising of chickens, ducks and geese because of bird flu for example. Wan confirmed that, 'if there is anything risky… especially for peasants they won't have a try.'

6.2 Rural Income

6.2.1 Agricultural Production

Per capita rural net income in Qinggang reached 2000 yuan after 2005. Wan believed rural income published in yearbooks for many counties have been underestimated. 'It is too little (much underestimated). Let's say a rural household has three people. They have 30 mu of cultivated land. 30 mu of land… a year…they should get 350 yuan per mu and about 10,000 for 30 mu. Then they should have over 3000 yuan per head. But that includes investment in land. Anyway, living in rural area shouldn't be too bad.' Vice governor Qin of the Zuogang township government provided a similar view, 'land at least will provide guaranteed food. If every member of the family gets four or five mu of land, usually production would be 1400 or 1500 jin. At the price of 0.5 yuan per jin, that goes to over 700 yuan per mu. For four mu of land, you get 2800 yuan. For peasants, income from land would be over 2000 yuan.' He continued that the non-rural population, on the other hand, had to work very hard in order to earn as much as 2000 yuan. He calculated, 'it is about 30 yuan every day, and only 900 each month. They have to work by selling labour for three months to earn up to the basic income as peasants.' Therefore, he concluded, 'what is the advantage of rural population? It is the land.'

'Land is the key issue in rural areas,' admitted Wan, 'because in recent years prices of grain have been increasing.' He pointed out that some rural households were in poverty due to a 'lack of land'. By lacking land, Wan referred to individual households rather than the local area as a whole. He insisted that Heilongjiang has the most cultivated land per head. Unlike some other provinces with large territories but not much farm land because of mountains, such as Guizhou (a province in southwest China), Heilongjiang is really rich in land. The reasons for having little or no land for some rural families were (1) there were fewer members in the households; (2) some migrated to work in the cities in the previous years and returned the land to the villages. When they failed to earn much in the cities and were forced back home, there was no land for them. In Zuogang and in many other rural places in recent years, much land has been occupied by constructions and buildings due to development. As Lin, the civil affairs assistant of the township government put it, 'that is what the government did, the government action! No one is able to do anything against it. You have no choice. I am telling you, once the government opens their mouth, the world could be swallowed...'

Because of emigration in recent years, much land has been concentrated within the hands of fewer people, making it more suitable for mechanized operation or scale management. Wan also noticed that some well-off rural households had appeared. He finally commented, 'it doesn't mean you cannot make money by farming. Some rural households are living a better life than those in the towns.' Wan's parents back in his home village in north Qinggang might be among the rich, as they had over 100 mu land for farming.

For the well-off peasants, per capita income could reach 5000 yuan.[3] Some could even earn up to the salary of the cadres in the township government. Lin estimated that at least 40% peasants would reach the level of 5000 yuan a year. These included people running their own small businesses, for example, a small shop or s grocery store. Some made a living from the collection and sale of grain, seeds, fertilizers and even vegetables. These people were called *shao zhangguide* (junior masters). When these people were married, they received financial support from both families. They then used the money 'to make a living earnestly'. Households like these were usually well-off, some even better-off than those living in the town as commented by Lin. Such people accounted for 30–40% of total population in Zuogang. Lin also estimated that the rest 20% were living 'with reasonable income', meaning they were just able to make ends meet.

---

[3]Gross income, according to Lin.

For ordinary peasants (living only on farming without doing any business), Lin admitted, they would certainly never starve to death, but a whole year's income would not be much. For example, if a peasant had 20 or 30 mu of land and he worked on it for a lifetime, it would be a great achievement if he could save 70,000 or 80,000 yuan by the time his son got married. Lin believed, 'in rural areas, in terms of farm and sideline products, there is nothing new, innovative or special. It is like a bottleneck at the moment. In Zuogang *Xiang*, maize production per mu is just as much as 1500 jin. Given that there comes a miraculous scientist...unless a special breed is invented...Otherwise, even if you put in 1000 jin of fertilizer, production won't be more than that.' Lin further explained that there are only dry fields, not suitable for growing rice. Besides, the soil is only suitable for maize, because when other cash crops are planted, production is not high. Considering these, income depending on agriculture is very limited.

In 2006, the average rural income was 2340 yuan for the whole county. In Zuogang, it was less, about 2100 yuan.[4] Qin also revealed how the figure was reached, or how local income was reported to the upper-level (county) government. For the reports he prepared, he had to adhere to the standard stipulated by the county government. If the county government said per capita income should be underreported according to a certain level, he had to follow the instruction. Unlike in the past when they wrote down whatever things were, and the county government provided some guidance only. Therefore, per capita income at county level was an indicator for reference only.

In terms of data collection, Wan mentioned the problem in statistics. Under the current system there is a statistic bureau in the county. Below it there is a statistician in each township or town, but their methods are not accurate. Take the investigation of the numbers of geese as an example, statisticians should normally visit door to door to get the number. But there is no way to do it as there is only one statistician in each township. They most probably give an estimated figure and multiple it by the number of households.

The first author witnessed how income data were collected for the national agricultural census. A group of peasants were called to the township government to fill in a questionnaire with detailed questions concerning income. These peasants (some became the author's interviewees) were almost all from well-off families, or at least with income at an intermediate level. The data collected were then sent to the statistics bureau of the county. Of course, the original data were subject to revision according to the requirement from the county government before they could be reported to an upper level (provincial) government.[5]

---

[4]According to Governor Qin.

[5]When the first author went to Zuogang to visit the statistician, she was told by Governor Qin that the statistician was at the Statistics Bureau of the county for the week. It was required that statistician from each township be present when original data were revised.

6.2.2   Migration Work and Earning Opportunities

The provincial government has encouraged migration to transfer excessive rural labour. More young people have decided to work outside their home villages. In every county there was an office for agricultural labour transfer. Such labour transfer centres had also been set up in some townships. According to Wan, such centres played a very important role in labour transfer. However, they were not responsible for finding working opportunities for rural labour. 'Say some enterprises need workers and the centres introduce some. It is not like that', commented Wan. Instead, they mainly gave political guidance and provided training. This indicated that ordinary people who had migrated to work in the cities mainly depended on kinship and friendships. Wan admitted some migrant workers were cheated and some were not paid by the year end. After the abolition of agricultural tax, there was an influx of migrants. Some went back to take back the land they had previously rented out. But after taking the subsidies, they rented out the land and left again.

In Lin's opinion, migration work did not help the peasants earn much income. He repeated one of the reasons Wan had mentioned that some 'black' (bad) contractors would not pay as promised. What is more, 'society is open now.' Some peasants would spend money earned on alcohol and some on prostitutes. All these would put migrant peasants into debts. They were people who finally managed to take some money back after working very hard for years. But according to Lin, they were very few in number.

Lin later challenged the state's policy to ensure migrant workers get paid on time, and the state would back migrant workers in pursuit of pay deserved through legal procedures. Lin was critical of the state, saying that it had no idea about the facts at all, 'it is too difficult for peasants to sue. After the lawsuit, the little money he claimed back would probably not be enough for the lawsuit expenses.'

As a native of Qinggang, Lin complained that the county had no other resources for making money. There are no rivers or mountains within the territory, no water resources to cultivate rice and develop fishery, nor mountains to develop tourism. Here people could only make a living by their physical strength. Some 'clever' people would have a small business. In Lin's words, 'you buy at the price of seven yuan here and sell at the price of eight yuan there... Save money little by little. If you depend on land, you could be no more than kept alive.'

6.3   Rural Poor and Expenditure

Similar to the views of peasants, officials also believed that much rural poverty was due to excessive expenditures such as medical care, gift money and bridewealth.

6.3.1 Medical Expenses

According to Lin, who had the most frequent and close contacts with peasants, there were two problems disturbing peasants, one was the problem of land and the other was the problem of illness. With these two problems solved peasants basically had no other problems in their lives. Meanwhile, Lin believed medical care remained the major problem, because it was too expensive.

Wei was the secretary of the Zuogang township government, responsible for drafting reports and speeches for township governors. He had been working for five years with a monthly income of 1000 yuan, much higher than the ordinary peasants. He complained how expensive medical care was. Once his child was ill and was treated in a hospital in the capital city of Harbin for a week. That cost him 10,000 yuan, equivalent to his salary for almost the year. For an ordinary peasant, this amount was completely unaffordable.

In Zuogang, many households in poverty were poor because of illnesses of family members who had no ability to work. Some families had been helped out of poverty, but a serious disease would send them back into it. For most peasants with diseases and disabilities, the priority was not medical treatment but survival.

There were stories of two families. One involved a family in which all of its members were mentally disabled. The parents were in their forties and unable to farm, because they were unable to understand how. If the others harvested 800 jin of grains, they could only get 20 or 30 jin. Their daughter, an eight-year-old girl had learning disabilities as well, always wearing the wrong shoes: one big and one small, or one in the right direction but the other not. Her problem was so serious that once got up (in the morning) she would simply put her feet into the shoes, without bothering to check whether they were in the right ones. Since no one was able to work, the family got all the shoes and clothes by donation from others. The family had been described as 'the house does not look like a house and rooms not like rooms'. There was nothing covering the *kang* (bed). Government officials had made three visits to the family, but no one could and dared get in. Finally, Lin rushed in and asked the family head to come out for a talk. The local government had tried to persuade them to move to a local care home for old people where everything was provided by state finance including free meals, but they refused. In despair, the government had applied for the title of 'five guaranteed households'[6] for them, thus the family would be eligible for 3600 yuan every year for survival.

The other family had four members, but three were paralysed and had to stay in bed. It is said that only the daughter-in-law was able to work, but she also had diabetes. Because the rural minimum living allowance was introduced in rural areas, the family got the highest allowance. Four members were given 2400 yuan every year and food stuff like flour was provided throughout the year. For such

---

[6]Household enjoying the five guarantees (childless and infirm old persons who are guaranteed with food, clothing, medical care, housing and burial expenses).

families, the only thing they could do was to stay alive. Medical treatment was out of the question.

Since 2006, new medical cooperation system has been carried out gradually in rural areas. It is believed the intention of the state policy was extremely good, but it was far from perfect. Once ill, peasants were first asked to go to clinics at township level. The write-off percentage at this level was between 20 and 30% according to Lin. The percentage was slightly lower at county hospitals and became less than 10% in the provincial hospitals. Since medical facilities and conditions at township level were extremely poor, people had to go to hospitals at provincial level for serious problems. However, only a small part of the expenses there were refundable.

It is said that the low income and unguaranteed salaries would not keep doctors or medical workers in local hospitals and clinics. The medical workers were not professional enough and most had no qualifications. One example was their application of the fourth-generation cephalosporin antibiotic on children. As a wide-spectrum antibiotic, it kills both good and bad cells. The disease might be cured this time, but once ill again the first three generations of antibiotics would never work on the children at all. They had to be sent to see experts in Harbin, the provincial capital. Treatments there were so expensive that they were described as 'robbers' in a local TV programme. But Lin commented,

> They are worse than robbers. In the Second Hospital of Harbin Medical University, a single chair would cost 30 yuan (so that a patient's family can stay overnight). As there was the news that a family spent five million yuan over the course of 60 days in that hospital. There were only 30 days in that month, but it was charged until 31st on the bill. What laws has the Communist Party stipulated? Had I, the civil affairs assistant dared to do that, I would have been handcuffed at the very least. I'd also have my job lost. But why in that hospital no one was blamed?...A robber would be sympathetic enough to leave you some money to go home and wouldn't strip you of your last item of clothing. How fierce are they (hospitals and doctors)! Nowadays, the problem of medical treatment is very serious'. (Interview on 20/06/2007 with Lin, civil affairs assistant of Zuogang township government, male)

In addition to this, the process of medical treatment under the cooperation system was extremely complicated. Peasants usually needed formalities if they would like to be transferred to a higher level hospital. They must apply to the county to do this. But it was highly possible that the person in charge would not be found in office in time. In this case, if a peasant went to the hospital without explicit approval, he had to pay everything himself. In Lin's opinion, such complexity was unnecessary, because it caused a delay which might lead to the person's death. To simplify the process, he suggested an ID card should be good enough to be used in the medical system. The person should be treated accordingly as soon as he showed the hospital that his identity was a peasant. What is more, Lin also believed more subsidies should be given for more serious diseases.

Many local people believed their real expenses were actually the same with or without the new medical cooperation. Lin stated very boldly: medical corruption made medical expenses too high. The problem of medical corruption existed in many hospitals. When doctors saw the characters 'medical insurance', which indicated that some part of the patient's expenses were refundable, some unnecessary medicines or facilities would be applied unless the patient or his family had a previous relationship or friendship with the doctor. Therefore, it was doctors and hospitals that took money from patients' medical insurance. Subsidies and benefits given by the state to peasants thus all went to the medical institutions.

6.3.2   Gift Money and Networking

Gift money giving has been a common practice in the rural areas of north China. It is found out during the fieldtrip that, for peasants, usually 30–50 yuan was given on each occasion. For a closer relationship, more would be necessary and 100 yuan was considered a 'big gift' among peasants. Such gift money exchange was expected to be at a higher price among officials and cadres. Take a wedding as an example, a typical gift was 100 yuan among township officials. 200 yuan was sometimes necessary in the case of a closer personal relationship. But for the wedding of a governor's child, the normal amount was 500 yuan. Wei remembered he once gave out 1400 yuan in 10 days as gifts, while his monthly salary at that time was only 630 yuan.

The purpose of gift money giving was almost the same for peasants and officials; to maintain and develop relationships. For peasants because of limited income, they were more reluctant to give the money, only to maintain existing relationships with their fellow villagers in most cases, while the cadres or officials would take every chance to extent their network perhaps because they had more wealth to mobilize. As a result, it appeared that cadres had always developed larger social networks than ordinary peasants. When a man who happened to be a village cadre (accountant) replied to our question about the amount of money he gave out every year, the two officials (in the township government) present corrected him almost at the same time, saying that the amount he mentioned had been underestimated because that was the amount for an ordinary rural household. As a local cadre, more gift money was needed because as a cadre he must have extended social connections.

It is important to notice that gift money exchanges between cadres and officials were not for personal relationships only. In some cases, they were for maintaining normal working relationship or in their words for doing 'zheng shi'er' (proper businesses). Once a cadre fails to give gift money to another official, next time he needs help with his work from that person, he might encounter some difficulties as it would be remembered that he did not give the gift money at proper time. Therefore the existing network is not maintained because of his actions.

For cadres and officials, social relations are more important. Lin described it as 'the greatest knowledge in China'. 'Once this is acquired, people do not have to be truly learned and genuinely talented.' According to him, in society one's mind was for most of the time occupied with interpersonal relationships. For example, one of the major duties of the Director of Finance Bureau is fund raising. Without a good relationship with the upper level government it is simply impossible. A 'no' from the upper level government would set him well back. But with a good relationship, he might be able to apply for more money for local people and pacify the ordinary peasants.

The problem lies in how to maintain or even extend the relationship. The first author witnessed an important way as to how local cadres and officials established their social network. There were a lot of small restaurants in the town centre, especially in the high street. It was said the restaurants were all supported by officials. During dinnertime, the restaurants would be filled with officials from various departments of the township and county governments, as well as their guests (mainly leaders from upper-level-governments). There had always been leaders for various inspections during the workdays. But they would not bother to pay for the meals in the restaurants, as everything had to be arranged well by the local officials. The social network was thus mostly established during meals.

The simplest lunch would cost 70–80 yuan for three people. If a goose feast was provided (Zuogang is famous for geese raising) at least 200–300 yuan would be needed. Such treatment was for ordinary officials from upper-level governments. For a VIP more money would be spent on meals. Money spent on meals would cost at least 60 or 70 thousand yuan each year in a single township. It is said there used to be much more such spending before agricultural tax was abolished, because at that time the township government had more money. Considering agricultural tax actually all went to the state, the money available for such expenditure on meals must be fees and charges collected from ordinary peasants. Lin's words later confirmed the suspicion. When talking about maintaining a good relationship, he said his principle was '*quzhiyumin, yongzhiyumin*' (to take from ordinary people for their own sake). He refused to elaborate on this principle, saying that 'this is something I shouldn't tell you. Otherwise, it is too bad'. But it can be inferred that money had to be taken from ordinary peasants for maintaining good relationships with upper level government so as to get more benefits for the local people. As he further commented, 'how is the relationship established? They (officials at different levels) are not relatives!' His principle clearly explained why he would take commissions from peasants for any funding he applied for, such as what he did to the sick girl's relief funds.

6.3.3 Marriage Expenses

In Qinggang as in other rural areas of north China, marriage would cost rural families a fortune. That's why Lin commented, for a peasant working in the field for a whole life it was a great achievement if he could help his son marry a wife without being in debt. He believed such a family would be considered 'middle class' in Zuogang. According to Wan, weddings usually did not cost much. In rural areas, even a luxury wedding would not be very expensive. What everybody mentioned was bridewealth and it had to be in cash.

Wan explained the change of bridewealth over the years. In the past when people were getting married, they asked for household items such as furniture, a television, a fridge and 'three golds'—a pair of gold earrings, a gold necklace and a gold ring. Later 'rural people might think it too much trouble' and they asked for money to 'build the house'. Some young couples certainly would not build a house for themselves (because they lived with the groom's parents), but the money had to be given. As for the amount, it was decided jointly by the two families. There was usually a matchmaker to set up contact between the families. Then the two parties would sit together and discuss how much to give. Marriage with the help of a matchmaker was found still popular in Qinggang, as free love was not very common for local youth, except those who had the experience of working away from home. The necessity of matchmakers might be due to the little contact between villages although villagers within the same one have been very familiar with each other. In recent years, young girls would not stay at home and many decided to work away. Wan noticed marriageable young girls in rural areas were few in number. This resulted in difficulties for young men to find a suitable girl locally.

There have been quite a few bachelors in rural areas unable to marry because of poverty. Wan found the phenomenon interesting that it was certain that a young man in a very poor family could not afford to marry. But once the young man had worked in the cities, it is highly possible that he would take a girl back. He attributed this to the widened horizon and extended social contact that helped the young man find a girlfriend. Yet Wan believed many boys staying behind in rural areas were actually better (or at least not worse) than those working away from the viewpoint of local people. He further explained, 'those going out might not have worked hard, but just muddled along outside for a while. However, they ended up taking a girl back (Laughed). It is really interesting. Later, I noticed some lads found the trick and went out (Laughed).' His words were partially echoed by Wei, that 'if they are doing well, adventuring away from home with some money saved, it becomes easier to marry a girl. If they are staying at home, they would pay a high price and end up having difficulties in finding a *xifu*.' In Wan's home village, until he went to the university, about half the young men did not have girlfriends, and some were 27 or 28 years old. In rural areas if a young man is 27 or 28 without a girlfriend, he is considered '*wanle*' (over), which means he will probably remain single for the whole life.

As to who takes the money (bridewealth), some officials' words might provide some clues. 'You just leave the money on the table, and your daughter-in-law collects it and saves it in her account. That's it.' And if there are a boy and a girl in one family who marry at the same time, 'parents won't get the money!' In addition, they had to pay the debt if the money was borrowed. It indicated that once married, money was transferred from parents to the new couples. Some might take the name of 'building a new house' although there were still many young couples who would like to live with groom's parents. It is commonly believed in rural areas that once the daughter-in-law is married in, the house would be hers eventually. So many young couple would not bother to build a new one with the bridewealth. Instead, they would rather set up a business and make money. Therefore, after the marriage of the young couple, Lin described the parents as '*za bo'er*' (having their neck at the point of being strangled).[7] Wan put it as 'this (bridewealth) makes one household poor and another one rich. But in general, it leads to poverty.'

The high level of bridewealth reflected the resource flow within the rural area from parents to the young generation. In a poor region like Qinggang, limited by income from other sources, young couples depend on money from their parents. Yet, rural parents would love to work hard for a whole life in exchange for some wealth for a better life of their next generation.

6.4 Local Finance

Local finance is an extremely sensitive issue. The officials visited tended to shun away from the topic. Therefore, we had to piece together the information obtained from the fieldtrip.

6.4.1 Transfer Income

Since there was no industry in Zuogang, the only income had to come from business taxes. With the limited revenue about 100,000 yuan every year, local finance was mainly dependent on transfer payment. According to the Director of the Finance Department in Zuogang, it included various items. Some were fixed such as staff salaries, office expenses and financial support for 'five guarantees households'. In Zuogang at the *xiang* level, office expenses were about 10,000 yuan each year for each village, support for 'five guarantees households' 16,000 yuan, and staff salaries 25,000 yuan. Teachers' salaries were not included as they had to be allocated within the educational system. These were called 'three funds' which added up to about 700,000 yuan per year for the whole township. The subsidies for seeds of good varieties and growing grains from the state government were also included in the category of transfer payment.

In addition to this, there were some ad hoc items within the transfer payment. These usually involved some individual projects so that the amount was not fixed. The funding for projects usually needed matching funds from the local government. For example, for the building of 'New Communist Countryside', each village was allocated 125,000 yuan, but villages had to make up the rest—200,000 yuan from individual villagers. Otherwise, the 125,000 yuan would not be given. Take road building as an example, according to the director all materials had to be ready (mixed up together) before the money was allocated from the upper-level government. It was not like in the past when villages were asked to match the funds

---

[7]To get one's neck strangled, meaning too poor to be alive.

allocated from above. Instead, according to the new requirement, local funding needed to be ready and monitored in advance so as to prevent any mistakes or anything faulty. The director emphasized that he was new in the office and had no idea how much transfer payment was allocated to the township each year, but 'it should be included in the final account statement'.

Although the title of 'state poor' county was removed for Qinggang, it had been designated as a poor county at a provincial level. It seemed no one knew exactly how much transfer payment the county would get every year from the provincial government (or those who really know would not release such information for whatever reason).

6.4.2   Final Account

Since some of the words from the director were quite confusing, we had to compare what he said with the information obtained from a woman officer in the same department but on a separate day. We found the director was not completely correct, either that or he was trying to confuse us deliberately. For example, the woman showed the first author that fiscal revenue in the final account was 3,219,240 yuan for 2006, and the expenditure was the same. Of the revenue, 197,000 yuan had been allocated to the *xiang* government as office expenses. 1,586,716 yuan was used for salaries for government staff (92 in total), the so-called 'population supported by public finance'. The rest was what was actually available for anything else in the *xiang* throughout the year, which was less than half of the total. It is noteworthy that people supported by public finance did not include teachers, households enjoying the five guarantees, nor families of revolutionary martyrs and military personnel. Teachers' salaries were allocated directly to the schools by the Education Bureau within the education system, and did not go through the accounts of the Finance Department. For households enjoying five guarantees, the 1200 yuan each year per head came from transfer payment. Money given to families of revolutionary martyrs and military personnel (7000 yuan per year per head) was also part of transfer payment. The rural minimum living allowance given in the previous year totalled 587,476 yuan, which was from transfer payment as well. In addition, subsidies given to peasants for growing grains totalled 3,765,629 yuan in 2006. They were under a special category of transfer payment from the central government. When the first author was in the office, she found the notice on grain subsidies in 2007 had been printed out. There was a large piece of white paper on a table, which showed the names of peasants, subsidies to be allocated and the area of their land. Of the hundreds of cases, the first author wrote down two pairs of numbers: 445.65-32.3 and 390.91-26.8. The former numbers indicated the amount of subsidies and the latter the land area (according to our calculation the unit of land area should be mu).

It gave a clearer picture when comparing the information from the director and the female officer. The director was wrong in that fiscal revenue or expenditure did not include transfer payment from the above. Meanwhile, it was confirmed that local revenue was limited and transfer payment did include numerous categories, relating to different departments.

Meanwhile, It was found out from the female officer that there were a lot of debts in the township accounts, which was far more than 10 million yuan, as Wei believed. The exact number was 29.15 million yuan indicated in the account book. Most of the debts had been accumulated over the years for unpaid salaries of individuals and for money owed to units and organizations. Lin complained that Zuogang was so poor that its ability to repay the debt was nil, so it had to depend on state funding to repay. But he doubted few would know whether the funding had been used for repayments, and it was possible that not a penny from the state was used for this purpose. For him it was quite normal and he believed that state policies were all good. Since General Secretary Hu Jintao and Premier Wen Jiabao took office, they had done all they could to benefit ordinary rural people. 'But for many policies, they were all up when carried out locally. Well before they were carried out locally, there had been interceptions and cut-offs, and policies were changed all over'.

The financial issue concerning Zuogang, as we believe in many other township governments at least in north China, is more mysterious than complex. After the first author left the Finance Department, the government official who was accompanying said that anything related to finance was sensitive. The female officer would not, should not and dared not tell us what we would like to know.

6.4.3   Agricultural Tax

The abolition of agricultural taxes is believed to have had a great impact on local finance. However, according to Wan, the influence on fiscal income at the county level was trivial. His statement was based on the fact that, at county level, local revenue had remained at about 70 million yuan for many years, regardless of whether agricultural taxes were collected or not. Fiscal revenue, from agricultural taxes used to be 30 million yuan each year. But after agricultural taxes were abolished the state allocated the same amount of money to the county to keep its fiscal income the same as before. In fact, the overall financial condition became worse because there had been more expenditure every year due to the increase of salaries for government staff.

At township level, the impact of tax abolition on local finance was greater. Together with agricultural taxes, *tiliu and tongchou* were scrapped at the same time so that the township government was put in such a financial difficulty that money was insufficient to develop local public services. Since finance was totally dependent on allocation from the above, the township government basically could do nothing but make applications for funding. However, there was no guarantee that the upper-level governments would allocate as much as needed. Investigators were usually sent to the local area for inspection before any funding was approved. It is highly possible that the upper-level governments would only provide part of the financial support as they also had tight budgets. If that is the case, the rest would have to depend on fundraising from peasants by *yishi yiyi* as stipulated in the agenda of 'building up new-typed socialist countryside'. But as noticed by the township governor, fundraising was difficult, because 'the government is not in control of peasants anymore'. He explained, 'in the past, peasants would do whatever they were required. But now, work with peasants has to be based on the principles of guiding, leading and helping instead of being coercive'. Taking the road building as an example, the governor believed peasants should offer money, work or service for their own sake. But some households would not offer any help and refused to pay, so that the local matching fund could hardly be raised. Nothing could be done with peasants at both village and township levels, just because of the new policy stipulating that fundraising from peasants should be on a voluntary basis.

Lin expressed the same view that after the abolishment of 'two labours' (voluntary labour and accumulated labour), provision of public goods of the local area could not be moved forward. He also gave the example of road building. Peasants' attitude would be, 'I will not do it anyway. Why bother me? It is better for me to have a rest.' In many *tuns* where the secretaries lack prestige, the road building and maintenance would be completely unable to realize.

The result was that after a soaking rain, vehicles had no access to some *tuns* for a whole month. Wan also confirmed that after it rained or snowed, there were still many villages which remained inaccessible. Some villages did not have roads at all. Since the 'building up of new socialist countryside,' there has been some investment in road maintenance. Before that 'some roads at the township level simply would not do, let alone those in the villages'. In 2006, a new bus route to Taiyang (a village) was opened, but for seven or eight months the poor road condition made buses impossible to get in.

Lin argued that if there were blacktop (or concrete) roads even brick roads in every village it was favourable for peasants so that when it was windy or rainy, harvested goods from the village could be transported out and exchanged for cash. One story was that, in the places of Liming and Xiangyang, peasants would interplant garlic and Chinese leaf because the soil there was not good enough. Sometimes when garlic and Chinese leaf were harvested but it rained, the peasants would simply pull them out and throw them directly into the trenches, because the products could not be transported out and sold. Besides, the village was 15 miles away from the market. Two '*four wheels*' were needed for the transport, in addition to a meal for the drivers and carriers. Garlic especially green garlic was extremely cheap, and usually a little income would be left after deducting all the expenses. Therefore, if the weather was not good, peasants would choose to throw the harvests away. With the limitation in public goods provision, development of rural economy was very much restricted.

The poor development of rural areas not only affected peasants' income, but also their personal life. Divorce rate has been on the rise in rural areas. There is no guarantee how long a marriage will last. Lin believed this is not necessarily have to be the result of long separation between couples due to migration. Instead, it was much related to poverty. Some would break up after only two or three months because the man was unable to support the family and the woman would develop a relationship with someone else. A contractor or a foreman with some money would be attractive enough. In Lin's view, 'even those who have made lovers' vows break up, never mind those without deep foundation of affection.' 'Didn't Master Lu Xun (the most famous writer in modern China) say that people have to be alive before love is provided? …You need economic foundation first, don't you? You have to fill the stomach, and eat well first. If you are unable to stay alive, who would want to live with you?'

6.5 Power, Local Resources and Corruption

6.5.1 Local Power

There is a saying that, 'shangao huangdiyuan' (the mountain is high and the emperor far away'. It indicates that Beijing is so far that the central government is in no control of remote areas. For individual rural areas it is local governments and the officials that implement policies. Thus, they are in direct control of the local areas and the people living there. In other words, they are the ones with 'power'.

Lin's comments provided answers to some questions concerning local officials, the local power. One question is about how powerful the communist officials are. As the saying goes, 'in control of heaven to the top and the ground at the bottom and everything in between'. The first author quoted Lin's words, 'the county governor or the secretary of the county committee is the magnate below the prefectural level. According to the official scale of the Qing Dynasty, he is fengjiangdali (the top official of the region, a magnate with conferred territory)'. They are in charge of the region and have the final say. Second, who exactly are the leaders? Since the Communist Party practices the 'leadership' institution that everything is under the control of the Party, anyone with a political title such as secretary of the Party Committee will be considered a leader. Lin further explained that this was not like a Party secretary in an enterprise or a Party secretary in a school, where the CEO or the headteacher was the real leader. Lin believed the governor and secretary of Party Committee as magnates in charge of the township. In the public sector, all secretaries of the Party committees are fengjiangdali.

Then a more interesting question arises as to how the power is exercised. In Qinggang County, for example, how does the secretary of the County Committee or the Party Committee exercise the power? Those with power do not literally control others or direct others to do something. For instance, they would not ask anyone to do anything illegal. There is a subtle word 'suggest'—I suggest you do something in this way. But in fact, once suggested you have to do it accordingly. The result of not doing so, as a state official one cannot be sacked easily, but one can be transferred (to another position). Lin illustrated that,

Suppose I am Secretary of the Party Committee of Zuogang township government. Imagine if I believe that what the Secretary of the County Committee says and asks me to do is an invasion to ordinary peoples' rights and tell him 'I can't do it'. The next day, the first person I receive would be someone from the Committee of Discipline Investigation of the Qinggang County. They would like to go over whatever I have. Is everything I have up to standard? Once a single one is found incorrect or illegal, I am over. What if they could not find anything wrong? They would then find some minor problems and hold a meeting to discuss it. They would usually say, XXX, Secretary of Party Committee of the Zuogang Township, works in this or that way, which is not proactive enough and so on, and has impeded the social and economic development. Then a document will be ratified for the transfer. Where to transfer then? To put it simply, the person will be transferred to a place or a bureau which is most famous for being messy in management. The person is still an official at the same administrative level, but the title will be changed to some 'inspector at the director level'. It basically means the person is actually retreated to the back line and is not in the leading position anymore. Therefore, senior officials are in control of the bowls (jobs) of those junior. One might hold a gold bowl, but he can be easily 'given' a clay one if he disregards the power overhead. (Interview on 12/06/2007 with Lin, local civil affairs assistant, male)

In reality, almost all local officials treat power respectfully in many extra-work activities. The first author was told about the work of chauffeurs. A chauffeur is a driver for a leader. But only driving would make a chauffeur far from good enough. A good chauffeur is supposed to undertake everything including bill paying for the leader, such as electricity bill and phone bill. For the living necessities, either the secretary (equivalent to a PA) or the chauffeur would be responsible. For instance, he would be responsible for the barrelled mineral water in the leader's home by topping it up on time. Thus, a good chauffeur always has a good relationship with the leader. As a reward, the chauffeur is empowered but in a more covert way. It is usually reflected by acquisition of certain resources. It is said the most expensive apartment at Pleasure Home in the town centre of Qinggang was bought by the chauffeur of the vehicle numbered one.[8] Also take the chauffeur as an example, he might get an extra refund for petrol expenses, vehicle repair and maintenance. When asked how much it would cost to maintain a government vehicle, we got the answer, 'they (government vehicles) are petrol drinkers! The expenses? The driver would do something (cheating), and you can't tell how much the expenses would be.' This became one of the ways to accrue resources.

6.5.2 Local Resources and Corruption

It is believed officials at any level would do the same thing—to worship power so as to accrue more resources. Officials from the Great Xing'an Mountains were said to go to the provincial department on business errands with two gunny bags of dragon

---

[8]Government vehicles are numbered according to the positions of the leaders the vehicles are serving at. The smaller the number is, the higher position of the leader holds. Therefore, the vehicle number one is for the top leader of a government.

birds.[9] The dragon birds are the special products of the Great Xing'an Mountains and are national second-grade protected animals. Killing and catching such birds is illegal, which would result in a prison sentence. However, it is the dragon birds that were taken in gunny bags to the provincial department for 'business purposes'. In return, several million yuan would be allocated.

The more common case is *songli* (money/gift giving) to officials at higher levels. It not only keeps the basic content of gift flow to maintain a good relationship, but also serves as a way to further develop it. Once accepting the gift/money, the higher-level official is believed to be in moral debt that he is expected to do a favour for the gift giver. Thanks to the various events in officials' families at higher levels, there are always many occasions for those inferiors to give. For those with high enough official positions, the amount to give is substantial. It is estimated that the salary for Secretary of the County Committee did not exceed 3000 yuan per month or about 30,000 yuan annually around 2006. When the child of the Secretary of Prefectural Committee was getting married, the county secretary's salary for the whole year was said to be not enough for a decent gift. During festivals and holidays, officials at lower levels would compete with each other in gift or money giving. During the exchange of power and resources, corruption has been cultivated. Lin argued,

> Sometimes, it doesn't mean that officials of the Communist Party have to be corrupt, have to occupy others' properties as their own…I am a college graduate and when I just started working, I was so inspired and daring, trying to do something for the ordinary people, and live a meaningful life. But you are here where all the ravens are black. Can you be the only white one? How can you refuse to go round to others to avoid *songli* during festivals and holidays? How can you refuse to give money when there are some big events for others? (Interview on 12/06/2007 with Lin, local civil affairs assistant, male)

With limited personal income to do this, some would think of public funds and properties. One local official seemed to be angry when talking about corruption. For example, in talking about the case of Chen Xitong,[10] who was accused of embezzling dozens of million public funds, He commented that, 'it is impossible! That's because the Communist Party is afraid of losing face. In fact, if they had a thorough investigation, for an official at such a high position, dozens of millions would be much underestimated. The money he put in his pocket would be several billion, and the money he embezzled, transferred and wasted would be at least up to 100 billion yuan.'

For local corruption, however, the officials would at most express their complaints in private, but keep silent in public. Government vehicles were mostly at the service of leaders. These vehicles were even used to send and pick up leaders' children from school. In a poor township as Zuogang, the vehicle would cost at

---

[9]Bonasa bonasia.

[10]Former mayor of Beijing Municipal Government, Secretary of Municipal Committee, was sentenced to 13 years' imprisonment because of corruption.

least 70,000–80,000 yuan each year. But for the county government one cannot imagine how much they would cost. Those vehicles were either Toyota 4500 or 2700 and were described as 'petrol drinkers'. Wei was very angry about this, as the state had stipulated that county leaders could not have at service *saloons* (because of their high emissions). But in fact, instead of having saloons, all of them have *jeeps* at service with extremely high emission standards. Wei said he once wrote a 100-thousand-word letter to one of the then top leaders of the State Council, but he later burnt it. He felt there was no use posting such a letter, as he said 'what choice do I have? I have to work here anyway'.

As mentioned in the previous chapter, Qinggang became known nationwide for the largest law case of 'buying official position'. When the first author was in the county, she was told that when Ma De was discovered guilty and arrested, his laptop was checked. It was found from the laptop that Wang Xuewu in Qinggang had sent a certain amount of money. It was also noted in the end that 'Wang would be assigned the position of county governor'. With such irrefutable evidence, he was caught and taken away from a meeting by people from the Provincial Discipline Inspection Commission. But according to the local officials, 'without such a sentence found from the laptop, he would have become the deputy governor as expected. Bribing for an official position would be nothing special. They are all the same. How did he (Wang) start? He started out as an ordinary official.' It is also common in Qinggang that some broke the law, but they bribed the officials in charge. In most cases, the victim would accept financial compensation from the offender to achieve a 'private resolution'. If the victim or his family decided to go through the legal procedure, he might not win the case, nor get any money.

Local officials blamed the Communist Party for the deteriorated ethos of society, because it does not have a good troop. There are too many idlers and they have wasted the state's resources. They should be made redundant step by step. For example, in a township government like Zuogang, a dozen or so officials would be enough. They also attributed corruption to the very low level of their income. Lin and Wei both said that their income had been increased to over 1000 yuan in 2006. Before that they earned about several hundred yuan monthly for the past few years. If they gave money for three occasions for the month, they would have nothing left for food. Officials also need money for maintenance. If China followed the example of Singapore and raised the income of officials to be high enough, there would not be corruption. The other suggestion they gave was to tighten up law stipulation. No matter how an official moved the public funds—eating, drinking, occupying or corrupting, they should be severely punished. Over 10,000 would deserve 10 years of imprisonment, and over 100,000 an execution. Then there would never be a single corrupt official. The reason that the local officials were still working there for a monthly salary of 1000 yuan was because the pensions and insurance were still attractive enough to them. If there was only 1000 yuan income without any other welfare, they said the local government would be empty as no one would work for such little money.

When the interview got further, we could not help asking a question: whether these officials interviewed were corrupt or not? Take Wan as an example, his parents back in his hometown could have over 100 mu of land to farm. But for Wan's position in the county government, an ordinary household could never acquire so much land. It might be too early to conclude that Wan was corrupt. But Lin certainly seemed to be. He once said he was not good as a son of a peasant. He described how he squandered the money his father gave him when he was in college. He would spend a term's (half a year) allowance within a week, going wherever he liked. He would go to Beijing to see his friends and spent a few days there, or go to Harbin just for a party, or buy some expensive clothes without thinking how much they were. At that time even in Harbin few students could afford those expensive clothes. After graduation his father even sent him to Japan, but he did not like the place and finally came back. He changed after he got married especially after he became a father. This change, according to him was from a few days' meditation. He first realize what he did was wrong. Then he started to think about his son and the future of the child before he started to save money for his child. During the talk, the first author got to know that apart from his salary he also earned money by being a local loan shark. At the interest rate of 10%, he admitted that he would earn more than 20,000 yuan each year. This means he would have at least 200,000 yuan. The first author was curious about what kind of rural family Lin was from. Another official said in private that his father had been working as a village secretary for many years. His family was almost the richest in Zuogang County. Besides, Lin was only in his early thirties. Taking his monthly income into consideration, to earn as much as 200,000 yuan for being a township official would seem impossible. He might have got some money from his father, but it was unlikely after his 'meditation'. He must have other ways to accrue wealth, as the 200,000 yuan has provided fairly strong evidence as well as the reason why he took commission from funding for peasants.

There is also a common belief in Zuogang that a rich father will have rich children. It is said to find a position in the local government would cost about 80,000 yuan around 2006, and it does not mean enough money would ensure a position in it. In addition to money, a good relationship has always been necessary. However, money would help to establish extensive relationship. Those young people working in the township government were all from rich rural families. Their parents exchanged resources (money) for a position which might be powerful enough in the future to further strengthen the economic foundation of the family. Thus, power and resources enhanced each other and became closely connected. By doing so, rich rural parents also successfully changed the registration status of their children from rural into town/urban to enjoy more benefits such as pensions and insurance. When the children were powerful and well-off enough they would most often buy an apartment for their parents in the town centre. In this way, the parents' rural status was changed as well.

However, ordinary peasants were excluded from the *guanxi* network involving power-resource exchange as they had neither power nor money. Even bank loans were not available for them as admitted by officials, because the credit association would not trust them. Peasants mostly depended on non-governmental loans with the high interest rate from 10 to 30%. Therefore, peasants have always been losers in the game of power and resource exchange especially in poor areas.

Chapter 7
Institutions, Urban Bias and Local Relations

This research has combined qualitative and quantitative methods to investigate rural–urban income disparities. Based on the results of these two methods, the findings are discussed below.

7.1 Institutions and Local Development

Both qualitative and quantitative methods have shown that counties like Qinggang in Heilongjiang are at a very low level of development. The interview data indicate that farming was almost the only source of peasants' income and maize as their major product. The peasants were largely confined to the land, with few income-generating opportunities, apart from agriculture. The quantitative results confirm that transferring the surplus labour out of agriculture will help to increase rural income, thus reducing the rural–urban income gap.

Interviews conducted in Qinggang revealed that, with modern technology, farming is no longer time-consuming. The whole year's work in the fields would add up to about a month. As Heilongjiang is located in the northeast of China, with its temperature in wintertime well below what is suitable for farming, there can be only one harvest per year. This leaves the peasants with a lot of spare time. According to the Lewis model, the surplus labour will be transferred out of agriculture when there is insufficient employment in the rural sector. Rural unemployment will be reduced, productivity increased and income improved. However, as far as can be seen in Qinggang, when the interviews were conducted, quite a few peasants were idling about with nothing in particular to do. Some men were playing Mah Jung and the women were sitting about in groups, chatting and gossiping.

There are certainly some young people who migrated to the cities. But during the 2006 fieldtrip, only two peasants admitted that they were better off because of

© Shanghai Jiao Tong University Press and Springer Nature Singapore Pte Ltd. 2018   149
Y. Gao and S. Fennell, *China's Rural–Urban Inequality in the Countryside*,
https://doi.org/10.1007/978-981-10-8273-3_7

migration work. Both had migrated to the city but changed registration by means of marrying a local person. It has confirmed that as long as the peasants were holding a rural registration, they were unable to obtain any of the benefits enjoyed by the urban residents, even if they migrated and found work in the cities. Therefore, what really prevents the peasants from benefiting from migration in China has been its *hukou* system, which effectively set up an institutional division to restrict free movement of labour. As such, what is suggested in the Lewis model cannot be realized in China, as household registration made the complete rural urban transfer almost impossible, even though the system has become less restrictive in the reform years. Labour was thus unable to move freely out of the rural areas into the cities and, accordingly, rural productivity remained low, as a great degree of under- or even unemployment persisted in the rural areas. The Pearson correlation result found in this study also indicates that areas with a lower urban rural productivity ratio tend to have smaller income inequality, as rural productivity is higher, but the institution of household registration becomes the biggest obstacle to reducing rural underemployment, increasing productivity as well as improving rural income.

It is argued by some Chinese scholars that, instead of a dual structure, there is a tri-structure in China so that, within the rural sector, there have developed rural industries. The township and village enterprises in many rural areas have been the driving force of local development and have absorbed much of the rural surplus labour, but in the field site of this study, the local industry did not develope well. As emerged from the interviews, several brick factories became the only places that absorb some of the surplus labour. When there were more workers than needed, the peasants would take turns to be hired by the factories, although the working conditions were harsh. The peasants were thus confined to the land in rural areas, which has greatly impeded their income growth.

The Theil index decomposition results of the study also suggest that, taking into consideration the homogenous nature of the overall low level of income at the county level, the constant high contribution of the rural–urban divide to the overall inequality throughout the years at least indicates that China's income inequality is due to the differences between the rural and urban sectors. Urban registration holders enjoyed secured jobs, subsidies, better social welfare and, above all, a far higher income, while the rural registration holders had to pay agricultural taxes and local charges, and had very little welfare protection, so they had to pay for their own medical costs and their children's education. In this sense, what really matters is the type of *hukou* held. The differentiated treatment enjoyed by the holders of different types of *hukou* have maintained and enlarged the rural-income divide, even within the rural setting.

Therefore, the Theil index decomposition results have provided quantitative evidence, which supports the argument of this study that rural–urban income inequality has been institutional. The division between the rural and urban population due to household registration system initially resulted in an income difference between the two sectors, and helped to maintain and enlarge the gap over the reform years. It not only restricted the free movement of rural labour but also ensured that urban household registration holders obtained sufficient benefits. As a consequence, the peasants' income growth was greatly restricted and the rural–urban income gap widened by a series of urban-biased policies set against such an institutional background.

7.2   Urban-Biased Public Policies and Resource Flows

Given the rural/urban division due to household registration, the benefits of the urban sector have been well protected, while those of the rural-dwellers largely neglected. At the very beginning of communist control, China decided to extract agriculture to ensure the rapid development of industry, adopting the development strategy of the Soviet Union. The policies adopted were believed to be highly urban-biased, as China used to set prices against agriculture in addition to extracting taxes from it. In addition to these, subsidies were given to the urban workers. Most domestic scholars believe that a large amount of resources were thus transferred out of agriculture to support urban industry under these urban-biased policies.

Such biased policies were thought to have been corrected since the 1978 reform; for example, grain procurement prices increased quite a few times, and urban subsidies were phased out. However, it is insisted in the present study that the legacy of the biased public policies is hard to be removed. Agricultural taxes were not abolished until after 2000. Public spending ensured a central financial control, but delegated many responsibilities to the localities, which worsened the financial difficulties of the local governments. It is the lowest level governments at the county and township levels that were most affected, and these governments have been responsible for most of the development in rural areas. When the local governments encountered financial difficulties, the peasants became the ultimate target for shouldering the burden, as the deficits had to be met through local charges (*tiliu and tongchou*) imposed on the rural residents. Even though the prices have been corrected since the reform to benefit the peasantry, as the Qinggang case shows, the peasants have to buy everything except maize. When the maize price rose, the prices for other products all increased substantially. As one female peasant commented, 'but for the good price (for maize) this year, we can hardly survive'. In addition, as the current policies encouraged by *hukou* system are still biased against the rural sector, the urban and rural residents have been differently treated in terms of social welfare. In townships like Zuogang in Qinggang, the overall social security system for peasants was virtually undeveloped. A disease could quickly return a family back into poverty. The peasants thus adopted the common view that they would rather wait for death than seek treatment, if they were seriously ill.

It is argued in this book that, since the reform, the policies have been corrected to some extent to benefit agriculture and the peasantry. Quantitative results have revealed that several pro-agricultural policies have had some effects on stabilizing and reducing the rural–urban income gap. However, the influence of such policies have been far from satisfactory, considering the high level, widening income inequality of recent years. This study suggests that, as long as the institutions to differentiate rural/urban sectors remain unchanged, the state policies will continue to be urban-biased. Therefore, the institutions and public policies have become the fundamental reason for the stagnated rural income and large rural–urban income inequality.

7.3 Local Resources, Cadre Activities and Corruption

In a province like Heilongjiang, with many rural areas in poverty, the resources are extremely limited and become the cause of conflicts among all of the parties involved. As a communist country, China's central government, the party-state, holds the absolute power over policy making. However, it is the officials in the lower-level governments who are working as the agents of the state to implement these policies. Since the reform and opening up, the state has delegated many of its obligations to the local governments. This has provided the local governments and their officials with more authority. That is, the local governments and officials are powerful in two ways. They function both as the agents of the state, representing the central government in policy implementation, and as the principals of the localities, responsible for the decision-making with regard to many local affairs. In both senses, they are playing an important role in mobilizing the local resources.

Firstly, as agents, the local officials must ensure the implementation of the state policies. In this process, they are certainly highly motivated by what is left over for themselves. For example, in the collection of agricultural taxes, every township in Qinggang had been very enthusiastic, as once they had fulfilled the task within the required time, they could obtain a certain amount as rebate from the county government. But compared with agricultural taxes, the local officials were more proactive in collecting *tiliu* and *tongchou*, over which they had more authority. There is no way of knowing how the collected *tiliu* and *tongchou* were actually used, as township finance accounts are a top secret of the government and few officials had access to them. During one of the visits to Zuogang government, the township accountant was constantly guarded in the presence of the first author. The peasants complained that they paid for the road construction (one of the most important items under *tiliu* and *tongchou*), but were still asked to join and offer labour in building the village roads. It is believed in this study that a certain amount must have been kept and used by the local officials. One local official admitted that, during the time when *tiliu* and *tongchou* was collected, they had more 'office funds'—money under their control, including expenses spent on entertaining leaders from the upper level government. The local cadres were so keen and coercive about collecting *tiliu* and *tongchou* that, sometimes, the local police were even mobilized. However, with regard to the introduction of a new rural cooperative medical system, the local officials made less effort, as they could not get any tangible benefits from it. The result is that most of the peasants in the field site still had no idea about how the new system actually worked. This confirms the finding of existing studies, that the implementation of state policies is selective, depending on whether the policies are of benefit to the local governments and officials.

Meanwhile, the local officials as agents do show their compliance with the state, for they depend on the latter for payments. Because of China's government bureaucracy, this is reflected by their compliance to their superiors in the upper-level governments, because the latter have direct control over their salaries and appointments. One official admitted that they had to set up good *guanxi* with the superiors in order to 'better serve the people', so money has to be taken from the peasants to maintain the good relationship. While a good *guanxi* with their superiors in the upper level governments might help the local officials to acquire more resources for local public use and thus 'better serve the people', it must be pointed out that, the local officials are doing this mostly for their own sake rather than for the ordinary peasants, as local officials need political achievements to secure their job or obtain promotion. The former Qinggang governor had a sufficient political record to be promoted as a prefectural level leader by falsely reporting the local income at a high level, regardless of the fact that most people were still living in poverty, and the county lost its central financial support because of his 'achievement in reducing poverty'. Compared with the peasants' benefits, promotion is more attractive, as it entitles them to wield more authority over the scarce resources, especially in poverty-stricken areas.

Apart from being agents, the local officials are also in direct control and management of the local development and whatever the peasants are making a living with. It is found in this study that, in Qinggang, land has been the hottest issue. Since land is not privately owned, the local cadres are decisive in the land contracts with peasants. Fairness has always been the focus concerning land. The initial distribution of land was said to be based on the number of household members, but, when the fieldwork was conducted, most of the peasants were complaining that land was scarce. Many households only have a few mu of land. In contrast, all of those with dozens or even hundreds of mu of land were found to be either village heads or other local cadres. It was explained by some officials that, with more peasants moving to the cities as migrant workers, much land has been left over for a smaller number of households, but the ordinary rural households could seldom contract much land to farm. They either had insufficient money for the rent or no access to the land available. According to the peasants, the local cadres accrued large tracts of land while in post, and much land was actually rent-free. The peasants were complaining about the dishonest deals that the local cadres made over land, that they had taken flexible land (public property) as their own. Somehow, more land has been transferred to the local power and the cadres, making them better-off. As the local principals, officials and cadres have reshuffled the local resources away from peasants towards themselves and the local power, with whom they have established and wish to maintain good *guanxi*.

The dual identities of the local officials also encouraged corruption in such a poor area. In Qinggang, the civil affairs assistant would take money as commission from the funding provided for peasants in need. The minimum living allowances for low-income households rarely went to those in real need of them. The process of choosing those eligible for the rural minimum allowance was a mysterious one in the eyes of the peasants. The lack of transparency could only result in unfairness and resentment. At least in Zuogang, the elections of the village heads and local cadres were not democratic at all. The candidates would go from household to household, asking the peasants to vote for them, while the peasants could not care less, as they believed that whoever took the position would do the same thing— embezzle the public property and exploit the ordinary villagers. Corruption was rampant in the area where the fieldwork was conducted. Limited by the sources of income, the local cadres secretly sold off the trees which had grown for many years in the villages, and other public properties, such as houses which were used as village offices. The officials regarded corruption as a result of their low income. Yet, somehow, after a few years in position, these officials as well as the local cadres such as the village heads (including former ones) had all become far better off than the ordinary villagers, with more land, bigger houses and better living conditions.

It is suggested in this study that the ultimate goal of the local officials is to maximize their own benefits, either for promotion or becoming well-off, while local development and the peasants' welfare are not their primary concern. One village secretary, who was described as vicious by the villagers, was given an honorary title as a model for poverty relief, even though he was deeply hated by the peasants. In poor areas, a political position might mean access to more resources. One provincial official stated that, in some areas of Heilongjiang, people would spend 200,000 yuan to buy the post of village head. This has explained why, in such a poor county as Qinggang, there were so many corrupt officials involved in the biggest post-buying scandal in China. It is simply because the local officials seeked the opportunity to acquire the limited resources, and had the ultimate power in their reallocation. The result is that the resources and wealth were shuffled from the ordinary peasants to the officials and the local power, which has worsened the income level of the rural public. Meanwhile, this has also contributed to the rural–urban income divide in rural areas, because the cadres and the local power, in most cases, held urban rather than rural *hukou*, either by adopting the official positions or by acquiring an urban *hukou* with wealth.

Therefore, the local officials, as both the state agents and local principals, play an active role in resource reallocation in the way that the scarce resources have been extracted and moved away from peasants into the hands of the officials and the local power, which has deteriorated the rural income and also widened the income inequality in the rural sector.

---

[1]In Zuogang, to secure a job in the township government required about 80,000–100,000 yuan in 2006, on the condition that one had the right *guanxi* (the so-called backdoor or improper ways).

7.4 Local Guanxi, Gift Giving and Bridewealth

'Etiquette demands reciprocity' is the Chinese way of maintaining *guanxi* with others. Gifts play an important role during the process Generally, when a gift is given, an outstanding obligation is established. This places the giver in a morally superior position, because he has set up an outstanding obligation for the receiver to pay back in the future. The local officials use gift giving (bribery) to maintain a good *guanxi* with their superiors and the latter are expected to 'pay back' by allocating more resources to the locality or granting personal benefits to the local officials. Among the officials and cadres, money and power are exchanged to maintain such a *guanxi* network, which has encouraged corruption and nepotism.

The qualitative data show that the peasants were seldom involved in gift giving to the cadres and officials unless they had established certain *guanxi* previously. In the words of the peasants, 'without money and power, who would rap to you?' This indicates that the ordinary peasants are at the outer edge of the *guanxi* circle of cadres and officials, or even excluded from it.

However, the peasants do set up their own networks and spend much on gift giving. The interview data revealed that the peasants generally considered gift giving necessary, and such a *guanxi* network was quite close-knit. This is seen not only in the way in which the villagers addressed each other as if they were relatives but also in the way that they helped each other when needed. A woman whose husband had migrated to find work could seek help from her neighbours with her household chores. When a girl was diagnosed with leukaemia, the whole village financed her initial treatment when government relief funding was unavailable.

Apart from the reasons for gift giving that have been analysed by anthropologists and other social scientists, it is suggested in the present research that gift giving in the *guanxi* network should be studied with regard to the real economic situation of the locality. While for the cadres and local power, the exchange of gift money might be for the establishment and maintenance of *guanxi* relationship to gain more information and opportunities from each other and obtain mutual benefits, the peasants had to maintain their own *guanxi* in order to seek mutual help and consolation, when no resources or other external support were available. Such a *guanxi* network, maintained by gift giving, seems very important for the peasants, in that it will probably provide a lifeline when they are in difficulty. In this sense, gift money giving provides a powerful backup for the peasants, who have no other resources to depend upon.

Generally speaking, the effect of gift giving on resource flow is horizontal in that the resources are moving among the peasants within the rural sector. In the long-term, all that is paid out will be returned to the individual households, simply because the gift giving is mutual. However, as shown by the qualitative data, over the years, people have been spending more on gift giving, as the money given out on each occasion had been far more than before, and people seemed to look for more gift giving occasions because some had no patience to wait, but wished to get their 'gift money' back quickly. This would eventually diminish rural income, because taking rural society as a whole, more resources have been spent as gift money and much on dinners and banquets. It is argued in this study that to maintain a *guanxi* network through gift money giving is necessary for peasants, but there are extreme cases when the peasants seek the opportunity to get their gifted money back, which would create a vicious circle and finally end up in waste, as money would be spent on excessive amount of drinks and banquets rather than on necessities more urgently needed.

Bridewealth is the most unexpected finding of the study. During the fieldtrip it was an unavoidable topic when rural income was mentioned. It is perhaps because bridewealth constitutes, for most rural households, the biggest one-off expenditure of their lives. It is found from the fieldwork that, in Qinggang, there were quite a few bachelors who could not find girlfriends because they were too poor to afford the bridewealth. Some were forced to leave home and work in the cities. One official interviewed found it interesting that those young men who migrated would in most cases find a girlfriend and get married without paying any bridewealth, but those back home remained bachelors, unable to afford the bridewealth and so get married. It is suggested that the issue of bridewealth also has to be examined against the local poverty background.

For most ordinary rural families, bridewealth might be one of the few possessions that parents can pass down to their sons, if not the only one. Constrained by their low income and the limited income-generating opportunities, most rural parents have to keep working hard over the years to save up some bridewealth, so that, with such a lump sum, the new couple would have a better life. The parents would usually consider it their duty to save enough bridewealth for their sons when other resources were not available locally. An old couple interviewed were even feeling guilty and blamed themselves for being useless for not being able to save decent bridewealth for their sons. Meanwhile, rural youth took it as the only chance to get some capital invested for their future life. A young couple interviewed were thus better off, due to having bought a vehicle for goods transport with the money given to them as bridewealth. However, for those who migrated to the cities, the situation would be different, as outside the villages, young people could find more opportunities. Whether or not these are accessible, these young people are presented with more resources and income-generating opportunities. Thus, they will not cling to bridewealth as the sole possible resource like their counterparts, who still remain in the home villages.

Of course, the study of bridewealth has to be related to cultural development. According to Chinese tradition, sons are supposed to support the parents after they get married. In this sense, bridewealth might be considered as an investment for the parents who may be expecting to receive future care from their sons and daughter-in-laws. However, with the changes in culture and society, Chinese rural families are tending to separate into nuclear ones (Yan, 2003, 2010), since many young couples are no longer living with their parents. As was found in this study, for many rural households, the parents have been deprived of everything after the marriage of their offspring.

Bridewealth is not the focus of this book, which certainly deserves further examination. However, in this study, bridewealth has been found to have caused resources to move around within the rural sector, in a vertical way, from the older generation to the younger one. This has resulted in some becoming richer and others poorer.

References

Yan, Y. (2003). *Private life under socialism: Love, intimacy, and family change in a Chinese village, 1949–1999*. Stanford University Press.

Yan, Y. (2010). The Chinese path to individualization. *The British Journal of Sociology, 61*(3), 489–512.

Chapter 8
Qinggang—Ten Years on

8.1 Overview of the County

In 2016, the first author had a follow-up visit to Qinggang to see how it is developed in recent years. On entering Qinggang, a catchy slogan by the road came into sight, saying 'precise poverty alleviation to initiate motivity; three-year decisive battle for moderate prosperity ahead of schedule'.[1] While the first author still could not remove out of the mind the image of Qinggang in 2006, a question came up immediately: is it still the county in poverty as ten years ago?

8.1.1 Recent Development

The answer seems no, because at least it looks different, and much busier. The main road from Harbin to Qinggang is under construction, making the temporary side-ways very crowded with all sorts of vehicles. The mini-buses once travelled between Qinggang and other cities have been replaced by coaches, and a new coach station has been built in the town centre, although rail services are still unavailable in the county. Local transport is also updated, with the four-wheels replaced by small automobiles. There also appear taxis and many private cars. Both sides of the roads are busy too. There are some construction sites by the main road, invested by different companies. Besides, there are more lively streets in Qinggang. The prosperity has been spread from the central to nearby districts. Over the past ten years, the changes in Qinggang have been substantial.

Official figures have shown the changes as well. In 2015, local GDP in Qinggang reached 5790 million yuan, nearly five times the level in 2006, with per capita GDP increased from 2644 to 11,286 yuan. As a grain producing county with agriculture still playing an essential role, accounting for half of its local GDP, its grain

---

[1] 精准扶贫, 激发内生动力; 决战三年, 提前奔向小康.

© Shanghai Jiao Tong University Press and Springer Nature Singapore Pte Ltd. 2018   159
Y. Gao and S. Fennell, *China's Rural–Urban Inequality in the Countryside*,
https://doi.org/10.1007/978-981-10-8273-3_8

production in 2015 reached 2.6 billion jin, almost 1.2 billion more than the 2006 level. Accordingly, fiscal income reached 199 million yuan in 2015 compared with only 21 million yuan in 2006. During the ten years, rural per capita income increased from around 2000 to over 8000 yuan.

The local government has attributed the achievements to both investment in industry, especially in industrial cluster development, and the development of modern agriculture in the rural sector. Meanwhile, the government has focused on the development of small towns and new countryside under the direction of the central government.

8.1.2 Contribution from the Rural Elites

We believe the development of Qinggang cannot be achieved without some rural elites. These people used to be migrant workers in different cities. Since the reform and opening up, some have seized the opportunities to get rich. For instance, one of them invested in real estate in Hainan in early years, and became a successful real estate developer. He invested in hotels in Qinggang, and these hotels are doing well. In addition to accommodating visitors, the hotels are also ideal places for weddings. During the recent visit right before the National Day holiday in 2016, the first author was kindly reminded by the hotel reception that there would be no room left during the holiday, because all the rooms had been booked in advance for weddings.

Dadong Agriculture Co. Ltd. is another typical example. Dong Zhanhe, a native of Zuoxiang Township in Qinggang is the founder and owner of Fanghao Group in Daqing City. Through decades of efforts, his business has been extended into the fields of real estate, road and bridge construction, food processing, as well as property management. In 2012, as a successful businessman he came back to his hometown. He first invested 1200 million yuan and built 21 apartment buildings in his home village of Minzhong, which attracted 276 households out of 320 in the village to move in. Meanwhile, he set up Dadong Agriculture Co. Ltd. in Zuoxiang. His son, a young entrepreneur once studied in Australia came back to help him with modern techniques and management ideology. The enterprise is engaged in food processing, including sweet corn and some green vegetables such as runner bean, asparagus and broccoli. In 2014, the enterprise introduced Yubari melon from Hokkaido, Japan. It is said to be a special species of honey dew melon produced out of Japan for the first time, and that a normal melon could be sold for up to 1000 yuan. Currently, the annual production capacity at Dadong is about 30,000, accounting for 10% of its total production in the world.

Dadong has also benefited the villagers and the local rural development. For a normal rural household, income from rural land and rural labor from Dadong could reach 53,000 yuan. First, the mechanism 'to join with land and ensure dividend' has enabled villagers to join the enterprise with their contracted land, so that in addition to land rent as guaranteed income and two subsidies (for grains and fines seeds) from the government, villagers could get bonus from the enterprise. It is estimated that the income per mu could reach 718 yuan, and each household could get an average of 17,000 yuan only for land rental. In addition, the enterprise needs 200 permanent and over 1000 temporary workers. Based on the salary of 1500 yuan per month, each household is able to earn an income of 36,000 yuan from the enterprise. Accordingly, in 2015, rural per capita income in Minzhong realized 12,721 yuan, 4386 yuan higher than the county average.

For rural development, after the relocation of villagers, the enterprise reclaimed 1100 mu of rural residential land, and signed a 12-year contract for land transfer (rental), so that the village collective got a lump sum of 10 million yuan. Minzhong thus became a rich village immediately. Besides, Dadong has changed the way of local farming. By land transfer, the enterprise collected farming land of over 8000 mu from Minzhong and 4000 mu from nearby villages, thus realized scale farming. In recent years, Minzhong Village (and even Zuoxiang Town) has been set up as a model for new countryside development, much due to its tidy rural environment as a result of investment by Dadong.

In recent years, there has appeared the trend for migrant workers to return home. They use their knowledge, skills and wealth that gained while working in the cities to start their own businesses in their home villages/towns. By doing so, they have also made great contributions to the development of the countryside.

8.1.3 Battle Against Rural Poverty

Despite of the achievements, however, Qinggang is still a poor county compared with other regions. In 2006 when the previous fieldwork was carried out, Qinggang was at the bottom of all counties in Heilongjiang in terms of economic development. In 2011, Qinggang was designated to be one of the eleven poverty counties with special difficulties in the contiguous area[2] on the southern side of the Great Xing'an Mountains. In 2016, when the follow-up visit was made, there were still 20,158 rural households, or 77,591 rural residents living under the poverty line, accounting for over 20.6% of its rural population. In other terms, of the 165 villages, 90 were villages under poverty.[3]

The county has recently set up a poverty-alleviation responsibility system. Each leader of the county government is required to be in direct contact with one town/township. 77 departments/organizations of the county and 13 enterprises are responsible for 90 villages for poverty alleviation, while 4132 officials and staff of government organizations are directly responsible for 20,158 households. During

---

[2]There are altogether eleven such contiguous areas throughout China.
[3]The national poverty line has been set at 2855 yuan per year since 2015.

the follow-up visit, the first author was told by some officials that they had visited the poor households under their responsibility earlier that year. Their assignment was to help the rural families out of poverty with whatever methods they could think of by themselves. Therefore, some had given a few goslings to their partner households, and some tried to find working opportunities for them. But they had to bear in mind that no cash should be given. The purpose was to 'teach them fishing, rather than give them fish'.

Whereas the state has decided to lift all of its rural population out of poverty by 2020, Qinggang has wowed to achieve the goal by 2018, three years ahead of the national schedule. To be specific, Qinggang has drafted the practice plan for winning the three-year tough battle against rural poverty. To be specific, it aims to lift the population of 28,360 out of poverty in 2016, 27,631 in 2017, and 21,600 in 2018.

It is obvious that the government has been determined to win the battle against poverty. However, based on the observation of the first author, the battle does not appear as tough as claimed. In practice, the identification of poor population is not strictly based on per capita income against the poverty line. A local officer told the author that it has been difficult for local cadres to know the exact income of a rural household. It is certainly easy to estimate the income from land. However, no one could tell how much a family could get from local off-farm work and from migrant labour. According to villagers, it has been much easier to make money. A person with working capacity would easily make a few thousand yuan each year. There do exist poor households without capable labour, but the number is very small. Therefore, the poverty list is actually worked out according to who is worse off in the village, rather than their real annual income. According to the local officer, the vulnerable group including the elderly and the disabled is indeed in need of constant support. However, he also indicated that most poor households are in fact already living above the poverty line, so that it would not be a problem to report the poverty alleviation achievement when necessary. Besides, as the deputy director of Qinggang Agricultural Bureau said, 'if worse comes to worse (we are unable to achieve the goal of poverty alleviation already set up), we would include the poor in the minimum living allowance program (MLA), because financial support from the MLA is higher than the poverty line'. Thus, Qinggang is almost certain to win the battle against rural poverty.

8.2 Insight from a Village

During the follow-up visit, the first author attended a group discussion in one of the villages in Qinggang. The village head and some of his fellow villagers were invited to attend in the village meeting room. Some officials from both the township government and the county government were also present.

8.2.1 Income Sources

According to the village head, there are 6 *tun*s in this village, with 552 households and 1642 registered residents. Since the reform and opening up, villagers have been allocated with 6 mu of land per head. They only produce maize and the average production per mu is between 1200 and 1400 jin. Due to the limited income of maize production, villagers started to raise animals. A few years ago, villagers raised pigs, but it was difficult to earn money. So they have changed to cattle. In recent years, nearly 80% of the households engage in husbandry. Cattle used to be sold at 13–14 yuan per jin gross weight. Nowadays the price has dropped to 12–13 yuan. But it is generally good, as cattle raising is on-going. The cattle are sold when big enough and calves would be bought back. Each selling would worth 10,000–20,000 yuan. The work of cattle raising is usually carried out by women. In addition, women in this village will also do farm work for others during the busy farming season. They are paid on daily or monthly basis. The daily income is usually 200–300 yuan. The lowest would be 100 yuan per day. While women are busy at home taking care of children, and gain extra income with husbandry and occasional farm work, their men usually migrate to work. Nowadays, about 200–300 villagers have migrated to work in cities. In generally, one could earn 8000–10,000 yuan per year. For those who have worked in the city for a long time, the annual income could be 20,000 yuan.

Villagers believe the changes in recent years have been great. The days are gone when "the village depended on loans for expenditure and villagers depended on return selling for food".[4] The biggest change over the past years has been the increase of local employment opportunities. The popular brick factories ten years ago have been basically removed and replaced by more productive and profitable industries. For example, a villager once worked in Harbin and became successful. In 2015, he came back home and set up a livestock farm of 30,000 m², of which 3000 m² are used as sheep cot. Currently, there are 4000 sheep and it is expected he would need more rural labour for his farm. In addition, by inviting outside investment, rural tourism has started in the village. There is one household in the village, which earned over 100,000 yuan within three years. The father and two sons have been working on the leisure farm, and they could earn over 30,000 yuan each year. Besides, there is a construction company. The headquarters is in Harbin, and is engaged in bridge construction and road repair. The company usually needs 40–50 workers locally, and sometimes it needs over 100 workers. They have all provide local working opportunities for the villagers.

Thus, the per capita rural income in this village reached 11,000 yuan in 2015. The village secretary attributed the better living condition to three factors. The first

---

[4]Returned grains refer to the grains which were sold back to the agricultural production units by the state. In narrow sense, they were grain rations, seeds and feed grains the state sold back to regions without sufficient production (due to natural disasters, local poverty or over purchase by the state).

is the preferential policies from the state, so that villagers nowadays need not worry about their land input and output, and are able to concentrate on other income earning opportunities. The second is the diligence of the local people. There is no one idling about in the village, and everybody is busy working. The third would be the increased employment opportunities in recent years. Therefore, it is apparent that the living condition nowadays is much better than a few years ago. According to a villager, 'the village road has been built and lamps installed. The environment has been improved. What else can you expect? If you say your income is not as much as others, it might be because you haven't worked as hard as others. You haven't made so many efforts!'

However, the villagers did mention that rural land is an important issue waiting to be solved. Nowadays, some villagers at 18–19 years old still have not been allocated with land. Because during the last round of land allocation, they were too young. Meanwhile, some villagers had long deceased but still have land entitled to them. The village secretary admitted, 'high school students in our village do not have land. We once raised the problem when a research team came last time. The old (deceased) have land but have been lying under the ground for years, and could do nothing, whereas students are of the tremendous promise for the state yet they have no land. This will make people feel unhappy.' He emphasized, 'until now the problem has been there for over ten years. Northeast China is different from southern part of the country where there is limited amount of land and is easy for minor land adjustments. Self-adjustment of so much rural land in our village would mess things up. Because our village doesn't have the authority, and neither does the township. We have to adhere to the No. 1 documents. Therefore, we have to depend on the state regulations and policies to pacify the general public in rural areas.'

8.2.2   Expenditure Pressure

Having discussed the better living condition, the village secretary admitted there are still households in poverty in his village. He gave the number of 173 target households for targeted poverty alleviation, and it was expected 168 of them would be lift out of poverty by the end of 2016.

In general, there are three main reasons for rural poverty. The first is poverty due to illness, especially chronic and serious diseases. The rural medical cooperation helps, but it depends on how much one pays and where the person is treated. According to villagers, if one spends 100,000 or 200,000 yuan, the highest reimburse level would be 5000 yuan. If a person is treated in the county hospital, 90% of the medical expenses will be covered, or only 5% if one is treated in a hospital in Harbin, the capital city. Villagers believe the reimburse rate especially for serious diseases is set too low. However, they do agree that this is better than before, as one had to pay everything himself in the past. What is more important, more diseases and treatments have been included in the medical insurance scheme. They gave an example of a young man in their village, who needs regular dialysis. Dialysis used to be costly, but it is totally free nowadays. Besides, there is a meal provided for each time. Therefore, villagers believe although there are still vulnerable people in the village, state policies are getting more preferential.

The second is poverty due to marriage. Similar to ten years ago, parents would borrow money for their sons' marriage, and afterwards all debts are to be undertaken by the parents. It is expected that the new couple could live a better life with the lump sum of bridewealth. The two major changes in recent year are that groom's family would be expected to buy an apartment in the town, and marriage has become less stable.

To be specific, decent bridewealth should include an apartment in the town seat. It is not for the change of urban *hukou*, as purchase of properties would not be entitled to a non-agricultural household registration anymore. With more properties developed in the town, however, young people are not satisfied living in the home villages. Besides, the ownership of an apartment in the town seat is considered beneficial for their children's education in the future. Therefore, if the apartment is included, the bridewealth is usually higher than 200,000 yuan. A recent research carried out in five provinces in China shows that in Hailun, a poverty county very close to Qinggang, bridewealth averages 300,000–500,000 yuan, of which cash is between 250,000 and 300,000 yuan. If a car and an apartment in the town are included, the total amount would reach 500,000 yuan.[5]

However, such financial contribution might not keep the marriage stable. According to villagers, if the man is not good or capable enough, the wife would easily run away, and his parents would be put into deeper debts for his second or third marriage. Bridewealth has thus become one of the major reasons for rural poverty. A villager at the meeting talked about women's household status, 'you have the money and your wife is with you. If you have no money, she leaves. Nowadays, it is the wife who has final say at home! Regardless of in south or north China, the wife plays a dominant role, because money is in her hands. If you need money for the family occasions of others, you have to discuss with the wife (as to how much to give).'

Meanwhile, during the discussion villagers admitted that the cost of bridewealth to much extent depends on the groom's capability. If the young man is outstanding, for example, succeeds in his career, or gets well-educated and well paid, he could easily get married without spending much. One of the villagers commented, 'girls would consider the potential of young men. If you have the potential, I will ask less. Otherwise, I have to ask more for assurance.' The problem lies in how to be outstanding and capable. According to the village secretary, 'education is the only way out for rural children. If one is not educated, he is doomed to be a drudge in the future.'

In terms of education, the related cost has become the third reason for rural poverty. The education here means education beyond junior high school. In other words, villagers consider the nine-year compulsory education insufficient, so that

---

[5]http://leaders.people.com.cn/GB/n1/2016/0927/c58278-28742249.html.

one has to receive higher and better education, even though such education is not free at the moment. This has led some households fall in poverty. Currently, a student needs 70,000–80,000 yuan to finish high school locally. A cadre is responsible to help a poor household with a high school girl. She lives a life, pinching and scraping. She told the cadre that her annual expense was at least 26,000 yuan. In addition to accommodation and food, she had to pay extra classes, for 200 yuan per hour, and she had to buy revision and exercise materials. If a student continues to receive higher education, the cost would be 100,000 yuan in total. One of the villagers did the calculation, 'every year, tuition and accommodation would cost 10,000 yuan. For food, 20 yuan per day wouldn't be enough, and 1000 yuan per month is necessary. So food and miscellaneous expenses will add up to 15,000 yuan. That goes to 25,000 yuan per year, or 100,000 yuan for four years (to finish higher education)'. '100,000 (yuan) is an enormous figure in rural area,' the village secretary commented, 'that is on the condition that the child is sensitive enough to know his family is poor, for those thoughtless children, the cost will be 150,000 yuan.'

Although education is costly, villagers still consider education the best way for their children to get out of rural areas. So after graduation, none of them would come back. However, they would seldom forget their home villages. For example, when a village was about to build an entertainment square and short of capital, the villager secretary called those graduates from the village, asking them to contribute as much as they could. As a result, some contributed cash and some offered materials. The square was soon built. The village secretary was very proud that wherever he goes, such as Harbin, Beijing or Shanghai, he will get picked up, and his train or flight tickets sorted out as long as there are graduates from his village in the city. He believes not only the family, but also the village and fellow villagers will eventually benefit from these graduates. Therefore, his village committee has decided to award newly-admitted university students with cash, for up to 10,000 yuan depending on the admitting institutions. Besides, those poor families with high school and university students have also been supported by the MLA scheme.

8.3   Family Story of the Guans

For the past ten years, we have been unable to imagine what has happened to the Guans. How is their younger daughter? How is the family getting along? With these questions in mind, the first author hoped to find them during the visit after ten years. However, it was not straight forward as their contact information ten years ago has been changed. Besides, great changes have taken place in Guan's village in that due to the new countryside construction, rural houses by the main road have been removed. When the first author arrived at the location of Guan's Village, it was totally unrecognizable as there appeared rows of new apartment buildings and a new office building of the township government (Picture 8.1).

Picture 8.1 Change of a village over ten years. *Source* Authors

Walking along the road in front of the township government, and stepping deep into the village, rural houses started to look familiar. The major changes are that the village road has been rebuilt and not bumpy anymore, and that some houses are rebuilt with blue or grey roofs, made of the so-called "colourful steel" by local people. It was in the inner part of the village that the first author got to know a woman who happened to be wife of a former village secretary, Zhao. According to her, some rural households have been relocated to live in the apartment buildings including the Guans.

She said she did see Guan pass her house to the village clinic frequently, and she could see Guan's wife sometimes. But she did not mention anything in particular about Guan's family, nor did she say anything about their daughters. It seems the Guans is living a normal life and nothing special has happened to the family recently. It was with her help that the Guans were found.

8.3.1 The Current Situation

Guan has not changed much, but gained some weight. But the change of Guan's wife has been substantial. She is much slimmer and fitter, and looks even younger than ten years ago. They took the first author to their home. After the removal of their house, they were given two apartments, door to door on the same floor in a new building. According to the compensation regulation, apartment is allocated in square meters according to the condition of villagers' old houses. Therefore, owners were expected to get up to 100% of the original housing space. Guan's house was

Guan's Old House in early 2007   Guan's New Apartment in late 2016

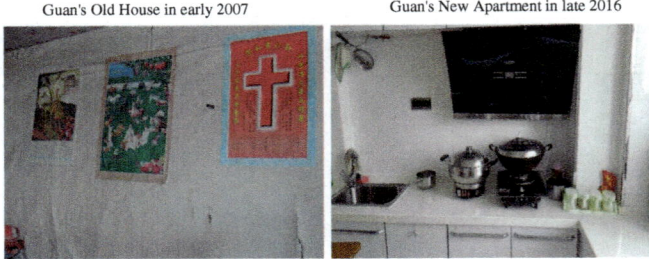

Picture 8.2 Changes of the Guans' living condition over ten years. *Source* Authors

newly built before it was removed, so they were allocated the full space. The Guans did the indoor decoration themselves, and they made the new apartment tidy and fashionable (Picture 8.2).

The construction of the apartment buildings occupied the farmland of some households, who were compensated with 21,000 yuan per mu for good, and given town-level pension insurance (with change of household registration). The construction, however, left the Guans' contracted land untouched. Therefore, the Guans still keep their original household registration, and more importantly their contracted land. According to Guan, to keep the land in hand is good because land price is increasing. He and his wife have rented the land like many of his fellow villagers. For villagers, the net income from farming is about 400 yuan per mu, similar to the land rent. As a consequence, villages capable to do some off-farm work would all love to take the rent rather than engage in farming. Guan and his wife are currently working on a nearby construction site of a factory, where Guan is responsible for fixing machines and his wife is hired to cook meals for the workers on site. Guan was proud, 'but for my leg, I could be a very skilful person. Everybody nearby knows me. They call me Guan, the capable cripple.' In fact, he is not only able to fix machines, but also able to repair his artificial leg. The current one has been assembled by himself with parts of the broken ones.

8.3.2 Efforts for a Better Life Out of Poverty

The miracle of the Guans is that the younger daughter is fully recovered. She is not only married but also has baby boy. During the past years, she had chemo-treatments every three months, and it lasted six years until she was nineteen when the doctor announced that she did not need treatment anymore. The Guans were overjoyed and rushed out of the hospital, without even asking whether she was able to marry and had children like a normal girl. According to Guan, the treatment was over 3000 yuan each time. The couple would raise the money each time in advance. Guan's wife was very grateful, as the director of Civil Affairs Bureau in the county government had much sympathy with their family. Each time he would try to get them some relief fund, or asked officials at the lower level to offer some help. He was one of the four people responsible for local civil affairs, who gave the family great support with the girl's treatments.

Besides, the Guan couple has not stopped working these years. Guan's wife said she could not imagine how they survived those years, as they worked day and night just for paying off the debts, which was nearly 250,000 yuan in total. Guan described the hardest time when they were working in a brick factory, responsible for delivery of bricks. The factory closed at 7 p.m. but the Guan couple begged the person in charge to issue another delivery. The work was to deliver the bricks to different rural buyers who needed bricks for construction, such as building a house. The couple would then do the delivery with their four-wheels. They were also responsible for loading and uploading, so they would come back by mid-night, but could earn an extra 100 yuan. They asked every day for an extra delivery, the person in charge once got impatient and was about to leave. Then, Guan followed him lamely, kept asking, until the person agreed with a comment, 'you are just an iron cripple!'

Guan's elder daughter, the once youngest migrant worker from the village came back after a few years, when a successful migrant from Qinggang returned to the home town and opened a superstore. She was hired and worked as a shop assistant in the next five years. The superstore had two assessments every year. If one had a good result during the assessment, he/she would be promoted with income improved. She had done well in the assessments of the initial years and her salary was once increased to 3000 yuan per month. However, she failed in the last one and got her salary decreased to 2000 yuan per month. So she quit the job and migrated to Dalian with her husband, where she could join her sister and work together. She left her daughter to be taken care of by the Guan couple. The little girl is four years old. She goes to the nursery during the day when the Guan couple could go out to work.

Having experienced the hardships, Guan was not scared even though he spent a lot on medical expenses over the years. In addition to his daughter's illness, he once suffered from myocardial infarction, and needs over 10,000 yuan every year for medicines. He also paid over 30,000 yuan for his granddaughter as she was born with aproctia, and has to take another operation at the age of sixteen for a full recovery. Besides, his wife has a few lymphoid tumours, and might need an operation in the future. However, according to Guan, all these eventually will be solved as long as he is able to work with income as he did before.

Over the past ten years, he not only paid off the debts, but also managed to rebuild their house with 40,000 yuan. After the house was removed and compensated with two apartments, he spent almost the same amount on the decoration of their new apartments. Besides, when his younger daughter and her husband started a business for indoor decoration in Dalian of Liaoning Province, he worked two years there helping them make window frames and install suspended ceilings for clients. The income was about 200 yuan per day. According to Guan, he had to help his children because their business foundation was too weak.

8.3.3 Further Comments

Ten years later, the first author had another meal in the Guans. This time the dinner was like a feast for the spring festival, with fish, pork, chicken and quite a few vegetables. Everybody was pleased about the changes over the years. During the conversation, the Guan couple said they were lucky because they had two daughters. If there were two sons, there would be a different story. Guan continued, 'I might have no place to live, and have to sell my own apartments.' He said because of his younger daughter's illness, no one would like to introduce her a boyfriend when she was over twenty. She later migrated to work in a factory in Dalian where she met her husband. Guan would expect her to ask more (bride-wealth) from the young man's family for future assurance. But she was grateful that he would cherish her as fiancée regardless of her serious illness in the past. Besides, the young man is also from a poor rural family who was raised up by his mother alone. So the Guans asked only 50,000 yuan, the same amount as they did for their elder daughter. If they had a son, the Guan couple said they would have to pay 170,000–180,000 in cash. In addition, an apartment of 60–70 m^2 in the town seat would cost over 200,000 yuan, and the new couple also needs a car bought by the groom's parents. That goes well beyond 400,000 yuan, which is more expensive than any medical treatment.

8.4 Inequality in the Countryside

8.4.1 Institutional Change

Previously we have found out that until the institutional apartheid, i.e. the *hukou* system, remains unchanged, the influence of any policies to reduce the rural–urban inequality would be very much limited even in the countryside. Nowadays, it appears that it is time for a great change. In July 2014, the state decided to practice reform on the controversial *hukou* system. One of the major decisions has been to remove the distinction between urban and rural registration by introducing an urban-rural integrated residential registration system, indicating the end of the dual registration system.

Over the decades when migration became an irresistible trend, the *hukou* system was gradually relaxed. However, its disadvantage became more prominent. It not only reduced free flow of labour, but also prevented urbanization procedure of the country. Most importantly, it remained the biggest obstacle to the integrated rural and urban development. In 2014, when the state set a goal to urbanize 100 million rural Chinese, it seemed impossible to achieve the goal without reforming the prolonged *hukou* system. Such a goal is part of the state's efforts to shift China's economic growth to a more consumption and demand focused model, because urban residents play a more important role in increasing the country's aggregate demand. Accordingly, the state has decided to remove the limits on registration in townships and small cities, relax restrictions in medium-sized cities, and set standards for registration in big cities. Meanwhile, under the reform the state would safeguard the rights and benefits of residents who do not have urban ID records in the city where they live.

It appears the institutional change is more apparent in the rural–urban interface, especially for migrants in the cities. However, the role of *hukou* in the countryside has never remained static. It has been widely noticed that during the process of urbanization, urban *hukou* has become less desirable. Wong found out that in 1980s, to allocate urban *hukou* as a compensation of land requisition was like winning the lottery. Distributing such *hukou* depended on one's status that veterans and village carders were given the priority. The rest would be sold to villagers by public auctions. Since the 1990s, the price of each urban *hukou* had decreased from 20,000 to 4000 yuan within a decade. He even recorded when a village was assigned a quota of converting ten agricultural *hukou* into urban ones, the village collective had to provide a subsidy of nearly 5000 yuan to each villager who agreed with the conversion (Wong, 2015).

There are two major reasons for the changing status of *hukou* in the countryside. First, in addition to abolition of agricultural taxes and subsidies for grain growers in the countryside, the pro-agricultural policies especially over the years have provided more support to the rural residents. Take the new cooperative medical scheme as an example, it has helped to ease the situation of insufficient medical insurance in rural China since established in 2003. Although the level of medical support is still low (Husain, 2016), modifications have been made constantly to increase the reimbursement level and to incorporate more serious diseases, so that the scheme has been able to play a more important role in reducing catastrophic medical spending for rural residents. Another example is the support with rural education. Since 2006, Chinese government began to provide free nine-year compulsory education in rural areas, which was later introduced to the urban areas in 2010 so that nine-year free education has become available to all children nationwide. In order to reduce the regional inequality in education, the state has implemented a 15-year free education program in northwest China's Qinghai Province since 2016. The free education covers three-year preschool, nine-year compulsory education and three-year secondary or secondary vocation school. An initial total of 860,000 students will be benefitted.[6] These have greatly reduced the rural–urban divide, thus making the urban *hukou* less attractive.

Second, for safety and security, Chinese peasants would like to cling to their entitlements of land, especially as insurance in case of migrant failure (He, 2013; Murphy, 2002). Meanwhile, the economic development and rapid urbanization in recent years have pushed up land price so that rural residents consider their agricultural household registrations more valuable because of farming and rural residential land entitled. It is widely acknowledged that rural landholdings function

---

[6]http://news.xinhuanet.com/english/2016-03/23/c_135216617.htm.

more as assets than a means of livelihood (Tang, Hao, & Huang, 2016). Therefore, migrants prefer to work in the cities while retain their rural *hukou*.

8.4.2 Inequality in the Countryside

With such institutional changes, it is expected that rural–urban income inequality will decline and even phase out at last. In Shanghai, for example, peasants' children born after January 1st, 2001 are universally registered as urban.[7] In such cases, it is meaningless to discuss rural–urban inequality anymore as the dichotomy of the rural and urban sectors is gradually removed with the state's intention to realize the integrated development.

Whereas rural urban inequality fades in the countryside, the disparity in other forms do exist and emerge. In previous discussions based on the observations ten years ago, we found that local officials enjoyed privileged status in the countryside, thus were able to manipulate *guanxi* to reallocate limited rural resources and benefit themselves. Since they mostly held urban *hukou* the inequality between local officials and villagers appeared to be overlapping with rural–urban disparity. Despite the change of urban-rural inequality, the gap between local officials and villagers exit and officials still enjoy a privileged status, as there are stories about local misuse of public funds and collective properties. However, it has to be pointed out that in recent years, institutional development has been progressed so that there has been less leeway for local officials to do so. For example, the first author was told Lin, the civil affairs assistant in the Guans' township quit the job in 2015. According to the vice director of Qinggang Agricultural Bureau, working in the countryside has been more and more complex. What might be more important, nowadays relief payments to villagers have to be credited to their individual cards or their own deposit booklets. Therefore, there is no cash to be dealt with, and chances are less that one can accumulate resources with this post.

Local entrepreneurs have emerged as a new elite group in the countryside. They have brought in investment, working opportunities and prosperity to the local economy. In terms of income, the inequality between the entrepreneurs and villagers has been substantial. As the case of Dadong indicates, the owner has changed the economic condition of the whole village. In reality, the disparity between rural elites and villagers has been very much enlarged because the former have more capital and resources for further development. In Qingang, some return migrants have become new local powers economically, and perhaps politically. Accordingly, there have appeared new questions as whether they can replace the original official group to be the new power, or how they interact with local officials. These are

---

[7]According to *The Practice Guides on Changing Part of Agricultural Population into Non-Agricultural* issued by the Municipal Government of Shanghai.

definitely issues waiting to be answered in future research. What seems certain is that there will appear new inequality within the countryside.

8.4.3 The Role of Rural Guanxi

Finally, during the follow-up visit in 2016, it is surprising to notice that the once prominent *guanxi* is seldom mentioned, and accordingly the maintenance of *guanxi* seems no longer considered one of the major expenditure burdens for villagers.

There might be several reasons for this. First, by moving to live in the apartment buildings, it is spatially inconvenient for villagers to keep a close relationship as before. Life in an apartment has become much confined, so that some villagers including Guan still miss their self-built houses, saying they were more spacious, sunny and warm where they had more communications with others.

Second, the development of local economy, and increasing employment opportunities have keep villagers busy with earning more income. During the fieldtrip ten years ago, the visit of an outsider would easily attract quite a few villagers to join the conversation, indicating that many of them actually had little to do. However, nowadays villagers have been mostly busy with taking more opportunities to earn extra money. In other words, the villagers have less time to spend on maintaining *guanxi*, because their minds are much less occupied with local *guanxi*.

Thirdly, and most importantly, institutional and economic development has played a more important role so that the role of *guanxi* has been replaced to some extent. This corresponds to the scholarly view that *guanxi* can be seen as an informal institution which substitutes for the market economy (Hendrischke, 2004; Xin & Pearce, 1996). As market mechanisms are developed, informal institutions will gradually diminish and will eventually be replaced by formal ones built on market rules (Putnam, 1995). In studies of Chinese society, similar views are expressed: where the state has established market mechanisms, there is a decline in *guanxi* practices (Guthrie, 2001). Based on our observations in Qinggang, we argue that where there is a low level of economic development, villagers tend to turn to informal institutions such as *guanxi* as one of the few remaining coping strategies available to them in times of need. In context of better economic development and better developed institutions, however, *guanxi* would play a less prominent role in rural life.

References

Guthrie, D. (2001). *Dragon in a three-piece suit: The emergence of capitalism in China.* Princeton University Press.

He, X. (2013). *Xin xiangtu Zhongguo (Rural China in the 21st century).* Beijing: Beijing Univerisity Press.

Hendrischke, H. (2004). The role of social capital, networks and property rights in China's privatization process. *China's Rational Entrepreneurs,* 97–113.

Husain, L. (2016). Looking for 'New Ideas That Work': County innovation in China's health system reforms—The case of the New Cooperative Medical Scheme. *Journal of Contemporary China, 25*(99), 438–452.

Murphy, R. (2002). *How migrant labor is changing rural China*. Cambridge University Press.

Putnam, R. D. (1995). Bowling alone: America's declining social capital. *Journal of democracy, 6* (1), 65–78.

Tang, S., Hao, P., & Huang, X. (2016). Land conversion and urban settlement intentions of the rural population in China: A case study of suburban Nanjing. *Habitat International, 51,* 149–158.

Wong, S. W. (2015). Land requisitions and state-village power restructuring in southern China. *The China Quarterly, 224,* 888.

Xin, K. K., & Pearce, J. L. (1996). Guanxi: Connections as substitutes for formal institutional support. *Academy of Management Journal, 39*(6), 1641–1658.

Glossary

Term	Term in Chinese	Meaning
buxing	不行	No way
chaogou jiage	超购价格	Above-quota price
dagong	打工	To work for others
eiyamaya (eiya)	哎呀妈呀(哎呀)	Interjection
fenji banxue, fenji guanli	分级办学, 分级管理	To run and manage different schools in accordance with various administrative levels
fengjiangdali	封疆大吏	Governor of a province
gongliang	公粮	State grain
guanxi	关系	Relationship
guniang	姑娘	Daughter, girl
huangliang guoshui	皇粮国税	Emperor's grains and state's taxes
hukou	户口	Household registration
jidongdi	机动地	Flexible land
jin	斤	Measurement unit of weight 1 jin = 500 g
kang	炕	Bed in northeast China
kuai	块	Colloquial language for RMB, yuan
leijigong	累积工	Accumulated work
liangbu	两补	Double subsidies
lishangwanglai	礼尚往来	Etiquette demands reciprocity
mao	毛	10 cents in RMB
mianzi	面子	Face
mu	亩	Measurement unite of area 1 mu = 1/15 hectare
nianchi nianyong	年吃年用	To consume what is produced within a year
paigou	派购	Allocated purchase
quxifu	娶媳妇	To marry a girl into the groom's family
		To take from the ordinary people for their own sake

(continued)

© Shanghai Jiao Tong University Press and Springer Nature Singapore Pte Ltd. 2018 175
Y. Gao and S. Fennell, *China's Rural–Urban Inequality in the Countryside*,
https://doi.org/10.1007/978-981-10-8273-3

(continued)

Term	Term in Chinese	Meaning
quzhiyumin, yongzhiyumin	取之于民用之于民	
renqing	人情	People's feeling
shangao huangdiyuan	山高皇帝远	The mountain is high and the emperor far away
shao zhangguide	少掌柜的	Junior master
shichang jiage	市场价格	Market price
shougou jiage	收购价格	Purchase price
silunzi	四轮子	A tractor-like vehicle with four wheels
songli	送礼	To send gifts to others
tiao and kuai	条块	Vertical and horizontal
tiliu and tongchou	提留统筹	Remained and unified planned fees
tonggou	统购	Planned/unified purchase
tun	屯	Natural village
tunqin	屯亲	Fellow villagers living in the same *tun*
tuyibalü	秃尾巴驴	A donkey without a tail
wanle	完了	All over
xiafang	下放	Be sent down
xiang	乡	Township
xifu	媳妇	Colloquial language for wife
yigong daizhen	以工代赈	To provide working opportunities rather than relief funds
yigou	议购	Negotiated purchase
yigou jiage	议购价格	Price for negotiated purchase
yishi yiyi	一事一议	One discussion over one issue
yiwugong	义务工	Voluntary work
yuan	元	Chinese currency
zabo'er	扎脖儿	Colloquial language for ending one's life
zaofu	造福	To benefit
zheng she'er	正事儿	Proper business
zhibian	支边	To support the construction of the frontiers
zilikouliang	自理口粮	Food grain self-supplied

Conclusion

This study has investigated rural–urban income disparities in post-reform China, taking Heilongjiang, a province in the northeast, as a case-study. The aims of this research has been that: (1) to explore the problem from the perspectives of both the macro and micro-economy with much analysis based on data at the province, county, township and household levels; (2) to combine quantitative and qualitative methods through a mixed method approach to gain a more comprehensive understanding of this widely discussed issue; (3) to extend the economic analysis of income disparities to their sociological background with a consideration of the influence of non-economic factors on the issue; (4) to measure the overall inequality as well as its composition in Heilongjiang province on a consistent basis for over 20 years.

The results from the inequality measurement have found that the rural–urban income disparities have been on the rise. The Gini coefficient calculation results have indicated that, at the provincial level, income inequality has been increasing, although it shows a milder trend in Heilongjiang Province and is subject to some policy changes, such as increases in prices, and preferential policies in recent years. The Theil decomposition results based on county data have showed a similar pattern of income gap growth. The impact of price changes concerning agricultural products has been more pronounced in the Theil index calculation results. With the help of the Theil index, it is found that the rural–urban income difference has contributed much to the inequality. The Pearson correlation calculation set up the statistical relationships between the rural–urban income gap and other economic indicators. The results show that the income gap is correlated with per capita GDP, urbanization, the ratio of urban labour productivity against rural, as well as high school enrolment. It tends to indicate that a better developing area with more opportunities would have a larger rural–urban income gap and more young people still at school age would be attracted to the income earning opportunities. It is suggested to transfer the surplus rural labour out of agriculture (to increase rural labour productivity) is helpful in reducing rural–urban income disparities.

The indications from interviews with the peasants show that there existed few income earning opportunities for peasants. Limited by land resources, agricultural income for ordinary peasants could hardly make ends meet. Due to the lack of local industry, the income from off-farm activities was greatly restricted. Most peasants

© Shanghai Jiao Tong University Press and Springer Nature Singapore Pte Ltd. 2018 177
Y. Gao and S. Fennell, *China's Rural–Urban Inequality in the Countryside*,
https://doi.org/10.1007/978-981-10-8273-3

would have to depend on small-scale animal raising to supplement their family income. Even though more rural youths would migrate to work in the cities, the chances were few that they could end up earning money. On the other hand, the peasants' expenditure was substantial. The agricultural tax and the affiliated local charge used to take away much rural income. Differentiated social welfare between the rural and urban sectors, such as the medical system, deteriorated the situation, by weakening the rural income. In addition, bridewealth and gift money giving within the rural *guanxi* network both imposed a financial burden on rural households. In addition, the peasants also complained about the corruption of the officials and cadres, that they accrued the public properties and scarce local resources for themselves, leaving the ordinary peasants more impoverished. From the perspective of the local officials and cadres, they generally believed that the peasants were basically able to make ends meet by farming, although they admitted that such income was limited. They also addressed the medical costs as one of the major reasons for rural poverty. In terms of corruption, they attributed it to their low level of income and the necessity for maintaining a good *guanxi* relationship with their superiors in order to 'better serve and pacify the peasants'. As corruption was interwoven in the *guanxi* network, to which everyone belonged, the officials believed that it has a societal problem from which they could not be shielded.

It is found out from the study that the enlarged inequality is due to the stagnation in rural income growth, as a consequence of limited resources coming in and much expenditure out for individuals and rural households. Based on qualitative and quantitative methods, it is argued that the enlarged rural–urban income disparities can be explained by both institutional and policy factors as well as non-economic reasons.

Firstly, at the national level, the institutions and urban-biased government policies have decided the overall allocation of resources. To be specific, the household registration system, grain procurement prices, agricultural taxes and public spending policies have all once ensured that resources are extracted from the rural sector to support urban industrial development. It is argued in this book that the institutions have provided the fundamental divide between the rural and urban sectors. They have not only prevented the free movement of labour to confine the surplus rural labour to the land, thus reducing their income earning opportunities, but also sustained a bundle of policies against the rural sector while supporting and protecting the urban residents and therefore further deepened the income inequality between the two sectors. During the reform years, urban-biased polices have been gradually corrected to favour the rural sector, such as increases in grain prices, the abolition of agricultural taxes and local charges, and the provision of subsidies to the grain growers in recent years. However, the high level income inequality at least suggests that the magnitude of the bias correction is far from satisfactory. We argue that a biased legacy against the rural sector still exists, as the institutions continue to withhold rural populations from becoming urban populations. As long as such institutions remain unchanged, the influence of any policies to reduce rural–urban income disparities would be greatly limited.

Secondly, at the local level, the officials and cadres play an important role in resource reallocation. As both state agencies and local provincials, low level officials are in direct control of the implementation of the state policies and the management of local affairs. What is more important, they have absolute authority over the scarce local resources in such an poverty-stricken area. Their power over the resources has created opportunities for them to accrue assets and wealth. Corruption was rampant in Qinggang, resulted in the scarce resources gradually being reshuffled to the rural elite—the rich and the powerful, with whom the local cadres and officials would like to maintain and develop a good *guanxi* relationship, while ordinary peasants were generally excluded from such *guanxi* networks. The resource reallocation manipulated by the local officials and cadres has enlarged the income inequality within the rural sector, which also contributed to the deterioration of the rural–urban divide in the countryside, as the local cadres and officials as well as the rural rich and powerful were, in most cases, holding urban *hukou*, either by being in an official position or through an exchange of wealth.

Thirdly, influenced by both the institutions and policies at the national level, as well as *guanxi* and corruption involving local officials and cadres, the peasants experienced stagnation in income growth. Under this circumstance of limited resources and income generating opportunities, ordinary rural households maintained their own *guanxi* network, supported by gift money giving, in order to seek mutual help, and the peasants would normally regard bridewealth as one of the few possible ways to help their younger generation better off. While maintaining *guanxi* by gift money giving will cause local resources to circulate around rural households, it eventually deteriorated rural income as in the whole rural area, bridewealth might help some to become richer, but at the expense of their parents' well-being by passing resources down to the next generation.

The pro-agricultural policies after 2004 helped increase rural income, but the low level officials were more concerned about the local financial difficulties, as the abolition of agricultural taxes deprived the localities of much of their income-generating capability. This would deteriorate the local financial situation, which would result in less investment in local public services, and eventually restrict rural income growth. Therefore, since the introduction of the preferential policies to increase rural income, the overall impact on income inequality reduction is not evident. What might be more important, again as argued in this book, as long as the institutions exist to confine the peasants to the land and maintain the differentiated treatment between the rural and urban sectors, the impact of any pro-agricultural policies to reduce the rural–urban income inequality would be greatly limited.

Some new evidence that emerged from the study deserves further discussion. Scholars within China and overseas have extensively examined the influence of the biased policies against the rural sector (Knight & Song, 1999; Lin, Tao, Liu, & Zhang, 2002; Wu & Perloff, 2005; Yang & Cai, 2003). Researchers also provide examples of how the migrant workers have been discriminated against in the cities (Hare & Zhao, 2000; Solinger, 1999; Zhao, 2000). The findings of the current study have confirmed the role of the urban-biased policies and institutions in restricting rural income growth. However, contrary to the descriptions and analysis of most studies on migration, it is found in this study that the peasants in Zuogang mostly find city work less harsh than working in their home villages. Those who migrated to the cities would mostly like to work there because of the long-term employment and on-going income, taking it for granted that there would be prejudice in the cities. The deterioration of the local economic situation made the peasants very much concerned about their survival but cared little about the unfair treatment. Therefore, the link is to be further explored between the impoverishment of the local peasantry and villagers' intention to find urban employment, whenever and wherever possible, regardless of unfair treatments.

In addition, the examination of *guanxi* and bridewealth in the specific local context also provides new implications for the coping strategies of those remaining in the rural communities. The growing importance of these local and informal forms of finance became an indication of the inadequacy of financial flows prevalent in agricultural production and the local economy. However, such conclusions, especially in terms of *guanxi* and bridewealth, deserve much in-depth research.

In fact, until 2017, the Chinese government has issued No. 1 documents focused on rural development for 14 years consecutively, indicating the determination of the authorities to regenerate the rural sector. Meanwhile, a major reform on household registration has been on the way. Since 2004 when the state decided to advance further reform on household registration, 30 provinces have drafted the plans by 2017 to abolish the distinction of rural and urban *hukou*, and replace by a unified residential permit system. This might eventually remove the institutional barrier on rural–urban income inequality. The *hukou* reform is another implicated issue, which must have great impacts on many aspects of social and economic life, including putting an end to the rural–urban income inequality. However, it is almost certain that there will appear other forms of income disparities and there are further issues to be explored.

While this research is based on the case study of Heilongjiang Province and its findings and conclusions cannot be generalized to other parts of the country, the study does provide some new thinking and understanding of income inequality and resource flows between the rural and urban sectors, especially from the rural perspective.

References

Hare, D., & Zhao, S. (2000). Labor migration as a rural development strategy: A view from the migration origin. *Rural Labor Flows in China* (42), 148.

Knight, J., & Song, L. (1999). The rural-urban divide: Economic disparities and interactions in China. Oxford: OUP Catalogue.

Lin, J., Tao, R., Liu, M., & Zhang, Q. (2002). *Urban and rural household taxation in China: Measurement and stylized facts*. Peking University, Beijing: China Centre for Economic Research.

Solinger, D. J. (1999). *Contesting citizenship in urban China: Peasant migrants, the state, and the logic of the market*. USA: University of California Press.

Wu, X., & Perloff, J. M. (2005). China's income distribution, 1985–2001. *Review of Economics and Statistics, 87*(4), 763–775.

Yang, D. T., & Cai, F. (2003). The political economy of China's rural-urban divide. *How Far Across the River*, 389–416.

Zhao, Y. (2000). Rural-to-urban labor migration in China: The past and the present. *Rural labor flows in China, 15,* 33.

Printed by Printforce, the Netherlands